CONDUCT AND THE SUPERNATURAL

CONDUCT AND
THE SUPERNATURAL

BEING

THE NORRISIAN PRIZE ESSAY

FOR THE YEAR 1913

BY

LIONEL SPENCER THORNTON, M.A.

OF THE COMMUNITY OF THE RESURRECTION, MIRFIELD ;
LATE SCHOLAR OF EMMANUEL COLLEGE, CAMBRIDGE
CARUS PRIZEMAN

LONGMANS, GREEN AND CO.
39 PATERNOSTER ROW, LONDON
FOURTH AVENUE & 30TH STREET, NEW YORK
BOMBAY, CALCUTTA, AND MADRAS
1915

JOHANNI NEVILLE FIGGIS

MAGISTRO

DISCIPULUS

GRATO ANIMO

DEDICAT

AUCTOR

PREFACE

THE original draft of this Essay was written with a view to the Cambridge Norrisian Prize. The subject chosen by those in authority was "Christian Ethical Ideals and Modern Reactions from Them." In preparing the book for publication it was found necessary to make some additions and to re-write and enlarge certain passages. The Essay remains, however, substantially the same. The writer has had a double purpose before him throughout: first, to examine and criticize certain ethical systems which illustrate the modern reaction against Christian ideals, and, secondly, to offer in apologetic form an argument for the supremacy of the Christian ethic.

Considerable attention has been paid to the writings of Friedrich Nietzsche and Mr. Houston Stewart Chamberlain, two of the prophets of modern Teutonic *Kultur*. The completed manuscript of this book, however, was in the hands of the publishers before the present war broke out; and I have thought it best to let it remain as it was. The bearing of current events upon what has been said in criticism of these and other writers will not be far to seek. It is to be hoped that Nietzsche's individualism will receive a considerable set-back from the present course of events in Europe. The full significance of his teaching is now laid bare as never before, and the world recoils from the sight of it. But those to whom Nietzsche was most opposed are faring no better. The camp-followers of the Utilitarians have received a rude awakening from their dreams. The peaceful approach of the earthly millennium has once more been indefinitely postponed. To some of us these things have scarcely brought surprise. Only, we are more than ever convinced that Christianity alone provides the solution to the problems which lie before the human race.

I am much indebted to the following authors and publishers, who have courteously given me permission to make considerable quotations from the works indicated :—

Dr. F. W. Bussell and Messrs. Methuen & Co. (*Christian Theology and Social Progress*) : Mr. H. S. Chamberlain and Mr. John Lane, The Bodley Head (*Foundations of the Nineteenth Century*, English translation by Dr. John Lees) : Dr. F. W. Foerster and Messrs. Wells Gardner, Darton & Co. (*Marriage and the Sex Problem*, translated from the German by Dr. Meyrick Booth) : Mr. T. Fisher Unwin (*Thus Spake Zarathustra* and *A Genealogy of Morals*, by Friedrich Nietzsche ; English translation edited by Dr. Alexander Tille) : Mr. T. N. Foulis (the following works by Friedrich Nietzsche, English translation edited by Dr. Oscar Levy :—*The Dawn of Day, Beyond Good and Evil, The Twilight of the*

Idols with *The Antichrist*, and *The Will to Power*) :
Mr. H. W. Garrod and Messrs. Constable & Co.
(*The Religion of all Good Men*) : Messrs Grant
Richards (*The Triumph of Mammon* and *Mammon
and his Message*, by John Davidson) : Miss Ellen
Key and Messrs. G. P. Putnam's Sons (*Love and
Marriage*) : Messrs. Kegan Paul, Trench, Trübner
& Co. (*A System of Ethics*, by Friedrich Paulsen ;
English translation by Prof. Frank Thilly) : Mr.
Benjamin Kidd and Messrs. Macmillan & Co.
(*Principles of Western Civilisation*) : Messrs. Mac-
millan & Co. (*The Renaissance*, by Walter Pater) :
Prof. Karl Pearson and Messrs. A. & C. Black (*The
Ethic of Freethought*) : Mr. G. Bernard Shaw and
Messrs. Constable & Co. (*Man and Superman* and
Three Plays for Puritans) : Prof. W. R. Sorley and
Messrs. William Blackwood & Sons (*The Ethics of
Naturalism*) : and Mr. H. G. Wells with the follow-
ing publishers :—Messrs. Constable & Co. (*First
and Last Things*), Messrs. Macmillan & Co. (*Tono-
Bungay*), Messrs. Thomas Nelson & Sons (*The Food
of the Gods*).

Detailed references will be found in footnotes on
the pages where the quotations occur.

I am very deeply indebted to the Rev. G. W.
Hart, C.R., and the Rev. Cyprian Rudolf, who have
kindly read the proofs with great care, and have
helped to eliminate errors and to smooth away
obscurities.   I am grateful to the Rev. W. H.
Freestone for some useful suggestions.   I must
also mention the Rev. Prof. Stanton of Cambridge,

who gave me some helpful guidance when I first took up the study of the subject, and Prof. F. C. Burkitt of Cambridge, whose very valuable criticism of the Essay in its original form contributed much to the subsequent elucidation of some points in the argument.

But, above all, my gratitude is due to him to whom this work has been dedicated. Without his encouragement and guidance it would never have been undertaken. He, more than any other, has furnished the inspiration and the point of view which have equipped the author for his task.

L. S. THORNTON, C.R.

HOUSE OF THE RESURRECTION,
    MIRFIELD.
    September 1915.

CONTENTS

xi

CHAPTER IV

ETHICAL FOUNDATIONS

PART II

THE CHRISTIAN ETHIC

CHAPTER V

THE OTHERWORLDLY PRINCIPLE

CHAPTER VI

THE ASCETIC PRINCIPLE

CHAPTER VII

THE SUPERNATURAL SYNTHESIS

CHAPTER VIII

THE SEX IDEAL

APPENDIX

CONDUCT AND THE SUPERNATURAL

CHAPTER I

INTRODUCTORY

CHRISTIANITY claims to be true for all men, and to be true for the whole field of human life and conduct; to be true, not only as to its foundation facts, but also as to the ideals which it sets before us as the goal of human striving; and the truth of these ideals includes their possibility of attainment. As Christians, we cannot admit, even in respect of the smallest detail of human conduct, that the Christian way of life is in the least degree inadequate, unpractical, or ephemeral;—either that it fails to meet all the needs of human nature, or that it is rendered obsolete by the changes which time brings. Still less can we allow that its outlook is gloomy, morbid, or vicious.

Yet every one of these charges has been made of recent years; and some or all of them are being accepted as true by an increasing body of people who have definitely turned their backs not only upon the Christian faith but, in a greater or less degree, upon the traditional ideals of conduct as well. The universal claim which Christianity puts forward in the sphere of practice (as in all else) makes it a primary duty to examine carefully the grounds upon which this wholesale rejection has been, and is, taking place amongst such a great variety of modern thinkers and writers. The Christian apologist must take the field in every sphere of thought where truth is challenged; and at the present time there is no branch of truth more openly assailed, or more urgently in need of his attention, than the Christian ethic itself, the sacred science of conduct.

The task which the present writer has set himself is to examine the grounds which have been put forward of recent years for rejecting, in one degree or another, the Christian way of life; and at the same time to criticise the various systems which have been proposed by way of substitute. An attempt will be made, in the first place, to show the inadequacy of these systems, and the failure of their authors to get at the real roots of moral life and to satisfy the persistent demands of ordinary human nature. I shall, then, seek to remove those misapprehensions which hide from many the real strength of Christianity, and, if it may be, to set before men's eyes afresh those elements in the Christian scheme which seem to meet these mistakes and correct them—those great sustaining realities which make Christianity both possible and reasonable in the sphere of conduct. I shall strive, indeed, to direct attention to the one comprehensive and satisfying principle of life, to know which and to understand the ways of its working, however feebly, is to be conscious of holding the key to personal existence.

If we are to come to an understanding about the nature of this reactionary movement in the sphere of morals, we must glance at some of the contributory causes which prepared the ground and made such a thing possible.

Survey of the Causes leading to the Reaction.

For is it not a fact worth weighing that, for some two hundred years or more after the Reformation and the rise of modern philosophy, no one ever questioned the supremacy of the Christian ethic, though from every other quarter inroads were being made upon the received traditions?

The contributory causes may perhaps be grouped somewhat as follows :—

(1) *Rationalism.*— In his *Social Evolution* Mr Benjamin Kidd has said that one of the principal functions of religion is to preserve human nature from an excessive intellectualism, which, by the undue place given to the intellect, endangers the welfare of the personality as a whole.[1] We are still suffering from the long supremacy of "reason" which swayed the eighteenth century; it is everywhere taken for granted that the ordinary man can come by the light of his own unaided intellect to safe and healthy opinions about the deepest and most mysterious things in personal experience. We probably pay less lip-service to naked logic than our fathers did; but that may only mean that our unwarranted assumptions have hidden themselves, and so are less easy to detect.

---

[1] See chapters v. and ix. of his book. *Cf.* the following remark by F. W. Foerster (*Marriage and the Sex Problem*, p. 186, note): "Kidd maintains that the invasion of the whole sphere of life by the intellect is fatal to the evolution of the race; religion, on the other hand, stands guard over the future of humanity, one of its prime functions being to keep the intellect in check."

(2) *The Theory of Evolution.*—Loud and self-assured as it was in those days, the rationalism of the eighteenth and early nineteenth centuries was notwithstanding held within limits by the fact that science was still in its infancy. The Deists had left a legacy of faith in some sort of over-ruling Providence ; and, above all, the gap between man and the rest of the natural order was as yet un-bridged. The promulgation of the Theory of Evolution brought this state of things to an end. When the full significance of this began to come to light, it was seen that many things once wrapt in mystery might after all be capable of an entirely simple and natural explanation. All life is a unity ; the world is moving through a great cosmic process, at the heart of which is the ceaseless unfolding of life. This principle of life is one—the same for man as for the protoplasm and for everything that lies between them. It follows that man's complex nature is no longer wrapt in dark clouds of mystery which hide its beginnings and its goal. All is plain. Moral consciousness is no longer a divine enigma sent down from heaven into an animal organism, from which it is entirely distinct and different. Man's moral nature, from which proceed his self-made schemes of conduct, is itself a thing evolved ; or perhaps rather a mass of evolved instincts, each and all stretching their roots down and back into the lower realms of nature. From such a stand-point the evolutionist surveyed the landscape behind him. The conservative attitude of hedonists and utilitarians, who clung to a traditional morality built upon such precarious foundations, might well be dismissed with contempt. Yet their opponents,

the intuitionalists, could scarcely have been expected to fare better; for from the new point of view they would seem merely to have played with their subject. There could be no return to the naïve belief in "natural affection" and "moral sense" exhibited by Shaftesbury and his school.[1] The attempts of these schools of thought to find a basis for morality always broke down over the dualism of self-interest and social obligation. Hedonists and utilitarians thought that all conduct could be based upon the desire for pleasure; intuitionalists, upon natural affection and a moral sense which was inherent. Looking back to-day, we may well ask :—How could the unbridged gulf which lies between the desire for personal pleasure and the accepted practice of altruism be justified on a naturalistic view of the origin of conscience? As long as the origins of conscience were admittedly unknown, that mysterious sense of social solidarity and its corollary of social duty which have become so firmly planted in our civilization must somehow be shown to be "natural." If the whole of conduct does not proceed directly from the desire for pleasure, it must be shown that the claim of pleasure for all follows from the experience of pleasure's value for the individual; or else it must be assumed (as by the intuitionalists) that altruism is as natural and instinctive as self-interest. But when the evolution of conscience out of animal

[1] Shaftesbury "is concerned to shew the independence of morality : 'there is no speculative opinion, persuasion or belief, which is capable immediately or directly to exclude or destroy it'; for 'sense of right and wrong' is 'as natural to us as natural affection itself,' and is 'a first principle in our constitution and make.'"—*The Ethics of Naturalism*, by W. R. Sorley (p. 93, 2nd edition), quoting from Shaftesbury's *Inquiry concerning Virtue and Merit*, I. iii. 2.

instinct became an axiom, its lowly origin might seem to justify criticism of the demands which it makes; and, if individual and social ends conflict, the way is always open to the rejection of one of the two. The altruistic instinct came to men with religious sanctions of long standing and universal acceptance. But if morality can be put on an evolutionary basis, may it not be true that where irreconcilable difficulties occur they may be due to false prejudices, wrongly derived from religion? As one reads Nietzsche's *Genealogy of Morals*, one is constrained to sympathize with his emphatic repudiation of that prudence which has no sure basis, that desperate defence of the moral sense by men like Hutcheson on the one hand and Mill on the other. It could only be done, as has been well said, "by making every juror stand aside unless he has pledged himself to morality." [1]

Now the evolutionary hypothesis in itself might not necessarily have produced a revolution in ideas about morality. But, as we have already seen, it did not stand alone; the rationalistic spirit at once saw in it a valuable ally. The clearing up of things hitherto thought mysterious and baffling to the reason was a signal proof, so it seemed, of the rationalistic contention that the human intellect will, unaided, solve infallibly all mysteries and unlock all doors. This new impetus is seen at work even as early as David Strauss, and later in Prof. Karl Pearson as well as in Nietzsche. The easy-going fashion in which Strauss picked the historic creed to pieces in his last work [2] by a process of shallow logic

[1] Sorley, *The Ethics of Naturalism*, p. 105.
[2] *The Old Faith and the New.*

reaches its climax in the few pages towards the end of
the book, in which he dismisses the ethical teaching of
our Lord.   Here we find the rationalist's blind faith in
the intellect ; and this unwholesome temper, wielding
the newly forged weapon of naturalism, relies upon
nature to supply a basis for morality, without respect
to existing moral standards or to the sanctions from
which their authority has hitherto been derived.

(3) *Idealist Philosophy.*—Meanwhile the whole
course of philosophy during the nineteenth century
has been of such a character as to undermine the
foundations of Christian moral standards.[1]   Modern
philosophy began with Descartes, who showed an
intense interest in the worth and meaning of the individual ;—*Cogito, ergo sum.*   That healthy tendency,
which was the result of all that was best in the
Reformation movement, reached its high-water mark
in Immanuel Kant.   But Kant sowed the seeds
of distrust ; and henceforth the centre of interest
shifted from the individual to the universal.   Hegel
took over from Kant his work upon reason ; and,
since the human reason no longer seemed so objective and concrete a thing as it was formerly held
to be, it was set aside as an unsatisfactory starting-
point, the Universal Reason becoming the centre
of interest.   But let us note well the result of this
change.   When once men lose faith in the objective
value of their own personality as a separate independent reasoning power and seek to form a
philosophical system which deals primarily in uni-
versals, the result always seems to be fatal ; the

[1] In this section the writer is much indebted to Dr F. W.
Bussell's book, *Christian Theology and Social Progress*, especially
Lecture vii. (Methuen).

individual ceases to be of interest, and the vision is filled with a great cosmic power which moves through the ages, fulfilling its inscrutable destiny regardless of pigmy man and his little struggles. This is the course which things have taken during the past century. How far such a phenomenon is the outcome of the tone and temperament of society, or in turn shapes the latter, it is impossible to say; nor does it matter much. The point of importance is that here we have an intellectual tone and trend which, the farther it is pursued, will become more and more plainly destructive of healthy moral standards.

No scheme of ethics can satisfy human nature, if it merges personality in some larger irresistible power. The influence of this tendency of thought is plainly evident in much of the literature with which we shall have to deal. But even so the worst has not been said. As rationalism and naturalism rushed into alliance in hostility to religious tradition, so now these two streams are enlarged by a third; especially significant is the union of forces which has taken place between pantheistic philosophy and the doctrine of evolution.[1] The age when idealism and

---

[1] *Cf.* Bussell, *op. cit.*, vii. § 2 (p. 110): "There have been two tendencies in Modern Thought answering naturally to the two sides of the eternal contrast, mind and matter, thought and things, ego and non-ego. In the search for a third principle which should explain the origin of this dualism, Idealist and Naturalist combined; or rather shall we say they pursued their independent study until that wider association of reflection and experience, that publicity and easy interchange of ideas which, with growing independence of special spheres, marks our time, brought them at last from opposite poles, not merely within hailing distance, but even to a common ground of agreement." And again, referring to Hegelianism, (p. 112): "We are now entering upon that brilliant period of philosophy in which the purely Idealist and the purely Naturalist view meet, not in a *compromise* but in an *identity* of opinion."

materialism were set up against one another as irreconcilable extremes is passing; or at least, if the controversy remains, it is ceasing to have any special religious significance. For all practical purposes the attitude taken up from both sides towards the distinctively Christian valuations is fundamentally the same. In either case a great cosmic movement (whether regarded as immanent in the world, or as the world-process itself) completely overshadows the significance of human personality. The rationalist movement was sufficiently dangerous in that it exaggerated the importance of one side of human nature; but a combination of forces which empties the individual personality of all permanent worth is infinitely worse. By such a process all the different elements in personality are decried in turn. The rationalist says that conduct is to be based upon reason and despises all emotion, whilst he assumes that the will is always ready to follow a clear track when reason has provided one.[1] The naturalist declares that conscience is only the aggregate of a number of prejudices and instincts, mainly hereditary, which have been evolved from the humblest beginnings, and cannot therefore, when united under one name, be placed in the seat of authority as though together they made up the Voice of God. The idealist starts by doubting the validity of the individual reason; but, as he has usually imbibed rationalistic suppositions to a greater or less degree, he proceeds, by means of reason, to build up a system in which there is no place for the freedom of the will.

These tendencies bore in themselves the seeds of

[1] A good example of this is to be found in *The Ethic of Freethought*, by Prof. Karl Pearson.

moral disaster; let us see how the evil fruit was brought forth from soil thus prepared. It has been said that the Hegelians took over from Kant the Universal Reason; it did not, however, in their hands long retain the Kantian shape. They still called it Reason; but it assumed with ever-increasing clearness certain darker features which we do not rightly associate with that idea.[1] It had no respect for the *individual* reason which had been left in such a precarious state; it was inscrutable; man could not hope to understand its purpose, if it had any. Then, too, the doubt was ever ready at the door that if it possessed such purposes—purposes which man could not control or even know—the Universal Reason was possibly in no better position than man; perhaps it could not control itself and was merely Fate after all. Thus the foundations of the distinction between good and evil were silently swept away.

But worse than this; pessimism reared its head and spoke through the mouth of the gloomy Schopenhauer, a veritable Caliban upon Setebos. It is said that Schopenhauer learnt his pessimism in the East,[2] and that through him the East found

---

[1] *Cf.* Bussell, *op. cit.*, p. 114: "'Reason' [in its Hegelian use] . . . bears a meaning which has scarcely a faint resemblance to current usage. The title itself was partly a heritage from the eighteenth century; partly the choice was due to the buoyant confidence of Hegel himself in his cardinal belief, *things* must agree to *thought*, and logic is ontology. But he was misled by their association, or swayed by a very natural bias. He might have styled it with greater correctness, 'Force,' or the 'Unconscious,' the 'Will-to-live.' Divorced from moral purpose, cosmic completeness is not far from the 'unknowable.'" And on p. 116: "The Real, said Hegel, is the Rational. The Real, declared the metaphysical pessimist and the empiric alike, is the work of a blind or malignant force, which man must *annihilate*, or *reverse*."

[2] He held Buddhism to be superior to Christianity.

her voice in the West. But he would hardly have been able to make this Eastern pessimism so popular had he not found allies in the disciples of Hegel. His system was based upon the conviction that the world was in the grip of an evil and malignant Force—a force which had no resemblance to the Universal Reason, for it was both wicked and ruthless. It follows, since we are all the slaves of this malignant Power, that life is essentially an evil thing, and on the face of it is not worth living; though it may be possible on reflection to discover some grounds for modifying this first impression.[1] This malignant Power still retains some shreds of personality. At least it may be given the name of Will; and all our little activities are merely instinctive reactions from the stimuli of this Will-Force.

We have now fairly traced the trend of thought which led up to Nietzsche and laid the mine for his revolution. He combined the pessimism of Schopenhauer,[2] the fatalism of the idealists and the arrogant logic of rationalism with the general outlook upon the world-process which is derived from evolutionist theory.

(4) *The Repudiation of Christian Dogma.*—Before we survey the revolution itself, there is one more cause of its appearance to be noticed; and that, it would seem, the most important of all. The repudiation of Christian moral standards is a direct and entirely natural result of the earlier rejection of Christian

---

[1] At any rate Schopenhauer himself seems to have lived a comfortable life and to have made no attempt to practise his principles.

[2] Although his conclusions were very different. Pessimism was for him the starting-point of a heroic view of life; whereas to Schopenhauer it was the justification for what Nietzsche called "Nihilism." See below, Chapter II. i. (i.).

dogma. No doubt far-seeing theologians foresaw all along that this would be the case; but those who repudiated the Christian creed did not themselves see it. It is indeed safe to say that they had no suspicion of it. There are still, perhaps, a few pedants who declare that the essence of Christianity is to be found in the Sermon on the Mount, and that one can be a good Christian by practising the imitation of Christ, without taking any notice of the traditional dogmas. Such people are living in a fools' paradise; for all around them at this moment are living proofs of the fallacy of their opinions. If there is one thing which can be said with absolute certainty about this whole movement with which we are dealing, it is that the revolt against the Christian ethic is due to the previous repudiation of the doctrines upon which it is founded. The two things, belief and conduct, are indissolubly bound together; they are parts of one whole, as the roots and the fruit are both alike parts of one tree, organically connected.

Yet, as has been said, all this was not realised at an earlier stage. We have already had occasion to notice the desperate efforts made by ethical philosophers to cling to traditional ideals. Their efforts were honest and well-intentioned; they bore witness to the divine spark of light in man—something over and above mere conservativism. But they were fighting an impossible battle; and that simply because the Christian religion is a unity, a supernatural way of living, based upon and inspired by supernatural facts and truths. Are there any martyrs for Christian principle, any devoted missionaries of the way of the cross, to be found in the ranks of those who accept Christian ideals without any of their dogmatic foundations? Even if we could point to a few here and there, would they bear comparison with the saints of all ages, whose devoted activities have been rooted in the Catholic creed? Only one answer to such questions can be found.

The earlier causes of change which we have noted were constantly accompanied by an undermining of faith in Christian dogma. The great central doctrines of Christianity became impossible to successive generations of thinkers from the time when the rationalistic point of view began to hold sway. But more than this : not only was supernaturalism set aside, but a wholly new point of view was suggested by the movements which we have considered. The shifting of interest from the individual to the universal rendered the whole idea of incarnation and personal redemption meaningless and grotesque. "What is man that thou art mindful of him?" What indeed? Nothing but a senseless atom tossed on to a wheel, which is not the potter's wheel of plan and purpose, but the wheel of relentless Fate. Moreover, it is not only that human personality pales before monist and naturalist philosophies ; with it go too, as we have seen, the reality of conscience and the distinction between good and evil. From this it is not a far step to make the whole history of moral consciousness a bad dream to be swept aside, whilst our new moralists usher in a golden age, in which man is henceforth to be interpreted "naturally"—a conveniently vague phrase which it will be necessary to examine in some detail hereafter. For the present it is sufficient to say that human conduct is to be based upon nature as interpreted by biology and psychology, without reference to any higher principle whatever. So we are asked to believe; and the results of these methods are before us.

The first thing which strikes the student of this modern revolution in morals is the extraordinary variety of the schemes put forward, and the amazing failure of their authors to agree upon the most important questions. There is no agreement to be found either as to the foundations upon which conduct is to be based, or as to the final aims towards which it is to direct itself. The writers indeed in many cases display individually glaring inconsistencies in their views of life; much less then can we expect them to agree with one another, so as to give us any one clear, definite, and coherent programme for humanity. They are in disagreement as to foundations. For many the great cosmic process of which we have spoken is at the background of everything. Strauss, for example, held that rationalistic faith comes to rest in the cosmic process; and for him the only legitimate religion is "dependence upon the Cosmos," a certain reverent sense of our connection with the universal scheme of things. He declared that man's reason has been set the task of co-operating with the Cosmos; and such co-operation, he thought, provides sufficient inspiration for altruistic conduct. For Prof. Karl Pearson the basis of conduct is to be reason, without the lingering piety towards the great Unknown which characterised Strauss; he is confident that reason has only to speak and the will must inevitably respond. Nietzsche set aside reason and her confident search for truth in favour

Survey of the modern situation.

of the Will-to-power; he believed that reason is always the servant of will, and that truth is to each man only that which he wills to believe. The enormous difference between this position and that of rationalistic moralists is obvious at once. From this point of view we have not to find out what is right, but rather to make sure what it is that we really want, and then to make ourselves masters of it. Nietzsche has a considerable following in his view that the key to the riddle of the life-process is to be found in will.[1] This is the foundation upon which several of the more reactionary writers of to-day have built.

Yet here again we meet with new differences when we come to the various superstructures. As far as his philosophical bases go, Mr. Bernard Shaw is in very close agreement with Nietzsche; yet their ethical schemes are really quite different. Both reject morality, as such, in theory; but in fact Mr. Shaw's conclusions are very much more akin to Christianity. The significance of all these differences will be considered in detail later; we are now only concerned to note their existence. These more radical revolutionaries are by no means, as might be supposed, all in favour of pure egoism; the balance of the different tendencies in human nature is just one of the points over which they are most at sea individually and in conflict amongst themselves. So again Mr. H. G. Wells, who strikes one as being far less of a philosopher than either of the above writers, shares their cosmic creed, but has for the most part placed his faith in education, that

[1] This was one of the leading ideas which Nietzsche derived from Schopenhauer.

is, in knowledge rather than in will. Like Prof. Karl Pearson, he seems to think that if only light can be shed around we shall have no difficulty in taking the true path. He, too, is—by conviction, at any rate—an altruist. On the other hand, John Davidson, the poet of materialism, has proclaimed with no uncertain voice the gospel of individualism in its most extreme form. He smiles at the Christian sentiments of Nietzsche. Though they start from similar presuppositions, their conclusions are poles apart; and to the present writer Davidson seems the more logical of the two. So much for the chaos amongst extremists.

We may notice next a group of writers who do not reach the extreme conclusions of the Nietzschean school. These may also be distinguished from the group considered above in that they appear to approach the subject more from the personal side— that is, rather from what has come to be their own taste and feeling than from a systematic will-philosophy or a large cosmic outlook. Into such a group would fall Prof. F. Paulsen, Mr. H. W. Garrod, Mr. G. Lowes Dickinson, and Mr. H. S. Chamberlain. One may say generally that in the case of these writers there is simply a re-vulsion of feeling against Christian conceptions of sin, moral law, and asceticism, and in favour of a return to the " Natural Man." Nature in this sense is held to be a safe guide as to what is best in conduct. But, once more, different superstructures are erected upon common foundations. Mr. Lowes Dickinson harks back to Hellenism,[1] bright and sunny in his

[1] See a further reference to this writer near the end of Chapter IV. p. 151.

eyes compared with the gloom of Christendom.
Prof. Paulsen seems to think that both Hellenism
and Christianity have had their heyday, and that
we are now in process of forming some new ethic,
which will include the best in both.   Mr. Garrod,
on the other hand, thinks that an attempt to do
this was made at the Renaissance, and that it
has not succeeded.[1]   Hellenism is too dangerous,
Christianity too unpractical.   He gives his allegiance
to a new "Teutonic" way of life, which is to be
better than both ; perhaps this idea was suggested
to him by Mr. Chamberlain's book, *Foundations
of the Nineteenth Century*.   But, once more, we
must notice the remarkable difference between these
two advocates of the new Teutonic religion.   Mr.
Garrod has thrown over Christianity ; whereas
Mr. Chamberlain loudly proclaims his whole-hearted
allegiance to the Gospel.   Of all the writers who
have been mentioned, he alone does lip-service to
Christianity ; yet, as will be shown, he shares their
presuppositions, and his Christianity suffers severely
in consequence.

There is one more distinction to be observed
before concluding this survey.   All the writers
mentioned thus far are *positive*, in the sense that
they all believe that their schemes of life would
leave the world better than they found it, with
the possible exception of Davidson, who stands by
himself.   All assume that man is here to enrich and
in some way to enlarge for the world the streams
of virtue and of life.   In so far as they do this
they are really on the side of Christianity.   Not so
long ago the Epicurean standpoint was revived by

[1] H. W. Garrod, *The Religion of all Good Men*, p. 134.

Walter Pater,[1] and by Edward FitzGerald in his version of the *Rubaiyát* of Omar Khayyám.   The outlook upon life displayed in their writings is negative. Things cannot really be altered one way or the other with any hope of permanence ; and the wisest counsel is that we should gather happiness while we may, each according to his taste.   Yet, at the back of this negative outlook is the very same fatalism which is responsible for so much that is to be found in the other groups mentioned.[2]

With such a chaos of conflicting opinions, where shall we begin ?   That we may arrive at some sort

Plan.

of order in a criticism of this literature, it will be necessary to follow the lines which the science of Christian ethics seems to demand. If their positive tenets spell confusion, these writers at least agree in their denial of certain great

---

[1] *E.g.* in *The Renaissance* (especially the Conclusion): "Not the fruit of experience, but experience itself, is the end."   "While all melts under our feet, we may well grasp at any exquisite passion, or any contribution to knowledge that seems by a lifted horizon to set the spirit free for a moment, or any stirring of the senses, strange dyes, strange colours, and curious odours, or work of the artist's hands, or the face of one's friend. . . . With this sense of the splendour of our experience and of its awful brevity, gathering all we are into one desperate effort to see and touch, we shall hardly have time to make theories about the things we see and touch."   Again, quoting Victor Hugo's "We are all under sentence of death but with a sort of indefinite reprieve," he adds : "We have an interval, and then our place knows us no more. Some spend this interval in listlessness, some in high passions, the wisest at least among 'the children of this world,' in art and song. For our one chance lies in expanding that interval, in getting as many pulsations as possible into the given time" (shilling edition, pp. 249–252 ; Macmillan).

[2] Davidson, the most individualistic of those referred to above, is really a connecting link between this modern Epicureanism and the group of writers with whom I have placed him above.   He can hardly, however, be called negative in his outlook, as he would not only gather personal happiness, but also mould the world to his liking (see Chapter II. II.).

principles which lie at the root of Christian conduct.
They repudiate three things :—the Christian view of
human nature, the moral law, and the Gospel itself,
in its claim to provide the true motive power of
conduct.   Let us therefore take these three words—
Nature, Law, Gospel—as the keynotes of this discussion ; and consider the anti-Christian schemes of
the present day, according as each seems to illustrate
the points to be emphasized under each of these
three divisions of the subject.[1]   Our plan then will
resolve itself somewhat as follows :—

The first question we have to consider in framing
our views on moral questions is, What is this
"nature" which we possess as individual beings? Is it simple or complex,
single or dual, trustworthy or unstable?   Can we
take for granted that we understand it, and therefore confidently build conduct upon instinct?   It
will be necessary to examine carefully the positions
taken up on this subject, for everything else will be
found to hinge upon it ; and it is useless to enter
upon a serious ethical inquiry without going right
down to the roots of things.   The view one takes of
human nature is, consciously or unconsciously, the
basis of one's whole outlook upon conduct.   Consequently the opinions held about human nature by
these writers, and especially by those more radically
anti-Christian, will first be considered ; we shall see
whether they are supported by the real facts of life or
not ; and if not, how far they fail to satisfy this test.

Nature.

[1] I reached this conception of " Nature, Law, Gospel," as the
best order of sequence to follow, before reading Dorner's *System
of Christian Ethics*.   I was glad to find that he follows the same
order and shows its necessity.   See pp. 51–53 of his book.

We shall find that in their schemes certain great fundamental realities are almost entirely left out of account, as, for example, the fact of sin and the necessity of a moral law, and therefore of a righteous, personal God. Where there is no grasp of the real significance of sin as a fact,—that is to say, not merely moral imperfection and failure, but something infinitely more serious and far-reaching,—there the whole idea of morality as a law binding upon conscience becomes meaningless and repulsive. But, since a true understanding of what sin is shows that there is something radically wrong with us, this conception of law coming to us with binding authority to redirect us is really a fundamental need of human nature. We cannot, however, stop here. If the fact of sin be true and the moral law a necessity, we must pass behind it and fall back upon a supreme, righteous Personality, a moral Governor whose authority we can accept as we cannot that of mere law in itself; and it is just here that the vital connection between theology and conduct comes in. Men reject the moral law just because they do not believe in the righteous, personal God behind it. His law seems to them a deadening, mechanical thing because they know not that it guards and represents life and truth. But more than this; disbelief in God means ignorance of the spiritual world of which He is the centre, and therefore ignorance of man's possibilities of attainment in the direction of fulfilling the law, when he is in contact with spiritual forces and has learnt how to use them. Thus far, then, the argument will have sought to show that the revolt is due (1) to shallow views of the meaning of human nature, (2) to the failure of the lawless spirit in human nature to appreciate law, (3) to ignorance of the spiritual world.

When men are encumbered by these three grave defects, it follows, in the first place, that they have no sense of spiritual need, and that con-

Gospel.

sequently they despise a gospel of deliverance. They are therefore unable to believe in the great world of spiritual possibilities which such a gospel of deliverance brings. The natural world is good; law is its suppression; a gospel which brings in a new kind of life from another world is unnecessary and mistaken, morbid, delusive, and world-weary. Christianity is pictured as the way of visionaries who have lost the sober balance of practical life. The whole meaning both of the Gospel itself, and of the present revolt against it, is that it is entirely "not of this world,"—a higher cross-current coming in from a different quarter, a fresh inrush of power, which by its otherworldliness is able to bring to fruition the life upon earth. From this it follows that all attacks upon Christian asceticism are wrong and beside the mark. It is a case of the blind attempting to criticise those who see, or of cripples scoffing at the training of athletes. Why is it that all the tirades upon this subject leave us Christians entirely unmoved? It is because we possess solid experience, which is confirmed, the longer we study our critics, by the amazing ignorance they reveal of sober, plain facts of which we are daily aware.

Christianity furnishes the key to the meaning of human personality in its entirety, and consequently the key to human conduct. This is perhaps most conspicuous at the present time in respect to the most profound of all ethical problems, namely, the problem of sex and marriage.   In the consideration of this question an attempt will be made to gather up all the principles which have been discussed in the course of this essay, and thus to bring the whole to a practical conclusion.

Part I.—NATURE AND LAW

CHAPTER II

THE FAILURE OF THE NATURAL MAN
(INDIVIDUALISM)

In this chapter and the next an attempt will be made to examine in turn the positive ideals of certain prominent writers and thinkers, of very diverse types, who have given expression to the cry, "Back to Nature!" so characteristic of the modern ethical revolt. The most important of these is, of course, Friedrich Nietzsche.

I

Nietzsche was the first thinker of modern times who deliberately advocated a return from Christian Friedrich to pagan morality. He saw that Christi-Nietzsche. anity claimed to be, not "natural," but "spiritual"; and it was on this ground that he condemned it. Nietzsche's early abandonment of Christianity, followed by that bitter hostility to it which he retained to the end, must have something deeply pathetic about it for the Christian who has endeavoured to study this writer sympathetically and who knows how close he really came to the Kingdom of God. He was exactly the sort of man who might have become a tower of strength to Christianity, if he had but once caught a glimpse of its

23

power. But his mind was fast closed against all
this through causes which have been traced in the
preceding chapter. He was early disillusioned as to
the value of "all-too-human" humanity as a character-
forming power; on the other hand, he passionately
desired an ideal and a great future for the race.
Thus there were in Nietzsche strong elements of
discord, — early disillusionment (*Human, all too
Human* was written at the beginning of his last ten
years of activity, the most important period of his life)
together with high aspiration. The real tragedy of
his life was that, with these conflicting tendencies, he
acquired a deep and lasting prejudice against Christianity, although it contains within itself the real solution of his problem, and indeed the only one. He
did not see the gigantic stature to which the spiritual
man may grow. He saw only negatives, when just
beyond them lay a rich life abounding in positive
energy. The whole dynamic force of Christianity
was hidden from him; and he turned back from
that avenue to construct a new gospel out of the
" Natural Man,"[1] that human-all-too-human in which
he was already ceasing to believe. The result, as
one looks back upon it, seems a likely conclusion for
such a temperament. The Natural Man must be re-
shaped in his hands by desperate methods, that he may
have a future; and when that future takes form, we
are unable to trace its continuity with its starting-point.
The Natural Man has been silently relinquished in
favour of a Supernatural Being whose very name
(" Beyond-man ") sounds treacherous to his origin.[2]

[1] This phrase is used in the Pauline sense throughout the
present work.
[2] On this point see further pp. 46 ff. below.

It is impossible to gain a fair impression of the significance of Nietzsche, unless one has first en-(i.) The Foun- deavoured to give sympathetic attention dation. to the positive message which he was seeking to deliver. For he was no mere cold and calculating philosopher building up a logical system; he was, like his child Zarathustra, a knight-errant and a prophet, passionately seeking after reality and proclaiming with conviction the truth which he believed he had discovered. Two strong influences contributed to the shaping of his view of life —Schopenhauer's philosophy and his own study of the phenomenon of ancient Greece. From Schopenhauer he derived his belief that the universe is to be explained as the manifestation of a Universal Will, which may be called the "Will-to-live." From the same source he accepted the pessimistic view of the world; when good and evil are weighed in the balance, the evil predominates, and this evil is directly due to the activities of the World-will. All this is reproduced in each individual, whose will is but a manifestation of the Universal Will. But at this point Nietzsche parted company with Schopenhauer. The latter concluded that the Will-to-live is something the existence of which we must entirely deplore, and that the best and happiest course is to say nay to life; the highest wisdom he found in the negation of the Will, in seeking Nirvana.

This conclusion was intolerable to Nietzsche; and, as he studied ancient Greece, his own solution of the problem gradually took shape. Its earliest form is to be found in his *Birth of Tragedy*. He believed that he had found in Greek poetry and thought a brilliant attempt, or rather series of attempts, to assert the goodness of life, in spite of all that darker side of things which seems to deny it. Whether the *Birth of Tragedy* gives a true estimate of Greek thought or not does not matter for our purpose; it describes what Nietzsche wished to believe about it, because in fact it represents his own way of escape from pessimism. First, then, in the Homeric literature and its Olympian mythology he saw a magnificent attempt to find satisfaction in æsthetic pleasures. Man is able, by virtue of his artistic and poetic powers, to create for himself a world of Apollonian visions, and thus by illusion to replace the world of fact by a world of beauty. The essential worth of this conception is that, while admittedly it does not do away with the world of evil, at least it vindicates some reality and independent dignity for the individual; while at the same time it assures to him some positive interest in life. For he is a creator of values;—no mere channel through which the Will-to-live flows, but a central point at which it becomes self-conscious. Man, then, a conscious centre of the Will-to-live, passes judgment upon the whole process and condemns it; and yet at the same moment he is able by creative power to secure for himself an inheritance of beauty in the midst of that which he has condemned. So great, then, is this individual man that he can rise above his surroundings and make a world of his own to dwell in.

Yet still the problem is unsolved. For man is still one with the whole world-order; and at times this sense of oneness with Nature comes upon him with irresistible force. He cannot separate himself from the universal Will-to-live, so as to escape sharing the pains and ills of the world; nor does he wish to do so.

His Apollonian vision cannot be final, for that would
be to turn too far aside from that Nature from which
he has sprung; æsthetic pleasure is but a temporary
hiding-place. He must come down again into the
arena of life and say *yea* to life—not merely to his
own self-made world of beauty, but to the world as
it is, the world of tragedy. So he makes his second
great venture, and embraces the Dionysian vision;
revelling, like the bacchants, in this vision, he becomes intoxicated with the universal Nature-Spirit.
Once more, one cannot but be impressed by the
prophet's message; for it declares that there is, not
only a personal happiness to be snatched out of the
midst of life's ills by the individual, but also a deeper,
more fundamental and universal satisfaction. This
larger treasure is to be reached by identification of
self with a far wider sphere of interest,—nothing less,
in fact, than the whole world-order, whose goodness
is thus so passionately asserted. Thus we seem to
obtain glimpses both of an individual good and of a
universal good, in which, by heroic sympathy, the
individual shares. Both are grounded in Nature,
so that by creative effort and heroic struggle the
world of evil is transformed into a world, not indeed
of unmixed good, but at least of something worthy
of the Will-to-live—a world in which there is room
for rich treasures of romance and heroism, and where
the joy of seeking and striving constitutes life. It
is thus the supreme merit of Nietzsche that he has
seen both the worst and the best in life perhaps as
clearly as they can be seen from the standpoint of
the Natural Man; he has appreciated both to the
full, and then has said, " I accept this life." What
was sketched out in the *Birth of Tragedy* burst

forth again in *Thus Spake Zarathustra*.   Here we find the same romantic outlook, the same conviction that the darker sides of life may be transfigured by a virtuous and heroic acceptance of the facts as they are—the facts of our common heritage.   Here too a future is unfolded ; yet no utopian illusions are held out to us.   A hand points to a hard rough way along which progress may be won by great sacrifices. Zarathustra is a knight-errant given to prophecy. We may be compelled to refuse his credentials as a prophet ; we shall at least do homage to his knightly bravery.

Yet it is as a prophet that he now speaks to the world ; and we must decide upon our attitude towards him.   We have discovered the foundation of Nietzsche's standpoint to be his passionate assertion of the goodness and sufficiency of the whole natural order, including the nature of man himself, which is the highest expression of that order.   The Will-to-live [1] justifies itself by the adequacy of human nature to find in life happiness, worth, and possibility of progress.   Bearing in mind, then, what has been said about the foundation, we are obliged to ask whether it will bear the weight of the system built upon it ; and in reply the following criticisms must be passed upon Nietzsche :—

(*a*) His confidence in "Nature" as a foundation sufficient for all human needs is completely contradicted by the way in which he depreciates human nature throughout his works.

---

[1] Nietzsche seems to have started with the "Will-to-live" as his keynote ; but later this passed into the darker and more stoical "Will-to-power."   Yet even his "Will-to-live" was never a passive acceptance of pleasure ; it had in it from the first the quality of heroism, which was the germ of the "Will-to-power."

(*b*) He does not really uphold the purely "natural" in man as self-sufficient.

(*c*) Thus a "natural" progress is precarious ; and, to avoid repeating the unprogressive conditions of classic paganism, something *not natural* is introduced ; yet even this is professedly built upon the natural.

(*d*) Finally, the very idea of progress, essential to the whole scheme, is completely nullified.

It was Nietzsche's misfortune that he was obliged to build up his whole system upon a foundation which was already in his own mind fundamentally weak. From the first he (ii.) A Weak Spot. mistrusted his materials. He did not really believe in ordinary human nature ; and yet it was the only material ready to hand, which he had no choice but to use. His poor opinion of human nature is writ large upon almost every page of his writings—or at least of human nature since history and civilization began. It is not at all clear at what stage his "blond beasts" (in whom indeed he does believe) appeared upon the scene ; apart from them, however, he has been at pains to give us his views of the mental and physical development of the race in his *Genealogy of Morals*. What do we find here ? Man, we are told, first appears as a good Nietzschean, hard and wild, loving cruelty ; but he soon deteriorates. His honest reverence for his departed ancestors soon becomes degraded into a belief in a spiritual world and in God ; and, above all, he is responsible for having invented that useless piece of lumber, now called "conscience," which has been his curse and his bugbear ever since. Finally, to crown this story of ever-darkening superstition, he has allowed himself to fall a prey to Christianity. He spent his pre-Christian days in inventing dismal bogies with which to frighten himself; and then he caught the Christian disease, the quintessence of folly and stupidity (*credo quia absurdus sum*). Thus it follows that the descendants of the primitive Nietzschean worship at the Ass-Festival.[1] So much for the value of ordinary human nature! This is not an unfair picture of what Nietzsche thought of it. If it be said that he denounced human nature in its present state, depraved through the influence of Christianity, what are we to make of all that pre-Christian degeneration, when conscience was invented, and religion too? What again must humanity, unperverted by Christianity, have been worth, if such a weak and absurd thing could succeed in overcoming it? Its fall from Nietzschean heights was surely as great as that of Adam from primeval innocence. Here we look into a very deep crevass in Nietzsche's system. His one and only standard of value is power or Will-to-power; the earlier Will-to-live became subordinate to this.[2] He declares that the strong is the good. What has been hitherto called " Evil " is good, if it possesses power; and what has been called " Good " is bad because it is weak—and this with special reference to Christianity.[3] And yet, as we have seen above, Christianity, supposed to be bad because it is weak, has succeeded in undermining the whole of

[1] *Thus Spake Zarathustra* (Tille's translation, pp. 464–472).

[2] *Beyond Good and Evil*, by F. Nietzsche (English trans. by Helen Zimmern, p. 52; T. N. Foulis): " . . . one would thus have acquired the right to define *all* active force unequivocally as *Will to Power*." See the note on p. 28, above.

[3] See *Genealogy of Morals*, Essay I.

the old "Evil" system of society; it has shown itself stronger, not weaker. If we are told that this victory of Christianity was like the poisonous bite of a serpent and cannot be said to be strong or powerful, one must reply that nowadays the old forms of brute strength are everywhere giving way before more subtle manifestations of power invented by the serpent-like cunning of man. The African lion falls before the sportsman's bullet; and one has a right to hold that the bullet is a greater manifestation of the universal Will-to-power than the strength of the lion. Nietzsche's attack upon Christianity will be discussed more fully in a later chapter; our present purpose is to examine his conception of human nature, and especially to inquire what he really meant by the term *power* as applied to his pagan heroes who succumbed to the influence of Christianity. He refuses to conquering Christianity this attribute "power," whilst he concedes it to those who were vanquished. Nietzsche has never once attempted to justify this arbitrary method. Even if it were granted that Christianity is bad and pernicious and the old paganism good and healthy, yet here we have the good which is weak calling itself good. It almost looks as if Nietzsche believed in a Nietzschean God, Who only allowed the title "virtuous" to those who agreed with Himself. But on Nietzschean presuppositions there is no overruling Providence; why then should not some malignant fate inoculate good pagans with the poison of Christianity? Moreover is it fair to deny to the latter the attribute of power? The real answer is perhaps that which Nietzsche gives in his *Antichrist*, where he makes it clear that he condemns the Christian sort of power as being destructive of what he conceives to be the only true kind of life.[1]   He hates Christianity, in other words, not because it is weak or deceitful, but because it is dangerous to his own particular conception of what powerful life ought to be.   He hates it—do we not see now?—because it would feign disillusion him as to the value of his foundations.   The history of religion, and especially of Christianity, has given him a poor opinion of human nature, which, as that history shows, has a strong spiritual element ever cropping up, just when our philosopher would have it show the strength of its innate paganism.   This spiritual element scarcely makes human nature a hopeful foundation upon which to build the gigantic figure of the superman.

In spite, however, of his own laments over the failures of ordinary human nature, and his dis-
(iii.) What is illusionment as to its value, Nietzsche
"Natural"? displayed a boundless confidence in the Natural Man. With all this in his mind to daunt him, he set the fashion (nowadays increasingly popular) of taking for granted that human nature, in its natural state with all its primitive instincts unchecked, can safely cut a pathway for itself to a supreme destiny. One can understand this point of view in our shallow optimists of to-day; but how was it possible in one who took such a dark view of history as Nietzsche did? The real reason is that he had ruled out the whole

---

[1] "After all the question is, to what *end* are falsehoods perpetrated?   The fact that, in Christianity, 'holy' ends are entirely absent, constitutes no objection to the means it employs.   Its ends are only *bad* ends. . . ." *The Antichrist*, by F. Nietzsche (English trans., by A. M. Ludovici, § 56, p. 214; T. N. Foulis).

spiritual side of man's nature as a diseased growth. If, then, he had allowed himself to mistrust the "natural" element he would have been obliged to give up his foundations, the only material left for him to build upon ; and, to do him justice, he did believe in them in spite of himself. He could not allow the dualism of human nature as portrayed by St. Paul or even by Plato ; he could not permit himself to acknowledge the struggle of flesh and spirit ; to do so would have been fatal to his whole position. He therefore assumed human nature to be one and simple; he took for granted that it is a harmonious entity, sure of what is best for itself and right in grasping it, able to correct instinctively any dangerous tendencies. For example, in *Thus Spake Zarathustra*[1] Nietzsche endeavours to show how "voluptuousness, thirst for power, and selfishness," though they have been given a bad name, are really good and human. Voluptuousness, we are told, is a fire to consume the filthy and degraded ;— a poison to the unhealthy, but pure joy and strength to the innocent, a good wine to be used sparingly, a prototype of a higher happiness. Again, thirst for power, the desire of the ego for self-expansion, is a natural instinct. To the hard-hearted, the cruel, and the vain, this instinct for self-expansion may, it is true, become a curse, an increasing hunger for tyranny, cruelty, and vanity. But it is a good thing, for it treads upon all poor-spiritedness. This human pride of spirit exposes all hypocrisy and shallowness as intolerable, and will not rest content with anything crude and premature. It is the human spirit

[1] Bk. iii., "Of the Three Evil Ones" (English trans., Tille, pp. 279–284).

striving after the fullest development of its will-power, and in its march condemning all low, servile, and contemptible standards of life. Nay, more, this desire of self-expansion becomes self-giving ; the ego desires to give of its abundant virtue to others and to bring them up to its level. Once again, selfishness, says Zarathustra, is the virtue of a great soul in a healthy body ; it is opposed to cowardice, to pessimism and mistrustful over-caution, to submissiveness and to patience. The assertion of self is an unqualified good.

In all this the ego is one, as opposed to the distinction between higher and lower, spiritual and natural, which Christianity makes. I have called Nietzsche's conception of human nature that of a harmonious entity in this sense, in that he assumes it to be self-contained and self-sufficing ; within this entity he will not allow of that deep-rooted civil war which St. Paul and St. Augustine found. The passions are to be gloried in, as in the passage from *Zarathustra* summarized above ; not only because they are, strangely enough, pictured as being under control of the ego, though the latter gives them the fullest rein, but also because the strength of the ego is to be measured by the extent to which they are allowed to flourish in richest abundance. This inevitably involves immense inward turmoil ; and Nietzsche does not shrink from the result, though he would refuse to identify it with the Pauline struggle of flesh and spirit. The distinction here made is very important. The Christian conceives of the higher self waging war to the death against the lower self ; and the end he looks for is the peace of victory, when the higher self alone is left. Nietzsche, on the other hand, conceives of the passions as being like a pack of hounds full of life and energy, jostling one another in their fullness of health and vigour, but only needing a firm whip-hand to direct all their energies into the right channels. For example, he says : " A man is productive only in so far as he is rich in contrasted instincts ; he can remain young only on condition that his soul does not begin to take things easy and to yearn for peace. Nothing has grown more alien to us than that old desire—'the peace of the soul,' which is the aim of Christianity. Nothing could make us less envious than the moral cow . . . the man who has renounced war has renounced a grand life."[1] We may pass by for the present his idea that "peace of the soul" is a sort of spiritual vacuum ;[2] the point he fails to see is that both the Christian and the Nietzschean have an inward turmoil going on in the soul. In the case of the Christian, it is a war in which the real ego of the man grows stronger daily in the fight against hostile influences, and thereby gains the peace, not of vacuity, but of victory ; although of course only progressively, for there is no expectation of a final and absolute state of peace this side of death. The turmoil in the soul of the Nietzschean, however, appears to have nothing either reasonable or hopeful about it ; for, the more conflicting elements there are, the better. Here there can be no unification by victory of spirit over flesh. The menagerie of motives and desires is obliged to keep company to the end ; whilst the restraints, which alone

---

[1] *The Twilight of the Idols*, by F. Nietzsche (English trans. by A. M. Ludovici, pp. 28, 29 ; T. N. Foulis).
[2] See Chapter VI., where this point is dealt with.

prevent an internecine conflict between them, are increasingly liable to break down. There is no hierarchy of values which may bring order by determining what may be pruned out, or subordinated; all must be allowed to flourish together, for all are manifestations of "life," sacred materials, of which Nature may be safely trusted to make good use. It is owing to this conception of human nature as being at its best when it is like a wild, over-luxuriant garden, that Nietzsche is so opposed to all idea of morality as controlling human life. Yet here as elsewhere he has displayed extraordinary inconsistency. In one passage he actually points out the amount of good which the world has derived from the principles of moral discipline. He says:—
"In contrast to *laisser-aller*, every system of morals is a sort of tyranny against 'nature' and also against 'reason'; that is, however, no objection, unless one should again decree, by some system of morals, that all kinds of tyranny and unreasonableness are unlawful. What is essential and invaluable in every system of morals, is that it is a long constraint. In order to understand Stoicism, or Port-Royal, or Puritanism, one should remember the constraint under which every language has attained to strength and freedom. . . . How much trouble have the poets and orators of every nation given themselves! . . . 'from submission to arbitrary laws,' as the anarchists say, and thereby fancy themselves 'free,' even free-spirited. The singular fact remains, however, that everything of the nature of freedom, elegance, boldness, dance, and masterly certainty, which exists or has existed, whether it be in thought itself or in administration, or in speaking

and persuading, in art just as in conduct, has only developed by means of the tyranny of such arbitrary law; and in all seriousness, it is not at all improbable that precisely this is 'nature' and 'natural' and not *laisser-aller*! . . . The essential thing 'in heaven and earth' is, apparently (to repeat it once more), that there should be long *obedience* in the same direction; there thereby results and has always resulted in the long run, something which has made life worth living; for instance virtue . . . reason, spirituality. . . . Slavery, both in the coarser and the finer sense, is apparently an indispensable means even of spiritual education and discipline. One may look at every system of morals in this light: it is 'nature' therein which teaches to hate the *laisser-aller*, the too great freedom, and implants the need for . . . immediate duties."[1] The whole of this passage is a very grave admission on the part of one who spent his life in warring against the whole idea of morality as a bad dream, alien to nature and subversive of man's true welfare. Nietzsche cannot have it both ways; if he was really prepared to stand by the passage just quoted, then his whole theory of human nature as self-contained and unified, as free from fundamental dualism, must fall to the ground. He in no way betters his case by declaring that this necessity of moral discipline is "natural" or implanted in us by nature; for it is in flat contradiction to his whole theory of nature in man, as for example in the passage from *Zarathustra* referred to above.[2] If

---

[1] *Beyond Good and Evil*, by F. Nietzsche (English trans. by Helen Zimmern, § 188, pp. 106–109; T. N. Foulis).

[2] p. 33.

it is of nature and natural, then there are two sorts
of nature in man after all (as Christians contend),
the "natural" and the "spiritual," and this on
Nietzsche's own showing; or else we must say, as
was said at the beginning,[1] that in the passage to
Beyond-man Nietzsche leaves his own foundation,
the purely "natural" man, because it is altogether
unable to bear the weight of the superstructure.
It is perhaps worth while to draw attention to the
concluding sentence of the section quoted above.
It is as follows: "'Thou must obey someone, and for
a long time; otherwise thou wilt come to grief, and
lose all respect for thyself'—this seems to me to be
the moral imperative of nature, . . . nor does it
address itself to the individual (what does nature
care for the individual!) but to nations, races, ages,
and ranks, above all, however, to the animal 'man'
generally, to *mankind*." This conclusion of the
sentence is a characteristically Nietzschean way of
trying to minimize his own concessions to the
enemy. Whenever the lower selfish side of the
individual is under consideration, he assumes that
it has the fullest right to be intensely individualistic; but when he is advocating obedience, this
would not do; it would be too unpleasantly like the
voice of "conscience" to make it so personal; and
so obedience is to be a general impersonal virtue
for nations, races, ages, and ranks. But "above all"
let us note that it applies "to the animal 'man'" and
(again as a minimizing afterthought) "generally to
mankind." So "the animal 'man'" must set about
learning to obey, in order that the more individualistic
superman may be born into a world where he need

[1] pp. 24, 29.

not obey. But let us notice carefully how this separates man from superman. The latter is in truth " beyond man," so much so that the whole race of man, it would seem, including the Nietzscheans, must practise "obedience" and the entire range of servile virtues before this new race can be born.

It has been said that Nietzsche assumed human nature to be a harmonious entity, self-contained, and free from the dualism of flesh and spirit ;—an assumption which was necessary, on account of his wholesale rejection of religious psychology. We have, however, seen that this is seriously inconsistent with his recognition of the necessity of discipline. Moreover, Nietzsche was intensely aware of some sort of struggle of different forces within the individual ; his whole idea of human life worthily lived is one of struggle and stress. He conceived of personality as composed of manifold forces, all rich in exuberant life ; and, though all contained within the one harmonious entity, yet requiring much delicate handling if Nature is to make use of them all. But he went even further than this. In his attempt to reconstruct the origins of morality, Nietzsche gave a large place to the love of cruelty which he supposed to be ingrained in primitive man.[1] Much of our moral outfit he held to be due to the fact that this primeval love of cruelty was in course of time turned inwards, so that it became a love of internal cruelty against oneself. He considered that Christian asceticism is an extreme development of this internal cruelty. Yet he by no means identified the two ; in many places he speaks as if this love of cruelty against oneself were a more or less uni-

[1] See especially *A Genealogy of Morals*, Essay II.

versal phenomenon, and he even admits that it has a certain value.[1] Now this (as the passage quoted in the note below clearly shows) amounts to an acknowledgment that by the strain of suffering and discipline some higher element in human nature may be called into activity to conquer the mere animal fear of pain. This, again, involves a warfare within the man, in which one element must seek to conquer another element for the sake of the personality as a whole. In one passage, indeed, his whole view of human nature approaches so closely to the Pauline doctrine of "flesh" and "spirit" that it is worth examining. This passage is to be found in his *Beyond Good and Evil*.[2] After speaking of the "cruel wild beast" which still remains in our civilisation, *i.e.* the love of cruelty, he turns to the enjoyment which is to be found "in causing one's own suffering." He finds this, not only in the practice of religion, but also in every seeker after knowledge :—" Even the seeker of knowledge operates as an artist and glorifier of cruelty, in that he compels his spirit to perceive *against* its own inclination and often enough against the wishes of his heart :—he forces it to say 'Nay,'

[1] Such a passage as *Dawn of Day*, by F. Nietzsche (English trans. by J. M. Kennedy, pp. 116 foll., § 114 ; T. N. Foulis), is significant in this connection. Describing the effect of sickness upon the mind of the invalid, he says : " He experiences delight in conjuring up this contempt [of the comfortable life of the healthy man] and thus inflicting the bitterest sufferings upon his soul : it is by this counterpoise that he bears up against physical suffering. . . . In one terrible moment of clearsightedness he says to himself, ' Be for once thine own accuser and hangman ; for once regard thy suffering as a punishment which thou hast inflicted on thyself ! Enjoy thy superiority as a judge ; better still, enjoy thine own will and pleasure, thy tyrannical arbitrariness ! Raise thyself above thy life as above thy suffering . . .'"

[2] *Beyond Good and Evil*, by F. Nietzsche (English trans., pp. 176–181, §§ 229, 230 ; T. N. Foulis).

where he would like to affirm, love, and adore;
indeed, every instance of taking a thing profoundly
and fundamentally is a violation, an intentional in-
juring of the fundamental will of the spirit, which
instinctively aims at appearance and superficiality,—
even in every desire for knowledge there is a drop
of cruelty." The "fundamental will of the spirit"
here spoken of is the untrained ego which, as we
have already seen, is elsewhere represented as self-
contained and trustworthy.[1] In this passage we are
told that it must be thwarted and contradicted; it
is to be compelled "*against* its own inclination,"
because that inclination, if followed, leads to mere
superficiality. We pass now to § 230,[2] where he
comes still nearer to the Christian conception of a
duality in human nature. For our present purpose
it does not matter that in this section the "fundamental will of the spirit" has changed its colour
somewhat, and has passed from being something to
be controlled and chastened into being the actual
controlling and regulating principle, the central pivot
of the personality. This is a natural confusion in
Nietzsche because the ego in his individual is such
a blurred and motley thing. But the point of importance is that in this section he develops the whole
antagonism within human nature until he actually
admits the existence of two opposing principles.
He says:—"That imperious something which is
popularly called 'the spirit' wishes to be master
internally and externally, and to feel itself master;
it has the will of a multiplicity for a simplicity. . . .
The power of the spirit to appropriate foreign elements reveals itself in a strong tendency . . . to

[1] See pp. 33, 34, above.　　　　[2] *Op. cit.*, p. 178.

simplify the manifold, to overlook or repudiate the absolutely contradictory. . . . *This same will has at its service an apparently opposed impulse of the spirit*,[1] a suddenly adopted preference of ignorance, of arbitrary shutting out, a closing of windows, an inner denial of this or that, a prohibition to approach, a sort of defensive attitude against much that is knowable, a contentment with obscurity, with the shutting-in horizon, an acceptance and approval of ignorance. . . ." And again :—" *Counter to this* propensity for appearance, for simplification, . . . there operates the sublime tendency of the man of knowledge, which takes, and *insists* on taking, things profoundly, variously, and thoroughly ; as a kind of cruelty of the intellectual conscience and taste, which every courageous thinker will acknowledge in himself, provided, as it ought to be, that he has sharpened and hardened his eye sufficiently long for introspection, and is accustomed to severe discipline and even severe words." He goes on to assure us that this heroic side of man's nature has no moral value, because it is only the innate love of cruelty coming out. This is the usual minimizing postscript, which does not diminish the significance of the passage quoted. Here we have two tendencies in human nature fundamentally opposed to one another ; the one is the spirit of gravity, by virtue of which we seek after and possess reality ; the other is the spirit of superficiality, which requires a severe chastening and discipline. One cannot help comparing all this with the latter half of *Thus Spake Zarathustra*, especially Book III., where the dualism of life's outlook is very strongly marked. Zarathustra desires

---

[1] The italics are mine here.

to be optimistic and to think only of the glorious approach of the superman ; but again and again a spirit of gravity oppresses him ; he wrestles with it, he denounces it, but all to no purpose. He desires to believe only in the great ascent of man ; but the thought of the Eternal Return comes back again and again, like a nightmare, to haunt him.

" . . . Thus my foot forced its way upwards.

" Upwards—in defiance of the spirit drawing it downwards into the abyss—the spirit of gravity, my devil and arch-enemy.

" Upwards—although that spirit sat upon me, half a dwarf, half a mole ; lame ; laming ; dropping lead through mine ear, thoughts as heavy as drops of lead into my brain.

" . . . His silence pressed me down ; and being thus by twos, verily, one is lonelier than being by one ! " [1]

We have now seen how the Natural Man becomes shaped into something very like a moral being, in whom is waged the perpetual conflict of flesh and spirit, energy and sloth, optimism and pessimism. Starting from the conception of a unity, we soon find that what we are invited to contemplate is in reality a manifoldness, striving hard to attain unity by way of a severe and prolonged disciplinary struggle ; whilst at times the whole thin disguise of realised harmony is broken through, and the struggle is seen to be a battle between opposing forces. Moreover, one is obliged to ask next, What is the value of this struggle ?—For, throughout his writings, Nietzsche is at pains to empty the concept of personality of all meaning and value. Free-will is

[1] *Thus Spake Zarathustra*, Part III. (English trans. by A. Tille, pp. 227, 228).

a superstition; Nature has nothing to say to the individual.[1] In spite of all his glorified egoism, the Nietzschean is less of a man than the Christian, for all his heroic striving is merely the work of Nature in him; he has no real say in the matter, for he possesses no conscience or power of choice, and therefore cannot be held responsible. "People speak of the 'combat of motives,'" he remarks, "but they designate by this expression that which is not a combat of motives at all"; he proceeds to de-personalise the whole combat, and then to express the conviction that possibly the whole world is governed by chance and hazard—"possibly there is neither will nor aim, and we may only have imagined these things." He does not say free-will, for it is an axiom in his system that our wills are not free; but possibly they are not worthy of being called wills at all. Possibly they do not exist, and we have read them into a world of universal hazard, where "the dice-box of chance" is perpetually shaken by "iron hands of necessity."[2] It is necessary to refer to these fatalistic presuppositions, because one may suppose that people have been largely attracted to this system by its promise of greater individuality, of an enlarged self. The master-morality is welcomed, because it seems likely to develop the will and give it a wider sphere of power. Christianity, on the other hand, with its frank recognition of

---

[1] *Cf.* p. 38 above: "What does Nature care for the individual!" and, *Dawn of Day*, by F. Nietzsche (English trans. by J. M. Kennedy, p. 132; T. N. Foulis): "We are really not responsible for our dreams any more than for our waking hours . . . the doctrine of free-will has as its parents man's pride and sense of power! Perhaps I say this too often . . ."

[2] *Ibid.*, pp. 132–137.

dualism in human nature, seems to introduce an unnecessary discord into life, breaking up its unity and creating the weakness of a divided house; whereas the superman, it is presumed, will have a "super-will." Those who think thus should read again the passage quoted above: " Possibly there is neither will nor aim, and we may only have imagined these things." Whatever, then, the will may accomplish is really, quite possibly, a matter of pure chance; in any case it is quite outside the control of the individual. It is difficult to see in what sense there can be any idea of individual progress under these conditions. Yet progress is essential to Nietzsche's whole scheme —not of course social progress, such as the Utilitarians desired, by which all the units of society are made happy,—but race progress in the person of individuals, who, however few in number, sum up in themselves the total advance of mankind—progress therefore of the most individual kind.

All this tends to show that the whole idea of individual progress is really an impossible one to maintain upon naturalistic presuppositions; the higher race cannot be produced by the Natural Man. The truth is, one wants to get away from this perpetual circle of "nature" from which there is no outlet. One may, perhaps, contrast the comparative merits of the Christian and the Nietzschean views of human nature with the help of an illustration. The difference between them is like that between a lake with running water passing through it and a stagnant pool. In the Christian scheme the waters of the fleshly life are kept pure and fresh by the constant inflow of a steady current of spiritual life, as the lake is continually cleansed and its waters renewed by the force of the stream running through it. Thus there is at once progress and simplification, because the higher nature corrects the lower and transforms it. But human nature as Nietzsche would have it (the self-contained entity) is a stagnant pool, a dreary circle with no ingress or egress, because it only contains one principle, the natural. Here the natural self finds itself in charge of a seething world from which there is no outlet; here then no cleansing process can go on, but only the foul fermenting of a multitude of passions. The "fundamental will of the spirit" may have "the will of a multiplicity for a simplicity", but there can be no simplification here, for there is no proper egress through which unhealthy elements can be carried out in an orderly flow. Thus enclosed, the passions of the natural life become destructive, throwing off noisome fumes which poison the surrounding atmosphere; whilst the false glamour of egoism, with its superficial attraction, is but the thin light of an *ignis fatuus* flickering over a scene of desolation and decay.

From this criticism of Nietzsche's material let us now pass to a consideration of the edifice which he sought to build out of it.

It was a habit of this writer to denounce religion, and especially Christianity, because it seemed to him (iv.) The Superman. to be upheld in the interest of world-weariness. Religious people, he thought, were obliged to desire heavenly things because, Difficulties in the Theory. through lack of a healthy, robust spirit, they had no taste for earthly things. "Body-despisers," "preachers of death," "back-worldsmen,"[1] were some of the epithets by which he

[1] See *Thus Spake Zarathustra*, Part I.

sought to show his contempt for this dissatisfaction
with the things of earth. He considered it a slander
upon all that is natural and human; the world is
good as it is, rich in goodness, and we ought to be
gladly content with it. Now if Nietzsche had
adhered to this point of view, he would at least
have been consistent; but his whole doctrine of the
superman nullifies his charge against others, seeing
that it commits him to the same crime himself. If
the world of men is so good, why this need for
a "Beyond-man"? On the one hand he cries,
"Back to the beasts! let us get nearer to the earthy
and the natural"; but on the other hand, if the
purely natural is so good, why this need of progress
to something which has not yet appeared within the
sphere of nature? The answer which Nietzsche had
to give was the Christian answer, little as he realized
it. Nature is incomplete because man is incomplete.
Progress is necessary, because we are dissatisfied
with human nature in its present condition; in all
this, Nietzsche and Christianity are at one. The
superman is a sort of counterfeit of the "spiritual
man," an outcast who repudiates heaven, and yet is
not at home upon earth, because he finds it too small
for him; whereas the spiritual man of Christianity
is equally at home in both. Nietzsche, then, desires
to go "beyond man" because man is a failure, and
must be given up in favour of something entirely
different. Superman is born of a despair over man,
as a new game is attempted by a child, because the
one it has been trying to play is too difficult; the
result is not usually any more satisfactory. Man,
then, is either so little that he is not worthy to endure,
or so big that he is unmanageable; to solve the

difficulty, the imaginary is made to take the place of the real. This, too, is the method of one who hates all idealism and metaphysics.

If now one inquires what method is to be employed in order to ensure the advent of the superman, the answer will hardly increase any one's faith in this doctrine. For in the first place, in order to make any advance at all, the clock of time must be put back two thousand years. The whole history of Christianity and of the European civilization which has accompanied it is, according to Nietzsche, the history of a retrograde movement, which has already enormously delayed the development of the race in the right direction. The nearest approach to the higher order that has yet appeared was far back in the old pagan civilizations; we must, therefore, go back to primitive man and begin again. When this point, however, has been decided, another difficulty presents itself. As we have already seen,[1] this primitive aristocracy, from which so much might have been expected, proved a failure; it was ensnared by Christianity, the first really hostile movement which it met. Moreover, we must not suppose that this happened by chance, through some unlucky accident, which one may hope will not occur again. On the contrary, it was precisely due to the very nature of aristocracy; for in Nietzsche's great and final work, *The Will to Power*, we read as follows:— " How constantly the aristocratic world shears and weakens itself ever more and more! *By means of its noble instincts* it abandons its privileges, and owing to its refined and excessive culture, it takes an interest in the people, the weak, the poor, and

[1] pp. 29–31 above.

the poetry of the lowly," etc.[1] Though he is speaking of the aristocracy of to-day, a Christianized aristocracy, he does not attribute the self-weakening process to their Christianity but to their "noble instincts." Truly this is not very hopeful for the production of the superman. It appears that the very type of man at present most like the higher race is doomed to betray itself habitually (as it has done in the past) by means of its noble instincts; yet these are presumably the very material out of which the super-race is to be developed. Thus the poison will continue to work endlessly; and the superman himself and all his race will similarly betray themselves into the hands of the weak and the botched upon whom they should be trampling. Besides, as the whole process is probably subject to blind chance, how do we know that the arrival of the superman will not be deferred, every time it draws near, by a set-back similar to that given by Christianity? Wise men do not readily consent to spend their life in rolling stones uphill, when it is more than probable that the stone is doomed to roll back every time, before the top can be reached.

Let us pass on now to ask, By what method is the superman to be produced? The answer to this

The Method: Discipline or Breeding? question is as unsatisfactory as everything else in this scheme. We are told that a certain type of virtuous character described as "noble" must be cultivated. But this at once raises another point. How is this noble

---

[1] *The Will to Power*, by F. Nietzsche (English trans. by A. M. Ludovici, § 938, vol. ii. pp. 351, 352; T. N. Foulis). The italics are my own.

type of character to be promoted?—to this question at least two answers are given, by the help of which Nietzsche argues in a circle. First, as we have already seen,[1] his whole system demands discipline. Life is to be hard; "learn to be hard" is the burden of Zarathustra's message to his disciples, or in other words the "noble" virtues must be acquired through long schooling. Besides the passages already examined, which bring out this point, I need only refer to one in *The Will to Power*,[2] where Nietzsche admits the necessity of " $\dot{\epsilon}\gamma\kappa\rho\dot{\alpha}\tau\epsilon\iota\alpha$ and $\ddot{\alpha}\sigma\kappa\eta\sigma\iota\varsigma$," though of course they "are only steps to higher things. Above them stands 'golden Nature.'" But on the very next page we read: "The only nobility is that of birth and blood . . . intellect alone does not ennoble; on the contrary, something is always needed *to ennoble intellect*. What then is needed?— Blood." And again at the end of the next section : "We hold the belief that no morality is possible without good birth."[3] Since, then, "the only nobility is that of birth and blood," it would seem to follow that, if one is of good birth and blood, one need not worry about any disciplinary process; for why should a man take trouble to obtain that which already belongs to him by birth? If, on the other hand, one has not the qualification of "birth and blood," the disciplinary process is useless, for it has no materials upon which to work; "no morality is possible." What then becomes of the whole training of Zara-

[1] See above, pp. 36 ff., and p. 42.
[2] *The Will to Power*, by F. Nietzsche (English trans. by A. M. Ludovici, § 940, vol. ii. p. 352 ; T. N. Foulis).
[3] *Ibid.*, § 943.

thustra's disciples? Either it is superfluous or else it is useless. Again, supposing there is no good blood left—a likely possibility on the Nietzschean view of European civilisation—then nobility of character cannot be inherited. It must be acquired; and this, as we have just seen, Nietzsche declares to be impossible. If, then, one must conclude that the only hope of finding a "bridge to beyond-man" lies in nobility of birth and blood, which cannot be acquired by discipline, the problem becomes one of breeding pure and simple;[1] and in that case Zarathustra was wasting his energies when he broke the Tables of the Mosaic Law and sought to set up New Tables of Virtue; for what have legal codes to do with breeding?[2]

What then was the conception of virtue that Nietzsche had in mind, when he spoke about his The Goal: "nobles" and the cultivation of virtuous nobility? A typical answer to this What is Virtue? ous nobility? A typical answer to this question is to be found in the following passage from *The Will to Power*: "The Noble Man — *Type:* real goodness, nobility, greatness of soul, as the result of vital wealth; which does not give in order to receive—and which has no desire to *elevate* itself by being good; *squandering* is typical of genuine goodness; vital *personal* wealth is its prerequisite."[3] This is called a typical answer, because it does not seem that Nietzsche ever reached anything more definite than this very general, almost

---

[1] Even "breeding" really involves moral discipline (see below, Chapter III. 1.). Nietzsche, however, wished to assume for "good blood" an entirely non-moral origin.

[2] *Thus Spake Zarathustra*, Part III. (English trans., Tille, pp. 292 ff.).

[3] *The Will to Power*, by F. Nietzsche, § 935 ; T. N. Foulis.

vague, outline.   It might have been written by any
religious-minded person, apart from the Nietzschean
presuppositions which lie behind the terminology
used.   For of course "vital wealth" means physiological health and vitality, "the good blood" as the
basis of "nobility"; and, in consequence of this,
progress is not due to the attraction of ideals or to
the desire of attaining moral ends, but is physio-
logically necessary.   But if we make allowance for
such presuppositions, this passage is simply a
statement that virtue is needed, that it can only
be displayed by personality out of a wealth which
is part of its life, and that such personality can
afford to expend itself freely.   All this was known
long before Nietzsche; it is in fact specially characteristic of the teaching of Christianity.

The only real category of virtue with which
Nietzsche himself was satisfied is that which forms
the burden of his later writings—namely, *Power*.
Power *is* virtue; nobility of character is for him in
reality power conscious of superiority and showing
itself genial and generous towards others, simply
because it is self-satisfied and self-contained.   His
four cardinal virtues illustrate the truth of this:
"Honest towards ourselves and to all and everything friendly to us; brave in the face of the
enemy; generous towards the vanquished; polite
at all times: such do the four cardinal virtues wish
us to be." [1]   Now, if these "virtues" are regarded
in the light of Nietzsche's writings as a whole,
"honesty" to self and friends is revealed as merely
the self-interest of power; in the same way

[1] *The Dawn of Day*, by F. Nietzsche (English trans., § 556;
T. N. Foulis).

"bravery" in the face of the enemy is the self-assertion of power; "generosity" to the vanquished is the contemptuous indifference of power towards weakness, when the latter does not provide good enough sport; "politeness" is either the geniality of animal spirits which power is able to squander without inconvenience, or else the self-interested caution shown towards equals in power. It may, perhaps, be said that this is not a fair treatment of four good pagan virtues which Nietzsche would fain make room for in his new tables. Just so; but the point is that, in so far as he allows these virtues to retain any moral colouring in his scheme, they are completely at variance with his supreme standard of egoistic power. If he intended them to have the significance which has been given to them above, then they are simply manifestations of non-moral power; if, on the other hand, he did not mean this, but something more human, he brought in another standard of value quite different from that of the Will-to-power. If honesty to self and others, and bravery against enemies, are not purely egoistic, then they are something like the Christian love of the higher self and of the neighbour to whom that self is inseparably linked. Again, if generosity and politeness are not due to contempt or self-interest, they are due to a real respect for other individuals, such as that which is specially characteristic of Christianity and entirely opposed to the Will-to-power philosophy.

Thus the whole search for virtue resolves itself into the command "Be Powerful." The New Tables of Zarathustra (which were discreetly left blank by that prophet, after all his destructive work) might be filled in with these two words, which sum up Nietzsche's doctrine of values in his later works. Yet when one asks, "How are we to become Powerful?" only two answers have been given, and they are mutually destructive. One must, on the one hand, be born noble, for nothing avails without that; and one must also acquire power by moral discipline. Thus the whole highway to the superman crumbles to pieces under examination.

When the Higher Race has come, what will the new order of things be like? Society will be like
The New a pyramid. On the lowest level will be
Order:
a Slave Foun- a great slave-population; next to them
dation. a middle-class mediocrity of commerce; and above that again a small and select aristocracy, the new race of the superman. Each class will trample upon the one below it. But, lest by this means the lower ranks should gradually be crushed and their life extinguished—in which case the pyramid would tumble down—they will be held together by a slave-morality of the Christian type,[1] which is thus strangely enough conceived of as promoting life, nay, indirectly even the life of the superman. Thus a certain utility is found for the slave-morality which ought not to be overlooked; it is apparently necessary to the existence even of the superman. This is a matter upon which Nietzsche seems to have left statements which may well appear mutually contradictory. As will be shown in a later chapter,[2] he saw a Will-to-power at work in Christianity which is really a Will-to-nothing. But, from the passages referred to above, it is clear that he also

[1] *The Will to Power*, by F. Nietzsche (English trans., vol. i. pp. 107, 323; T. N. Foulis).
[2] Chapter VI. § (ii.), pp. 212 ff., and the note on p. 213.

saw in it a slave-morality which represents the point of view suitable to slaves. By this point of view they may justify their existence ; and in this case there cannot be said to be a Will-to-nothing, but rather a Will-to-power making the best possible use of the worst materials—a will to live and not to die. It is at least clear that Nietzsche does not desire the extinction of the slave-race; for they provide materials which make the life of the superman possible. Thus he says :—" We take care to support the religions and the morality which we associate with the gregarious instinct ; for, by means of them, an order of men is, so to speak, being prepared, which must at some time or other fall into our hands, which must actually *crave* for our hands. Beyond Good and Evil,—certainly ; but we insist upon the unconditional and strict preservation of herd-morality."[1] For what reason ? Clearly to make men serviceable slaves.[2]

But not only does the superman require the slave-morality to provide him with good slaves. He has also himself to imbibe a little Christianity in order to climb to the top of the pyramid. In *The Genealogy of Morals* we learn that the "nobles" have two standards of conduct, one for use amongst them-

---

[1] *Will to Power*, by F. Nietzsche, i. p. 107 ; T. N. Foulis.

[2] *Cf. Will to Power* (English trans., vol. i. p. 323), a very significant passage in which he puts a mark of interrogation to his whole system :—" Is there not perhaps a stronger guarantee of life and of the species in this victory of the weak and the mediocre ? . . . Suppose the *strong* were masters in all respects, even in valuing : let us try and think what their attitude would be towards illness, suffering, and sacrifice ! *Self-contempt on the part of the weak* would be the result ; they would do their utmost to disappear and to extirpate their kind. And would this be *desirable* ?—should we really like a world in which the subtlety, the consideration, the intellectuality, the *plasticity*—in fact the whole influence of the weak—was lacking ? " A note added to this by the translator (A. M. Ludovici) shows that the passage gives him some uneasiness.

selves, and the other for their dealings with the slaves. Amongst their equals they are social, whereas to all others they are individualists: "Those very men, who by manners, reverence, usage, gratitude, and still more by mutual superintendence, by jealousy *inter pares*, are rigorously held within bounds, and who on the other hand, in their conduct among one another prove themselves so inventive in regardfulness, self-restraint, delicacy, faith, pride and friendship,—these same men are towards that which is without . . . not so much better than so many disencaged beasts of prey. Here they enjoy liberty from all social restraint ; the wilderness must compensate them for the tension produced by a long incarceration and impalement in the 'peace' of society. . . ."[1] Nietzsche pictures his "nobles" as being naturally lonely, loving isolation and antagonism rather than to herd together like slaves. Loneliness is as characteristic of the strong as herding is of the weak. But in their war against the slave-races they are obliged to combine together, against their natural instincts; "whenever the former [the nobles] enter into alliance with one another they do so . . . solely for the purpose of joint action and aggression. . . ."[2] Thus they conquer the world by making common cause. In other words, they find a little Christian altruism absolutely necessary to bolster up their otherwise helpless egoism. The noble cannot reach his true life without this device. He must "herd" in order to conquer the slaves ; but slaves are so called largely

[1] *A Genealogy of Morals*, I. p. 38 (English trans., edited by A. Tille).
[2] *Ibid.*, III. p. 185.

because they herd; so that the noble has, by his method of conquering them, relinquished his noble characteristics and become slavish; he must become a common man in order to reach the fruits of his nobility. Altruistic morality, then, is found to be the means by which the superman attains his position at the top of the pyramid; and at the same time it is the one thing which holds together the foundations upon which that exalted position rests.

Notwithstanding all this, however, when the race of the superman has come, it must still live under the Loneliness and principle of individualism: "The first Decay. condition which an aristocratic society must have in order to maintain a high degree of freedom among its members is that extreme tension which arises from the presence of the most *antagonistic* instincts in all its units: from their will to dominate. . . ."[1] And so the final act of the drama unfolds itself at the top of the pyramid. A pyramid must have an apex; there must be civil war amongst the race of the superman in order that one may dominate; for a will to dominate is in them all, which will not rest until one remains victorious and alone,—*the* superman.[2] And then what will *he* do? He will be lonely, which is what his race always desired; but perhaps his excessive loneliness will pall![3] At any rate we are told that nowadays man

[1] *The Will to Power*, by F. Nietzsche (§ 936; T. N. Foulis).
[2] I do not know that Nietzsche ever stated this; but it is the only possible conclusion of his system. Further, the lonely superman provides the necessary link between the race of supermen and the fatal equilibrium, which necessitates the Eternal Return.
[3] Paulsen has some useful remarks upon this point (*System of Ethics*, English trans., p. 152).

has become a wearisome object just because there is no longer anything to fear in him; that we have become tired of "man" since the disappearance of the "nobles."[1] But when the revived aristocracy has itself been trampled upon by the all-conquering superman, this nausea of contempt for ordinary humanity will be tenfold more unbearable to one so far superior. Moreover, he will have no more material upon which to exercise his powers; for there will no longer be any who are worthy to be his rivals, since all will be grovelling victims of the herd-morality beneath his feet. "The first condition of a high degree of freedom" will have gone.[2] The superman, then, it would seem, must lose his freedom in this intolerable solitude. He will be like a gladiator in corpulent old age with his muscles running to seed for lack of training; he will resemble those modern millionaires who, having spent their lives in amassing the means of possessing comfort and luxury, find themselves by their very life-training unfitted to enjoy it when it is within their grasp. Thus the gigantic egoism of the superman, having no more food for its all-devouring maw, must pass into decay.

So we are brought at last to what is, perhaps, the most amazing feature of all in this system—the conception of the Eternal Return. Apart from this it might be said that the whole superman philosophy was simply a wild romance, created by superficial optimism; but with this doctrine a deeply tragic note is struck. There is nothing more moving than the struggle revealed in Nietzsche's biography—the struggle between the two conflicting

(v.) The Eternal Return.

[1] *A Genealogy of Morals*, i. (English trans., pp. 41–43).
[2] See the quotation from *The Will to Power* above.

ideas of the Superman and the Eternal Return. In *Thus Spake Zarathustra* we watch the struggle growing to a head. The cheerful belief in progress which he seeks to maintain is always undermined by the haunting uncertainty as to the final goal. The superman is the creation of the artist who desires life in all its beauty and richness to grow ; *pereat veritas fiat vita.* But the philosopher could not rest satisfied with this result. One gathers that Nietzsche had intended to bring Zarathustra's wanderings to a close with a triumphant scene in which the people were to accept his New Tables of Morality.[1] But his intellectual honesty could not suffer this to be. Instead of it, the climax of the book really lies in his passionate acceptance of the Eternal Recurrence of all things, in the midnight song of Eternity.[2] This idea, which at first seemed

[1] See his biography.

[2] The growth of the doctrine of the Eternal Return in Nietzsche's mind is most vividly set forth in Part III. of *Thus Spake Zarathustra.* Driven forth by a Voice (end of Part II.), Zarathustra goes out into loneliness to muster courage to declare his whole prophecy, its darker as well as its brighter side. The spirit of gravity besets him in the shape of a dwarf by whom he is compelled to face the truth of the Eternal Return (English trans., edited by A. Tille, pp. 227 ff.). Immediately he sees a vision of a shepherd bitten by a snake (p. 232), which he understands to be himself labouring under the new-found and dangerous knowledge of the Eternal Return (*cf.* p. 325). At length, after all the old values have been spurned and broken (pp. 292–320) under the inspiration of his faith in the Superman to come, the dark truth comes once more before him demanding acceptance.

"Everything goeth, everything returneth. Forever rolleth the wheel of existence. Everything dieth, everything blossometh again. Forever runneth the years of existence.

"Everything breaketh, everything is joined anew. Forever the same house of existence buildeth itself. All things separate, all things greet each other again. Forever faithful unto itself the ring of existence remaineth."

"Alas, man recurreth eternally ! The small man recurreth eternally. . . That was my satiety of all existence "(pp. 324–327).

so intolerable, finally succeeded in fascinating
him :—

"I lay in sleep, in sleep :—From deep dream I woke to light.
The world is deep,—And deeper than ever day thought it might.
Deep is its woe,—And deeper still than woe—delight.
Saith woe : ' Pass, go !' Eternity's sought by all delight—
Eternity deep—by all delight ! " [1]

For what is this eternity of return ?   Is it not simply
the recurrence of Life unceasingly ?—that life which
he had loved so passionately,[2] that life of seeking
and striving and longing, and throwing dice with
gods for new values, and dancing after virtue, and
breaking all obsolete things?   If life is good[3] in
spite of all its ills, then the recurrence of life must
be good, though it means also a perpetual recurrence of decay.   Thus life and truth are reconciled.
This was a grand attempt to make the best of
things ; for the fact remains that in Nietzsche's
scheme life *must* wane and decay as soon as it
attains its full fruit.   He did not believe with the
utilitarians that the final resting-place of life is to be
found in an equilibrium ; nothing could have been
more distasteful to him than such an idea—for would
it not be " the peace of the moral cow " ?   Nor was
he ensnared by Herbert Spencer's device of a
"moving equilibrium," which would give all the
advantages of freedom from struggle without the
accompanying decay and death to which science
points.   Even Spencer was obliged to admit that
the "moving equilibrium " must at length become a
perfect equilibrium, static, and therefore already

---

[1] *Thus Spake Zarathustra*, pp. 339–340.
[2] See *The Second Dance-Song* (*ibid.*, pp. 335–340).
[3] *Cf.* what has been said under § 1. (i.) of this chapter.

hastening to its destruction.[1] So it was that Nietzsche in his stern pursuit of truth was driven to the idea of an eternal recurrence.[2] After all, life is not pursuing a permanent pathway of progress upwards, but rather describing an eternal circle; ascent is followed by descent and by return to the original starting-point.

What value, then, is left in the superman ideal? As we have seen, Nietzsche was driven to seek its value in the thought that there is a perpetual recurrence of the *ascent* of life; the decay which follows is necessary in order that the upward process may be enjoyed again. This, however, is to turn progress into a mere means to enjoyment. It no longer has any significance in itself; life becomes a vast Epicurean orgy, arranged for utilitarian purposes to minister to our pleasure. But pleasure, as the ultimate aim of existence, was to Nietzsche the heresy of heresies, the one inexcusable superstition which he conceived to be the special portion of Christians and Utilitarians! It is, then, hard to believe that he could have got any real satisfaction out of the practical destruction of his ideal

[1] W. R. Sorley, *The Ethics of Naturalism*, p. 257 (2nd edition).

[2] The struggle is represented in *Thus Spake Zarathustra* as the bitterness of a choice between two much-loved women, Life and Wisdom (pp. 338 ff.); then the situation changes, and the solution appears. Not Life in herself, but Eternity (which includes Life), is the one to be loved. Thus does Wisdom teach :—

"Oh! how could I fail to be eager for eternity, and for the marriage-ring of rings, the ring of recurrence?

"Never yet have I found the woman by whom I should have liked to have children, unless it be this woman I love.

" For I love thee, O Eternity !
For I love thee, O Eternity ! "

of progress, the one idol which he passionately
cherished.

It is significant that the intensely serious optimism
of this thinker should have broken down. From
Schopenhauer he learnt that life is serious; but he
utterly repudiated that philosopher's negative conclusions.[1] The positive assertion of life according
to the measure of the Natural Man has never been
more passionately preached; and yet (if this analysis
of his gospel has been at all near the truth) the
whole of it is deeply involved in inconsistencies,
marred by uncertainty of attainment, and darkened
by a strong note of pessimism. Nietzsche is, indeed,
rightly classed amongst the pessimistic philosophers.
In his biography we learn that his life was noticeable for its lack of joy. He struggled on manfully,
sometimes finding it necessary to assume an artificial
gaiety. He admitted that there should be a motive
for gaiety, yet he could find none. He felt the
absolute necessity for a self-made optimism, if only
to stave off Christianity, the consolation, as he
held, of weak pessimists. And yet in his case, in
spite of a brave attempt, the Natural Man failed to
provide the hopeful solution which he desired.

II

The poet John Davidson may perhaps be thought
to have held views so extreme as to be hardly worth
serious consideration. It is, however,
John Davidson.
necessary to say something about him
at this point; for he provides a fitting appendix
to all that has been said about the inconsistencies
inherent in Nietzsche's system. He has himself

[1] See above, § (i.).

seen these inconsistencies clearly and repudiated
them, just because he holds the same naturalistic
point of view as Nietzsche. This is what he has
to say on the subject :—

> " He posed as Zoroaster, and led us back
> To Dionysos : not our mark at all ;
> The past is past. And, for his prophecy ?—
> Why, Florimund, this Nietzsche was a Christian ;
> And that transvaluation of all values
> Was neither more nor less than transmutation
> Of transubstantiation :—grin, but grasp it :—
> His Antichrist is Christ, whose body and blood
> And doctrine of miraculous rebirth,
> Became the Overman : Back-of-beyond,
> Or—what's the phrase ?—Outside good-and-evil :
> That's his millennium, and we'll none of it.
> I want the world to be much more the world ;
> Men to be men ; and women, women—all
> Adventure, courage, instinct, passion, power." [1]

He denies everything which Nietzsche cherished
most. The latter believed in "progress," "the
future of the race," "Beyond-man"; but these are
all otherworldly ideas borrowed from Christianity.
We are not here to scheme for others who will
come after us, but to eat and drink, for to-morrow
we die. The individual must be our supreme care.
We are not to worry ourselves about the future of
society; the individual must seek to sate himself in
pleasure and selfishness, no matter what happens
to society. We are not to trouble about either
past or future, but simply to revel in the present.
Again, Nietzsche was a moralist hunting for a new

---

[1] *The Triumph of Mammon*, Act V. Scene 1 (p. 103), by John
Davidson (Grant Richards). The play is the first of a trilogy
entitled *God and Mammon*, in which the hero King Mammon
(representing the author's point of view) overthrows Christianity
in his native land, and expounds his own philosophy.

ethical code ; but Davidson has done with morals absolutely :—

> " A sense of sin is rust : go on to sin,
> And make the sense of it a constant joy :
> The sin's the man ; keep your soul bright with sin." [1]

Nietzsche made a careful distinction between the Evil and the Bad ; he would have his nobles refrain from the mean and petty sorts of wrong-doing, such as those which spring from resentment. But Davidson declares that no system of ethics can hope to live which does not minister to man's vanity and to his malice.[2] His hero King Mammon is crafty, malicious, and revengeful, torturing feeble old men, instead of keeping his blows for his equals, and not hesitating to wrong his best friends behind their backs. Again, Nietzsche pursued virtue and despised pleasure when sought for its own sake ; Davidson boldly declares for pleasure and mocks at virtue. The latter plays the Epicurean to the former's Stoic. But whilst Davidson thus shows us the weak spots in Nietzsche's philosophy, he cannot escape the very same charge of inconsistency which he thus levels against another. This comes out very clearly in his treatment of sex problems. In his *Testament of John Davidson* he declares virginity, and the age-long reverence shown for it by pagans and Christians alike, to be the greatest curse on earth. Moreover, since he makes no theoretical distinction between noble vices and those which are merely sordid, between the Evil and the Bad, one would think that—approaching this subject from the

[1] *Mammon and his Message*, Act I. Scene 3 (p. 22). This is the second part of the trilogy.
[2] See the epilogue to *Mammon and his Message*.

standpoint of extreme individualism, and the glorification of the bestial side of human nature—he would feel obliged to set no bounds to licentiousness. It is with considerable surprise, therefore, that one reads Act II. Scene 1 of *Mammon and his Message*. For in this passage King Mammon gathers the harlots of his capital into a hall and actually upbraids them for their sins in almost Christian tones. He bids them become pure, marry, and have children. He finds fault with them on the ground that their childlessness does injury to the world as he conceives it. But this is to revert to the Nietzschean ideal of seeking the welfare of the race and its future. He bids them sacrifice their individual inclination for the sake of others :—

> "Your cruellest pain is when you think of all
> The honied treasure of your bodies spent
> And no new life to show. O then you feel
> How people lift their hands against themselves,
> And taste the bitterest of the punishment
> Of those whom pleasure isolates. Sometimes
> When darkness, silence, and the sleeping world
> Give vision scope, you lie awake and see
> The pale sad faces of the little ones
> Who should have been your children, as they press
> Their cheeks against your windows, looking in
> With piteous wonder, homeless, famished babes,
> Denied your wombs and bosoms."

This is a moving passage, but it is so just because every word of it runs contrary to Davidson's theoretical code. In these few lines he finds it necessary to give up all his principles, in order to cope with one of the darker tragedies of human life. Moreover, in the context from which the above passage is quoted he finds himself falling into the Christian phraseology about "sin" and "sinners,"

5

holding the women responsible for their deeds.   Yet when a little later he corrects himself, he at once loses all ground for his reproaches :—

> "Sisters, I blame you not ; . . .
> I spoke of sin and sinner, using words
> That must be used until the common mind
> Escape from Christendom to the Universe.
> You have no souls, therefore you cannot sin."

Why then were they reproached for following what was to them the easiest path ?   King Mammon proceeds to preach to them his gospel of the Universe, which they cannot appreciate ; and seeing this he cries :—

> "They cannot grasp it, cannot bear to listen.
> The thing I have to tell, unthought before,
> Demands another language, another folk
> Than any earth contains : I fear it . . ."

These last words echo Nietzsche's doctrine of "Beyond-man." The speaker began with high hopes that the most degraded would be the readiest to understand him.

> "Ploughed up and harrowed and manured with sin,
> Their fallow souls are seasoned for my news."

If souls so sinful cannot follow his teaching, what hope is there that any will be found on earth who will respond to it ?   It would seem that the superman is necessary after all.   Then, since his own theories are found unsuitable when brought to a practical test, the king is obliged to fall back once more upon Christian exhortations ; he urges them to be—

> "A virtuous woman scorning man's embrace
> Except with passion and instinctive love,
> Obsequious and fruitful."

In the light of these passages it is hardly necessary to concern ourselves with Davidson's charge that profligacy is the "spirit and corner-stone of Christendom."[1] Only one more point needs to be noted. King Mammon goes on to say :—

> "You must be natural and chaste; like beasts,
> Unconsciously, devoutly bent on offspring."

Now, whenever the word *natural* is used by this class of writer one looks at once for utter confusion of thought; and one finds it here. In order to illustrate what he means by a chastity which is "natural," that is, instinctive,[2] this writer is obliged to go outside of human nature altogether, and refer to what, as he himself would admit, is a more primitive and rudimentary form of life. The necessity of going "back to the beast" is significant; it implies that chastity is not "natural" for normal human nature in the instinctive manner of animals; and the proof of this lies in the fact that Mammon finds it necessary to remonstrate with human beings for not being "natural." This plea to return to what is "natural" involves a strong assumption of the unreliability of human nature, which, as we have seen, was the real ground of Nietzsche's desire for the evolution of a higher race. Elsewhere Davidson uses the same plea of being "natural" as the justification of every kind of cruelty, perfidy, and anti-social conduct. Why too, after all, should his King Mammon be so anxious for the health and happiness of these poor women, and their becoming mothers of children, when the supreme principle of his life is belief in self and con-

---

[1] *Mammon and his Message*, p. 35 (immediately following the passage last quoted).
[2] *Cf.* line 9 of the same page.

tempt for all else, when murder is his daily amuse-
ment, and the well-being and worth of other lives
therefore count for nothing in his scheme of things?
If Nietzsche is to be condemned for subordinating
pleasure to the future of the race, then why not add
debauchery to the list of vices already practised?
For since, in this writer's eyes, it is only the
"present" enjoyment of the individual that matters,
the consequent deterioration of the race need not
have weighed upon his mind.

The argument of this chapter would seem to show
that the standpoint of individualism is an impossible
one to maintain.   It refuses to take account of the
facts of human nature : it ignores the social instinct,
so firmly planted in man.   We may, then, safely
set it aside in favour of some less radical solution of
the problem of conduct.

CHAPTER III

FROM writers whose principles of conduct are avowedly individualistic let us now pass on to examine two who, while frankly naturalistic in their presuppositions, come much nearer in spirit to the Christian standpoint.

I

It was pointed out in the first chapter that Mr. Bernard Shaw has close affinities with Nietzsche, Mr. Bernard because their philosophical bases are Shaw. much the same. Moreover, the fact that (i.) General Outlook. Mr. Shaw took up the superman theory has made him seem a close disciple of its originator. But in reality there are very important differences which render necessary a separate discussion of his

[1] The association of this word with those which precede it must not be taken to mean that the author is hereby condemning "Socialism" as a political doctrine. I use the word in a rather broader sense as complementary to "Individualism" in the title of Chapter II. Just as the writers examined in Chapter II. make the worth of all conduct to lie solely in the advantage which accrues to the individual, so the writers to be examined in this chapter make the welfare of society as a whole the objective towards which they would direct our energies, and by this they mean the happiness of *all* the individuals who compose society. The fact that they have moulded their ideas largely along the lines provided by the political Socialism of their day is significant, but it is not in itself my ground for the use of the word in the heading to this chapter.

point of view. The dominant fact about Nietzsche was his individualism; the dominant fact about Mr. Shaw is his socialism. Before the latter became known as a playwright and philosopher, he took an active part in propagating the political doctrine of socialism, which Nietzsche and all his school regard with whole-hearted repugnance, as one of the worst dangers threatening the human race.[1] Like Nietzsche, Mr. Shaw believes that progress is desirable and possible, but in his case it is to be social progress. The race is to be consummated in a social order, not in an individual who has absorbed its goodness into himself; in fact, the progress of the individual is, for him, bound up with that of the social order. Here, altruism is not allowed to be the tool of a devouring egoism;[2] on the contrary, the individual is to serve the best interests of society. So too Mr. Shaw's outlook upon life is far more humane and benevolent than that of Nietzsche. He seeks the happiness of the whole social body. He wants health and wealth for all; the removal of social ills, not by starving out the weak and the unfit, and eliminating them from the scene, but by compassionate care for their ills.[3] He would do away with all suffering, animal as well as human. He will have none of Nietzsche's tirade against

[1] *Cf.* Davidson, *The Triumph of Mammon*, Act V. Scene 1 (p. 116):—

> "This socialism is mere misanthropy
> Erected to a creed; the evil smell
> Of Christendom, long dead and rotten, kept
> In salts and sponges to resuscitate
> The hopes of hungry malice; the fishy glow
> Upon the putrid carcase of religion."

[2] See p. 56 above.
[3] *Cf.* G. K. Chesterton, *George Bernard Shaw*, p. 78.

pity. In short, he does not believe that man is to
follow ruthless " Nature " in casting the feeblest to
the wall for the sake of the strong, but rather that
man is social and that his task is to perfect himself
socially. He does not directly attack the supposition that happiness should be an end in itself, as
Nietzsche does ; he accepts "the greatest happiness
of the greatest number" as the supreme end for
which man should work. He actually became a
playwright by way of social propaganda ; his earliest
plays are tracts advocating social reform.[1] He
wishes the world to look poverty, oppression, and
the crushing of individual life in the face, and to do
away with them.

The possibility of improving human society as a
whole, without throwing over the weaker members,
(ii.) The Mean- would seem to presuppose a high esti-
ing of the mate of the worth of the individual—
Individual. and that in two ways. In the first
place, if the elements in society which appear to be
most useless are to be preserved, there must be
something unique and valuable in human personality
to justify such a course. Secondly, if the open
sores of modern civilization are to be healed, mankind must be acknowledged to possess, somehow
and somewhere, capabilities which show considerable promise of effecting something in the right
direction ; otherwise to hope and work for betterment would be an idle dream. Yet as a matter of
fact Mr. Shaw's estimate of human nature does not
satisfy these expectations. He shares with Nietzsche
and many others a strongly fatalistic standpoint, the
origin of which was traced in Chapter I. In his

[1] *Mrs. Warren's Profession* and *Widowers' Houses.*

earliest plays, referred to just now, which directly
deal with the question of individual responsibility
in its relation to society, the importance of the
individual is reduced to the smallest possible dimensions.   In *Mrs. Warren's Profession*,[1] for example,
the purpose of which is to show up the horrors of
the "white slave traffic," he labours to prove that
the woman responsible for the evil was forced into
her position by circumstances, and that from first
to last she was herself quite as much victimized as
her victims ; and that not by any other person, but
by the state of society and the conditions of her
early life.   This explanation is accepted in the story
by others as a matter of course.   Again, in *Widowers'*
Houses he does well to point out how many respect-
able members of society are living on the rents of
rotten slum houses, which are a plague-spot to the
community.   The conclusion of the matter, however, is not that things must be put right at all costs,
but that no individual, however well-intentioned,
has the power to lift a finger to put them right ;
all must wait with folded hands until some great
change takes place in the conditions of civilized life.
In this respect the position taken up is very similar
to that which one finds in his much later work,
Man and Superman.   "What is wrong with the
poor is their poverty," we are told ; they must be
made well-to-do and comfortable by some new social
device, for one cannot expect them, or anyone else,
as individuals to better their lot.   Machinery is
everywhere advocated as the supreme panacea ;
love working through human personality is of no
account.   There goes with all this a radical disbelief

[1] *Plays Pleasant and Unpleasant*, vol. i. (Constable).

in the power of the individual to free himself from the tyranny of circumstance. He cannot be expected to improve himself; his individuality is static, feeble, unprogressive, in the face of the difficulties of life. And yet the whole burden of Mr. Shaw's message is one which requires forceful and commanding individuality. His whole conception of the meaning of life is that it must be an unceasing struggle[1] on the part of each individual to co-operate in bringing in the better order. So then man, we are told, must struggle; and yet he is too fast-bound in the web of fate to be able to effect anything. All this comes to a climax in *Man and Superman*. Here the Don Juan philosophy is strangely out of place in the midst of a play in which all the leading characters belong to the "idle rich class," and are too much in love with ease and comfort to do anything in particular but cling tight to their riches.

But the most remarkable feature of Bernard Shaw's writings is his advocacy of a return from (iii.) Instinct the guidance of morality to that of and Morality. instinct. It is remarkable in him, because, as we have seen, his ideals are social, and not egoistic like those which have thus far been considered. In spite of this, however, he believes that morality is harmful. His advice is—" Be what you want to be"; so once more we are brought face to face with the question as to what is, and what is not, "natural" for man.[2] Mr. Shaw's view of morality is largely due to his puritan training, but the whole of his puritan outlook on this matter

---

[1] See *Man and Superman*, Act III. (the "Don Juan" interlude).
[2] See above, Chapter II. I. (iii.), pp. 32 ff.

is perverted by his anti-Christian view of human nature. Puritanism was a protest against the whole external side of religion, on the ground that it is a lifeless encumbrance, a dry form which hinders and stifles the spirit. It held that all moral practice which had this formal element in it was lifeless and useless, a dead weight which it were better for a man never to have possessed; "works without faith are dead." This is the burden of Bunyan's *Pilgrim's Progress*. But the puritan objection to formal morality was due, not to its stifling individual independence, but to its hindering the man's dependence upon God. Humble faith in God was what they desired to guard. To say, then, as Mr. Shaw does, that Bunyan's allegory is, from first to last, a tirade against morality,[1] is not true. It is rather a protest against mere decorative moral outworks which are not subordinated to the soul's inner principle of faith and on that account assimilated to its life. What Mr. Shaw really dislikes, and justly so, is the idea of a man being pulled this way or that by a purely external force; but he errs in thinking that morality is such an external thing. Puritanism, so long as it does not become antinomian, is a witness to the fact that morality was never intended to remain external; that, on the contrary, it can and ought to be assimilated by the inner self of man and to become part of it. In one of his characters, "Mrs. Dudgeon", Mr. Shaw recognizes that her repulsive, pharisaic type of puritanism is due to the fact that in her "the puritan religion has died."[2] If morality were an autonomous, self-

---

[1] *Man and Superman*, the Preface.
[2] *Three Plays for Puritans*, p. xxiv.

empowered thing, as Mr. Shaw professes to believe it to be, then it would have no living power of assimilating itself to human life. But morality never has stood by itself. It must always be vitalized by religion, otherwise it becomes a dry husk; Mrs. Dudgeon is intolerable as a strict puritan just because she has lost the religious spirit. It is significant that in this play Dick Dudgeon sets up his "diabolonian" ethics, not against a religious morality, but against this dead husk, long bereft of its religious inspiration. But to kick husks because they have lost their kernel is unprofitable; it were better to look for the kernel, that religion by which all true morality must be inspired.

Once more, Mr. Shaw's rejection of morality is fatal to his social ideals. Nietzsche was consistent to this extent, that he rejected morality on the ground that it made men social, which he held to be a curse; but Mr. Shaw desires the social order to become more and more of an organic unity. Now morality, taken at its lowest, is a thing fundamentally social. In its beginnings it is the will of the tribe enforcing the observance of certain rules and customs upon the individual, in the interests of the common welfare. The individual accepts them, because he also is social at bottom; but, apart from the limits set by this primitive social law, the social side of his nature would remain dormant, and his individualistic instincts would be uppermost. Morality then is social; but just for this very reason a moral community has about it certain features which have misled Mr. Shaw into thinking morality harmful. Just because a moral community is social, the individual in such a community is always more dependent upon the community than the latter is upon him.   A community, it is true, is upheld by the total morality of its individual members ; but each single individual owes more to all the rest of the community than the whole body can owe to one single individual.   Thus the weaker members are upheld by what is called public opinion ; in other words, they are restrained from their own retrograde proclivities by the stronger power of the standards of the whole community.   But the less moral members of the community do not necessarily accept this state of things willingly.   They find themselves in various ways dependent upon the whole body and bound to respect its standards of morality, while personally they have not assimilated those standards to themselves as part of their being.   Thus they conform outwardly without vital appropriation ; and the morality of the community is in their case only a formal and external morality.

Now, this state of things shows that the community is not a perfectly moral community—that is to say, that it has not assimilated into its being, in the person of all its members, the inward reality of the moral life.   But to make this a ground for rejecting all morality would be like saying that, because a tool we are using has become blunt, we will henceforth throw away tools and work without them.   So far from the presence of this element of formal morality in an imperfectly moral community being a signal for despair, it is, rightly understood, a real ground for hopefulness.   For the individual is a part of the community ; and if he can be restrained at all from a downward path by the fact that he is a part and not the whole, it is a reason for being thankful for the social nature of humanity, which makes a man dependent upon his fellows, and capable of being strengthened by that dependence.

Now, it is just at this point that one discovers the gravest defect in Mr. Shaw's whole system. All social schemes are useless, unless one can show the part which the individual is to play in bringing them to realization. We have already seen that Mr. Shaw's conception of individual responsibility and worth in dealing with social problems is gravely deficient on the *personal* side.[1] The conclusion of this inquiry into his dislike for morality is that his conception of the individual is likewise seriously amiss on the *social* side. He dislikes morality because it presupposes a social dependence of the individual upon the community ; and this appears to him to be a mark of weakness instead of strength. His preference of "instinct" to "morality" or "duty" is due to an anti-social idea of the individual. He would have him always independent, self-sufficing, and self-contained, and would build up his social Utopia exclusively out of such self-contained, wholly independent individuals.

There is undoubtedly a personal power which is at the root of all social strength ; but it is not the sort which Mr. Shaw has pictured. Nor is there ground for rejecting his contention that we must act upon instinct ; it all depends upon the quality of the instinct. But it is necessary, in order to form a fair judgment, to have before one the whole of Mr. Shaw's view as to the worth of the individual. He has pronounced the individual powerless on the whole to effect any serious change either in himself

[1] See pp. 71–73 above.

or in his environment,[1] and has pictured him as static and helpless under the heel of fate and circumstance. What value, then, can one attach to the same individual, when he acts upon his own unfettered instinct without moral guidance? He is admittedly weak and powerless in one sphere, held down by social fetters ; yet supreme licence is to be granted to him in another sphere, on the assumption of an independence and self-possession which do not exist. Moreover, when a man living in the twentieth century advocates a return from morality to instinct, one is constrained to ask, What does he know about instinct? He is living in the midst of a civilization in which, for centuries, instinct has been under the guidance of morality ; how can he judge whether his morally trained instincts can move forward alone without that guidance? Or how can he be sure that his own conclusions on these matters are not the result of that very morality which has been moulding his instincts and those of his ancestors for so many centuries, and, on his own showing, degrading them in the process? It is a common mistake of modern writers on these subjects to disregard the possible benefits which morality may have brought to themselves ; indeed, they can hardly have formed any idea as to the extent of their obligations in this direction. It is absurd to imagine for one moment that the majority of mankind, if bidden to follow their instincts, would choose the stern, disinterested path mapped out for them by Mr. Shaw.

It has already been said[2] that there is no need to quarrel with the idea of following instinct in itself, but only when this means putting instinct in the

[1] See pp. 72, 73, above.   [2] p. 77.

place of morality. It is probable that the larger part of our daily activities are instinctive; but what does this mean? Not that instinct is the supreme arbiter of our lives, but that, in the economy of nature, many things, which were not at first done upon instinct, pass into that sphere of operation in the course of repetition. Behind instincts in many cases lie motives; instinct is itself one form which motive takes, and motives which are constantly brought into play become themselves instinctive. In one of his plays, *The Devil's Disciple*, Mr. Shaw makes the hero sacrifice himself for the sake of a woman in whom he takes no particular interest. Motive appears to be absent, and he describes the action as instinctive and therefore "natural"; thus, we are told, it cannot be based upon morality.[1] He asks whether it is not true that many people do similar unselfish actions without any apparent motive—for a stranger, let us say. Once again the truth lies in the fact that the motive has become instinctive; the self-sacrificing motive has, to a considerable extent, been ground into the characters of the people of Christendom by the moulding influence of Christian ideals. Such actions, therefore, furnish no evidence of reliability attaching to instinct in itself, as Mr. Shaw would have it; they point rather to a power of becoming instinctive, possessed by morality. "Duty," then, so far from being opposed to the true use of instinct, is the means towards the true use of it. The "sense of duty" is the pressure of morality from without, seeking to pass by way of duty into the inner sphere, where, if admitted, it will become instinctive.

[1] *Three Plays for Puritans*, p. xxvi.

Mr. Shaw's heroes and heroines are all creatures of instinct, who do what they want to do ; but this (iv.) Natural is strangely inconsistent with that stern, Virtue. virtuous struggle to bring in the social Utopia, which is the best side of his conception of life. It has been set forth by him nowhere more nobly than in the "Don Juan" interlude.[1] There we are told that our true ideal must be found in the work of helping life in its struggle upward, and that the individual is to work for the furtherance of the purpose of life, "instead of thwarting it by setting up short-sighted personal aims instead." Humanity is itself to be the agent for the continual improvement of man and of his kind. Here we have a progressive view of the purpose of life ; man is to progress in the attainment of "virtue" as Mr. Shaw understands it—that is, virtue of the quality which furthers the life-purpose. All this is the necessary basis for social reformers and philanthropists, for whom he has such an all-important place in his system. But this stoical virtue preached by Don Juan is a most dutiful thing. It is extraordinary that this writer should have failed to see that it is the very embodiment of that "sense of duty" which he professes to despise ; that it has consequently nothing whatever in common with his whimsical, irresponsible heroes and heroines, who—whatever else may be said about them—certainly do not deliberately and conscientiously co-operate with the Life-force. It may of course be said that they co-operate unconsciously by following instinct ; but in that case the whole Don Juan philosophy is rendered meaningless. For if we can co-operate so successfully by merely

[1] *Man and Superman*, Act III. p. 115.

following our instincts, why is this task represented as a purposive work, which we are only too liable to thwart "by setting up short-sighted personal aims instead"?[1] If words mean anything, instinct is not merely short-sighted; it is in itself blind. It might indeed be none the less on the right track for all its blindness, provided it had incorporated into itself the fruits of purposive action in the past. But this is not what Mr. Shaw means by instinct; his heroes are actuated by an innate instinct, whose glory is this, that it is "natural" and free from all inoculation with moral "motives." Thus we find two conceptions of virtue side by side, unreconciled. The one which Mr. Shaw prefers is this "natural" virtue of the instincts; and this one may call "static," because its essential characteristic is that, being innate in man from the first, it has not to be progressively acquired. As, however, we have already seen, the Don Juan philosophy requires that man should progress in the attainment of those qualities which further the life-purpose; here we have the "progressive" virtue which belongs to morality. On the one hand we are told that the whole greatness of man lies in the fact that he issues forth ready-made, complete and independent. On the other hand his significance is said to consist in this—that he is not an end in himself, but an agent of the Life-force imperfectly and blunderingly made. Consequently he must be fashioned into something more complete and perfect, if he would not be left behind upon the scrap-heap of experiments for which there is no further use. Thus one concludes that Mr. Shaw is no more able than Nietzsche to do without morality.

[1] *Op. cit.*

His most attractive and efficient creation is Don Juan, the philosopher of progressive virtue. The other sort consists, either of sophistical will-o'-the-wisps, or else of purely mythical figures like his " Cæsar," having no correspondence with the facts of life. This mythical element he himself acknowledges with extraordinary frankness in an appendix to his *Cæsar and Cleopatra*, where he says :—" I follow the precedent of the ancient myths, which represent the hero as vanquishing his enemies, not in fair fight, but with enchanted sword, superequine horse and magical invulnerability, the possession of which, from the vulgar moralistic point of view, robs his exploits of any merit whatever."[1] Thus we find ourselves once more in the presence of that prefix "super" which, in the mouths of those who have raised the cry, " Back to Nature!" betrays a disbelief in their own foundations and a despair of finding them sufficient to support the superstructure.[2]

It is a pleasant and easy task to build these castles in the air, to depict the sort of men and women (v.) The Breed-with whom we should like the world to ing of be peopled, the supermen whose super-Supermen. equipment solves all problems automatically. But to go no further than this is to play at romance ; and this, Mr. Shaw, of all people, would consider a most intolerable occupation. So in *Man and Superman* he seeks to answer the question of questions. If it be granted that these self-contained, naturally virtuous heroes are the type whom it is most desirable to produce, how is it to be done? In what way is Nature likely to attain this con-

[1] *Three Plays for Puritans*, p. 210.
[2] See above, Chapter II. 1. pp. 24, 47, etc.

summation. Moreover, may man himself have any say in the matter?

In his early Fabian days Mr. Shaw would doubtless have said that all his hopes lay in progress through social reform. But from this early optimism he passed to an increasingly pessimistic view of human life. All the romance, glamour, and beauty, all the fine ideals and words lost their charm; he became a realist with a deep scepticism as to the value of things that are to other minds most attractive in human life. The crowning blow came when he reached at length the conviction that there has been no progress in the history of man, and that there is no immediate prospect of any, if it continues on its present lines.[1] He had reached this point when he wrote *Man and Superman*. The Life-force had blundered badly; its highest creation, man, was in danger of proving a failure, another *cul-de-sac*, like so many previous experiments in the evolutionary process.

The defect is clearly so radical that an entirely new start seems to offer the only hope of recovery. A new race must be brought into existence; and since, for all his education and art, religion and morality, politics and social propaganda, man is not one jot further advanced, there remains only one line of possible progress not yet systematically tried, namely, that of breeding. The race of supermen must be bred by careful selection; and this method has the special advantage of delivering us from the last vestiges of moral effort—at least so its originator appears to think. Nature will at last

[1] *Man and Superman, The Revolutionist's Handbook*; *cf.* G. K. Chesterton, *George Bernard Shaw*, pp. 207-11.

really get to work; for breeding is a matter of instinct and natural law, which man will be less likely to upset by his short-sighted aims than was the case with the older methods.   Besides, if the supermen are to be distinguished by the Shavian " natural virtue," it will be most likely to come this way.   Innate qualities can only come from good parentage.   Thus we reach the conclusion that the free, natural heroes and heroines who fill Mr. Shaw's pages have not yet arrived; that no moral or disciplinary efforts have been able to produce them, or can do so, and that they must be a "nobility of blood."   To this point Nietzsche also carried his conclusions.[1]   But the science of eugenics was hardly, perhaps, so sure of itself in his day; otherwise he might have been saved from substituting for it the Will-to-power morality, which, as we saw, is so entirely incompatible with the dictum that nobility can only be of "blood."   Now, however, we are taken a step further along the road; the supermen will come as soon as we have a national breeding organisation on strictly eugenic lines.[2]

At this point it is necessary to note that Mr. Shaw has placed himself on the horns of a dilemma.   The dilemma had been in preparation for some time; but in *Man and Superman* it is presented to us complete, and it is impossible to get rid of it.   Briefly, it consists in this, that one half of the book is in flat contradiction to the other half.   For if the *Revolutionist's Handbook* is right, the Don Juan philosophy is hopelessly wrong.   If supermen are

[1] See above, pp. 49–51.
[2] See *The Revolutionist's Handbook* (*Man and Superman*).

to come through breeding, that most dutiful philosopher of the other world, moralizing about the
necessity of our working to co-operate with the
Life-force, was merely wasting his time.

It may, however, be objected that the practice
of eugenic selection of partners will require a stern
sacrifice of individual proclivities; that sexual love
will henceforth have to be subordinated to physical
qualifications—in short, that breeding will involve
not less moral effort but more. In this case the
Revolutionist's Handbook would be in agreement
with Don Juan's passionate repudiation of romance,
beauty, and love as ends in themselves; and eugenics
would mean a subordination of individual pleasures
to the great social purposes of the Life-force. It
must be replied that all this is perfectly true; but
that, if Mr. Shaw intended this to be the meaning
of breeding as a way of progress, then he would
have been wiser if he had left out of the *Revolutionist's Handbook* the whole section which declares
progress hitherto to have been an illusion; for, after
all, his new method is no more secure than all the
others which have so conspicuously failed. There
has been no progress in the past, we are told, because we have employed the useless method of
morality. If, then, breeding involves moral discipline, it can be of no use to us. Mr. Shaw would
also have to tear up all those passages in his writings
where he has condemned morality in favour of a
return to instinct and nature, as, for example, the
preface to this very book (*Man and Superman*). For
if the *Revolutionist's Handbook* is really in agreement
with the Don Juan philosophy, then it is simply a
new handbook of morals, which happens to specialize

in questions of sex. It is not a return to natural instinct after all; and "natural virtue," innate in the superman, must be produced by the "moral virtue" or "goodness" painfully acquired amongst his ancestors.[1] If, on the other hand, the *Revolutionist's Handbook* is not to be interpreted morally, but breeding is in some way to be arranged, so that, as in the case of animals, it is a purely physical thing, then Don Juan had better not have spoken; for the one hope of the human race lies in paying no attention to him. He pleads that man must sternly deny his hedonistic inclinations in order that virtuous instincts may become innate in his race. Away with such homiletics! The Life-process is purely physical; let us, then, put ourselves blindly into the hands of the State breeding official.

In the actual play, *Man and Superman* itself, Mr. Shaw has apparently attempted to offer us a compromise between these two incompatible systems. For there the woman is a veritable disciple of Don Juan. She co-operates most energetically and successfully with the Life-force in her pursuit of the man. The latter, however, being the author of the redoubtable handbook, knows his business only too well, and is the picture of a helpless animal in the hands of Nature, the great breeder. Yet the woman, for all her scheming, is but following blind instinct, whilst the object of her desire is himself in the grip of Fate. Thus, after all, there is no place for morality in this scheme, for all are in the hands of Fate, which does with us as it wills; and, this being so, there hardly seems to be any necessity for us to think about the matter at all,—

[1] See *Three Plays for Puritans*, p. 210.

nor indeed for any of Mr. Shaw's books to have been written.

Looking back then upon this system, one cannot help feeling that, as in the case of Nietzsche, the prevailing note is one of despair. The whole of it is deeply involved in inconsistencies which go down to the roots ; and these inconsistencies arise from the notion, upon which the whole turns, that morality is harmful and must be replaced by instinct. The risk involved in this reversion to instinct is apparently realized in part; but Mr. Shaw is ready to accept it. If the following of instinct should destroy ninety per cent. of the human race, it were better, so he thinks, to bear with this loss, in the hope that the remaining ten should prove to be supermen. But this is a slip into Nietzschean individualism, the sacrifice of the many for the sake of the few ; that point of view, however, is not really character- istic of Mr. Shaw, unless indeed his sense of social solidarity has been killed by despair. Despair, in- deed, is likely to be the end of such a system ; and this pessimistic conclusion is another evidence of the failure of the Natural Man.

II

The discussion of Mr. H. G. Wells has been reserved to the last place in this section upon the Mr. H. G. Wells. Natural Man, because, though he should (i.) General undoubtedly be placed in this group, he Ideas of Human Nature. stands very much nearer to Christianity than any of those hitherto mentioned. He shares with the others a deeply rooted scepticism as to the validity of any objective moral standards ; he ap- proaches the matter, however, far less from the

universal, and far more from the personal, point of
view.   He has indeed a strong and clearly thought
out background for most of his beliefs; but in the
sphere of conduct he speaks in a singularly frank
and personal way, as one who is perfectly aware
that such a practical and yet intricate matter as conduct cannot be settled on preconceived theoretical
grounds.   It is here that he seems to be on so
much firmer a basis than any of those to whom we
have so far given our attention.   He does not
lightly wave away the whole history of morality
in favour of some vague following of "nature" or
"instinct."   At the same time, whilst he treats
morality with more respect, it is significant that he
has a much greater belief in human nature.

This may be seen in various ways.   His belief
in progress does not break down utterly, as is the
case with Nietzsche and with Mr. Shaw.   All the
three writers whom we have so far considered, take
their turn in scoffing at the very idea of progress.
Davidson thinks it foolish and "Christian," yet he
cannot altogether avoid falling back upon it.[1]
Nietzsche and Mr. Shaw both laugh at those who
still suppose the world to be steadily advancing in
civilization.   The former has devised a scheme
whereby all progress, even if possible, becomes a
useless sport for fools;[2] whilst the latter has decided that it will come by a new method which
man has no power of furthering.[3]   Mr. Wells is as
deeply conscious as anyone else of the terrible
confusion, sordidness, and failure of our so-called
civilization; yet he still clings tightly to his passionate belief in the significance and value of ordinary

[1] See above, pp. 65, 66.   [2] See pp. 58 ff.   [3] pp. 82 ff.

human nature. He has never resorted to that refuge of the destitute, the superman. He came near to it in his *Food of the Gods*;[1] but his heroes there were not a new race. They had the same mental and moral constitution as ordinary men; their limitations were on the whole the same, except in physical strength.

His refusal to adopt the superman theory is probably due to the fact that he takes up a much firmer stand upon ordinary human nature; his system is on a much broader basis. His belief in human nature is not vitiated by the sacrifice of the majority as unfit, or as tainted by a morality which must be cast out at the risk of ruin to multitudes.[2] Nor is it blighted by the declaration that pleasure —the objective of most human beings—is not to be sought for itself, as Nietzsche would have it; or again that the romantic and æsthetic instincts of man are harmful and ensnaring, as Mr. Shaw declares. In saying this no comment is here made as to the actual merits or demerits of Mr. Wells' view of human nature, but only as to its freedom from various unnatural encumbrances noticeable in the views of these others. There is nothing of the fanatical Stoic or Puritan about him. He believes in beauty, as well as power, as an end in itself. For Nietzsche, the enjoyment of beauty is only an evidence of power on certain sides of life. For Davidson, power is only the servant of pleasure. And for all of these three[3] there is no thought of goodness, except under the name of virtue as a minister to either power or pleasure. But Mr. Wells

[1] How near may be seen in the passage quoted below (p. 91).
[2] See above, p. 87. [3] Nietzsche, Davidson, and Mr. Shaw.

gives, theoretically at least, a fundamental place to all these things—power, pleasure, and goodness—in his view of the goal towards which we strive.[1] We are justified then in saying that he takes a wider view of life as a whole. He does not find it necessary, in his desire for the "natural," to repudiate one half at least of what men have found to be natural in their own experience.

In proportion to this saner and clearer view of humanity as a whole, Mr. Wells places a higher value both upon its social and upon its individual powers of advance. With Mr. Shaw he refuses to subordinate society to the principle of individualism. "The subordination of the will of the self-seeking individual to the idea of a racial well-being embodied in an organised state . . . upon that I seize."[2] He has a passionate belief in the absolute solidarity of the human race; he is convinced that we all win or fail together. The progress of the whole is regarded as being so absolutely identical with the progress of the individual that, even though the latter may have no conscious share in the result, he should consider it a sufficient incentive for effort, to know that his labours will ultimately benefit the whole body.[3] To this Mr. Wells adds something else of great value, which is absent from Mr. Shaw's line of thought. This great human scheme of social progress for which we are labouring is not, in his opinion, the work of blind Fate, or of blundering Life-force without shape or plan, which must necessarily involve repeated waste and mistake. It is essentially a Purpose, spelt with a capital P; and

---

[1] See *First and Last Things*, by H. G. Wells, pp. 76–79, 96–98.
[2] *Ibid.*, p. 99.　　　　[3] *Ibid.*, *passim.*

though, in a somewhat arbitrary fashion, Mr. Wells
refuses to admit definitely the existence of a personal
God behind this extremely personal word Purpose,
yet even so the adoption of the word is a great gain.
It follows from this conception of plan and purpose,
of solidarity and order, as distinct from the blundering
mistakes of blind force, that there is an immense gain
in the conception of the individual and his place in
the scheme. "I dismiss the idea that life is chaotic
because it leaves my life ineffectual, and I cannot
contemplate an ineffectual life patiently. . . . I assert
therefore that I am important in a scheme, that we
all are important in that scheme, that the wheel-
splashed frog in the road and the fly drowning in
the milk are important and correlated with me. . . .
All this is important, all this is profoundly significant."[1] Again, with Mr. Shaw, he repudiates the
idea that there is any nobility in trampling upon
others. Both uphold the ideal of service; like Don
Juan, the "Children of the Food" say :—"It is not
that we would oust the little people from the world,
in order that we, who are no more than one step
upward from their littleness, may hold their world for
ever. It is the step we fight for and not ourselves.
We are here, Brothers, to what end? To serve
the spirit and the purpose that has been breathed
into our lives. We fight not for ourselves. . . .
Through us and through the little folk the Spirit
looks and yearns. . . . This earth is no resting-place;
this earth is no playing-place. We fight not for ourselves but for growth—growth that goes on for ever
. . . till the earth is no more than a footstool."[2]

---

[1] *First and Last Things*, p. 48.
[2] *The Food of the Gods*, Nelson's edition, p. 286.

This passage constitutes an emphatic repudiation of individualism; and it is significant that in the midst of it we are told that this earth provides an insufficient platform for the future activities of humanity. In spite of his rejection of immortality, the writer seems to feel that the earthly sphere of social service is too cramped; but that is by the way. It is time to note another important point in which his conception of human nature differs especially from Mr. Shaw's. It has been remarked that, "while he treats morality with more respect, it is significant that he has a much greater belief in human nature."[1] These two clauses are purposely set down side by side; their juxtaposition may be justified by all the facts discovered in the course of the whole of this inquiry into "the failure of the Natural Man." Let us confine our attention to a comparison of Mr. Shaw and Mr. Wells on this point. It will be remembered that in the former's system it is not merely certain moral standards which are called in question, as is the case also with Mr. Wells; rather the actual value of any morality at all is denied in the case of the individual, and consequently in the case of society also. The result, as we saw, is that human nature is land-locked, as it were, in the defects of the social system; the latter can be reformed only by some economic or mechanical device, for the individual cannot free himself from the system. Keeping for the moment to this question of the individual in relation to social defects, let us see what Mr. Wells has to say on the matter. "The socialism of my beliefs," he declares, "rests on a profounder faith

[1] See above, p. 88.

and a broader proposition. . . . It holds persistently to the idea of men increasingly working in agreement. . . . Through this great body of mankind goes evermore an increasing understanding, an intensifying brotherhood. As Christians have dreamt of the New Jerusalem, so does Socialism, growing ever more temperate, patient, forgiving, and resolute, set its face to the World City of Mankind."[1] Once more, he desires "to change economic arrangements only by the way, as an aspect and outcome of a great change, a change in the spirit and method of human intercourse."[2] Much more like this may be found in his pages; but the above sentences are sufficiently typical to convey the main thought. The remedy for social defects is here represented not as lying in any material devices, as is always implied by Mr. Shaw, but in a spiritual change; and this change is made dependent, as indeed it must be, upon the moral and intellectual elevation of the mass of individuals who compose society. The present imperfection of society is here assumed to be something which can be set right only by more effort, and which calls for the constant exercise of moral qualities, such as love, patience, and persevering service on the part of every individual. The individual is significant because he is capable of contributing something to the moulding of society for the future. It is easy, too, to see how different are the ideas of these two writers upon the significance of the individual as a factor in social development. In Mr. Wells' writings we find no trace of Mr. Shaw's magic heroes who get what they want, and surmount all obstacles by innate virtues. On

[1] *First and Last Things*, p. 107.   [2] *Ibid.*, p. 105.

the contrary, everything has to be won by hard discipline and much labour. Everyone is to be ceaselessly at work striving to bring about the needed change in society as though everything depended upon his individual efforts. "The general duty of a man . . . is to educate, and chiefly to educate and develop himself. . . . He has to make and keep this idea of synthetic human effort and of conscious constructive effort clear first to himself and then clear in the general mind."[1] Consequently Mr. Wells does not give anything like the same place to "breeding" as is the case with Mr. Shaw. He holds it to be very important, of course, and thinks that it should become more so, but not all-important. In his *Mankind in the Making* he devotes one chapter to it; and then, after acknowledging our ignorance on the subject, gives the rest of his attention to education and the possibilities of man's own moral and intellectual efforts for the improvement of the race. He believes in *acquired* virtue; and in his opinion man must give his whole energies to acquiring it.

Considerable space has been devoted to the consideration of the optimism of this writer and the (ii.) The Personal Materials. saneness and largeness of his outlook, just because his failure, notwithstanding these qualities, to find a satisfactory solution to the problems of life is rendered all the more noticeable. It is now time to turn to an inquiry into the causes of this failure. And first we must give closer attention to his view of the more personal aspects of human life. In *First and Last Things*[2] he has given us a vivid picture of the inner life of man as

[1] *First and Last Things*, p. 114.   [2] pp. 56-65.

he understands it. It is for him a very much more complex and disturbing thing than it is for the other writers examined in this group. Mr. Shaw declares that "motives" have been largely invented for purposes of the stage and literature, and that they are mostly non-existent, at any rate in people of worth.[1] Here, however, we are told that "the problem of Motives is the real problem of Life."[2] And this problem of motives weighs heavily. The shallow simplicity of following instinct, advocated by Mr. Shaw, leads only to the most hopeless conclusions; the more virile faith in man to be found in Mr. Wells grows out of a stronger sense of the delicacy and complexity of man's moral mechanism. Thus the contention is again confirmed—"the more respect for morality, the greater belief in human nature."

For the "problem of Motives" *is* the moral problem; and, if it is not brushed aside superficially, this problem of motives in ordinary humanity will inevitably baffle any serious person who examines it by the unaided light of nature. Thus we read: " I confess I find myself a confusion of motives beside which my confusion of perceptions pales into insignificance."[3] An analysis of motives into different groups is made, but they still remain a " complex " in which there is a " conflict " at work; and we are told of this complex of motives, that " in every age its mêlée has been found insufficient in itself . . . it does not form in any sense a completed or balanced system, its constituents compete among themselves . . . the motives suggested to us fall into conflict with this element or that of our inti-

---

[1] *Cf.* p. 79 above. [2] *First and Last Things*, p. 56.
[3] *Ibid.*

mate and habitual selves.   We find all our instincts
are snares to excess. . . . So to us all, even for the
most balanced of us, come disappointments, regrets,
gaps; and for most of us who are ill-balanced,
miseries and despairs.   Nearly all of us want something to hold us together—something to dominate
this swarming confusion. . . . We want more oneness, some steadying thing that will afford an
escape from fluctuations."[1]   Of course this picture
is a familiar one in literature, and in our own
experience; we find it in Plato and in Aristotle as
well as in Mr. H. G. Wells.   I have already referred
to it under the figure of an uncontrolled menagerie,
or again of a gloomy marsh-lake which has no
outlet for its poisonous waters.   Once more it is
necessary to point out that the sense of failure in
coping with this situation, the sense of some harmonious principle wanting, is entirely due to the
naturalistic method of dealing with it.   All humanity
finds this internal discord, this fundamental antagonism of "motives suggested to us" with "this element
or that of our intimate and habitual selves."   These
last words of Mr. Wells should themselves have
suggested the real solution.   There *is* a "self" intimate, and desiring to become habitual and dominant.
If it is allowed to become so, it will then be that
very something which is required "to dominate this
swarming confusion."   It is distinct from and
opposed to all motives that are clearly hostile to
its peace and self-possession.   The harmonizing
principle is this truest self which has to be discovered and preserved from all else which is alien
to it within the sphere of personal existence.   It is

[1] *First and Last Things*, p. 63.

remarkable that Mr. Wells should have turned to Christianity for the phraseology which he requires in order to speak of the way out to a harmonious life. He himself finds his synthetic principle elsewhere in the one ruling motive of seeking to further the growth of Power and Beauty in the human race. But, as has been said, he uses the Christian phraseology of "salvation" to explain the desired harmonious state.[1] "I find," he says, "in the scheme of conversion and salvation, as it is presented by many Christian sects, a very exact statement of the mental processes I am trying to express." But he misses the point when he goes on : "This discontent with the complexity of life, upon which religion is based, is called the conviction of sin." It is here that the fundamental difference between the Christian method of "salvation" and that of Mr. Wells becomes clear. The former seeks to eradicate "sin," not because it constitutes a complexity which requires to be simplified, but because it is an alien thing, poisonous to the life of the true self, and therefore requiring to be utterly cast out. But Mr. Wells follows the old Greek idea that the motives within a man are all legitimate and necessary ; only they need ordering in a scale of relative importance, like chariot horses, which must not be allowed to tear apart or to outrun one another. This involves a dilemma ; for whilst undoubtedly there is a fundamental antagonism between motives,[2] they are all treated as true parts of the whole, none of which is to be sacrificed to the others. "I do not want to suppress and expel any motive at all."[3]

---

[1] See *First and Last Things*, p. 65.
[2] *Ibid.*, p. 63.   [3] *Ibid.*, p. 64.

In other words, there is no outlet from the stagnant marsh, and consequently no means of clearing away the poisonous gases. This becomes clear when an attempt is made to fit the language of Christian soteriology to Mr. Wells' solution of the problem. "I believe," he writes, "in the scheme, in the Project of all things, in the significance of myself and all life, and that my defects and ugliness and failures, just as much as my powers and successes, are things that are necessary and important and contributory in that scheme. . . ."[1] This is considered to be the peace of one who has found salvation, "an active peace and not a quiescence,"[2] but as a matter of fact it is exactly the opposite. It is a quiescent fatalism ; for it involves the assumption that sin and failure and all the discord which arises out of the "complex of motives" are things which must be, because they are part of ourselves. This does not seem to be a very promising basis for activity, which, presumably, is what is meant by an "active peace." It does in fact lead again and again in this writer's novels to a fatalistic quiescence, wherever the conflict of motives dominates the situation. The synthetic motive, then, is found in a certain attitude towards life, which really amounts to a determination to make the best of things, and to work for the progress of the race as a way of distraction from the inward turmoil. The only suggestion of a solution of this inward turmoil is that a balance should be struck—for example, between asceticism and sensuality.[3] The balance is to be struck by the sense of beauty, a conception

---

[1] *First and Last Things*, p. 66.
[2] *Ibid.*, p. 64.   [3] *Ibid.*, p. 58.

which is really equivalent to the Greek idea of a
beautiful moderation in enjoying the pleasures of
life. Yet it is difficult to see how this sense of
beauty, this mere holding of the balance between
conflicting motives, can provide that "something to
dominate this swarming confusion" which is to
create a lasting peace.

It will be seen at once that this balance struck by
the sense of beauty is a very different thing from
the self-control inculcated by religious discipline and
asceticism, and especially by the Christian asceticism.
The two ideas are really incompatible; the former
directs a compromise between two elements in life
which are held to be on the same plane, but incomplete the one without the other. The latter, asceticism, involves the complete subordination of pleasure
and sense to an altogether different principle, which
is conceived to be higher and on a separate plane,
and which therefore claims authority to control the
lower elements of life. Throughout his *First and
Last Things* Mr. Wells makes it clear that he dislikes the whole idea of asceticism, and the virtues
which it promotes,—as, for example, chastity—in so
far as they seem to be merely negative. He does
not notice how this vitiates the whole of his own
fundamental belief in the self-denial of the individual
for the sake of society. "Life is impure," he says,[1]
in its essence; so purity is impossible until death.
Employing his own method, one might reply: "Life
is selfish and self-assertive in its essence, so your
whole scheme of self-sacrificing devotion to the
race is impossible until death." Besides, he does
not succeed in eradicating the need for discipline

[1] *Op. cit.*, p. 182.

upon the purely personal side, apart from the
supreme discipline necessary for one to devote
oneself to the interests of the race.   " To make love
well one must be fit and gracious and sweet and
disciplined from top to toe,"[1] is an emphatic recognition of this need.

Now there are, as we have already seen, two
points of view which may be taken up with regard
to this whole question of discipline and self-control ;
roughly speaking they may be called the Greek and
the Christian.   On the whole this writer very much
prefers the former ; but in one instance there is a
very remarkable exception, namely, in his description of the Order of the Samurai in his *Modern
Utopia*.   It is worth our while to give some consideration to this scheme of life, for such it is.   The
" Order," as Mr. Wells conceived it, was to exist as
a select body of superior people who would govern
the State, form its backbone, and supply the salt of
its life.   To qualify them for this task they were to
be subject to a common rule, involving a severe
discipline of their whole life.   We are told that a
visitor to Utopia sees them "with faces strengthened
with discipline."[2]   The aim of the Rule is "to discipline the impulses and emotions, to develop a moral
habit and sustain a man in periods of stress. . . .
We forbid a good deal.   Many small pleasures do
no great harm, but we think it well to forbid them
none the less, so that we can weed out the self-
indulgent.   We think that a constant resistance to
little seductions is good for a man's quality. . . .

---

[1] *Op. cit.*, p. 59.
[2] Quoted in *First and Last Things*, p. 136, from which the
whole of this description is taken.

We forbid tobacco, wine, or any alcoholic drink, all narcotic drugs . . . [a member of the Order] must shave and dress and serve himself, carry his own food. . . ." A number of small regulations about the ordering of the personal life follow, and then this comment: " These minor obligations do not earmark more than an hour in the day. Yet they serve to break down isolations of sympathy, all sorts of physical and intellectual sluggishness and the development of unsocial preoccupations of many sorts." Most remarkable of all, perhaps, is the rule by which each member of the Order must go apart into complete solitude and silence, with only a minimum of equipment, to spend a week under the open sky. " This discipline was invented to secure a certain stoutness of heart and body in the Samurai. Otherwise the Order might have lain open to too many timorous, merely abstemious men and women."

It is extraordinary that Mr. Wells should apparently not have realized how extremely closely he has in all this simply copied the common life of discipline and rule which has for centuries been actively realized in the monasteries and convents of the Church, the analogy is close at almost every point even to the annual retreat spent in silence. Moreover, the whole is based upon the same assumption as its Christian prototype, namely, that ascetic rule, abstinence, and discipline are not weakening, but strengthening, because through these things the higher powers in human nature are set free from all kinds of lower obstructions, and are braced to greater vigour. This was Mr Wells' outlook when *A Modern Utopia* was written; but in *First*

and Last Things, a later book, he confesses that he
does not want to see this picture realized ; it appears
to him impracticable and unworkable—a dream, yet
a dream which suggests a principle. " They [the
Samurai] may be valuable as an ideal of attitude,
but not as an ideal of organisation." Yet this is
sufficient to involve a recognition of the value which
belongs to asceticism of the Christian sort. The
truth is that its value *is* recognized, but it is not found
attractive. Accordingly the ground is changed, and
we are told that " in itself abstinence seems to me a
refusal to experience, and that . . . is to say that
abstinence for its own sake is evil."[1] But once again
we are told that if it is a means to an end it is good ;
and in the picture of the Samurai Mr. Wells has
once for all shown us that it can and ought to be
made such a means, and that, when so made, it is a
principle of supreme value. We shall return to this
question of asceticism in a later chapter. For the
present it will be sufficient if it has been made clear
that this writer has, in a most definite and emphatic
way, shown its value and strength, and that along
lines which do not at all fit in with his general outlook upon life. It is, however, too foreign to his
conception of the individual to be able to secure a
firm footing in his scheme.

After reading any of Mr. Wells' writings, there is
always one impression left deeply upon the mind.
(iii.) Uncer-
tainty of Aim
and Method.
He seems to be in a state of very great
uncertainty, both as to the exact goal
towards which he is driving and also as
to the method by which he proposes to reach it.
First as to the goal : we have seen that he has as

[1] *First and Last Things*, p. 181.

a rule plenty of optimism ; but optimism without
any clear discrimination as to the great principles
upon which future developments are to be based is in
danger of being a shallow optimism. It is all very
well to talk vaguely of power and beauty, with goodness as an afterthought ; but these terms are quite
valueless as tests of direction. Indeed, they might
as well not be used at all, if one cannot define them
satisfactorily ; and that is just what Mr. Wells'
materials do not enable him to do. He shares with
Mr. Bernard Shaw that sceptical realistic outlook
which denies the value of all universal ideals, so that,
as he himself says, "pure Good and pure Beauty
are to me empty terms."[1] Such ideals do not exist
as ideals in themselves, but only as "synthetic
things . . . they arise out of the coming together
of contributory things and conditions, and vanish at
their dispersal." It is true, he allows that each one
may have in general terms "his idea of Good." In
his own case his idea both socially and individually
is the altruistic one of self-subordination to common
ends ; yet it remains only "the general expression
for right living."[2] With such vague outlines of what
is right, the individual is thrown almost entirely upon
himself, as the final deciding factor in discriminating
between possible lines of conduct. Yet, considering
how intricate are the subtleties of casuistry which
may arise in questions of conduct, there seems very
little safeguard against individual weaknesses and
eccentricities. Further, special emphasis is laid
upon the idea that what is right for one is not
necessarily right for another ; thus no one is justified
in calling any individual to account for conduct

[1] *First and Last Things*, p. 96.   [2] *Ibid.*, p. 97.

which there is no possibility of appraising by any objective standard. This conclusion is not actually stated by Mr. Wells; but there seems to be no escape from it. What is the use of eulogies upon social solidarity, if we have only a subjective and uncertain morality which is unable to enforce any universal standard upon individuals? If there is no universal element in the individual, then it is impossible to conceive upon what grounds social solidarity can be supposed to exist at all. If, however, it does exist, as Mr. Wells believes, then there must be some common universal element in the individual, and there should be some common standard of morality, which by virtue of that universal element is applicable to all. There is no getting away from this dilemma in which subjective morality finds itself. Mr. Shaw's "instinct" is more logical; both alike abolish all right in society to control the individual. Mr. Wells admits as much as this when he comes to the discussion of so important an element in social conduct as Justice.[1] Society, he declares, has no rights over the individual, nor has the latter any rights in society; it is for him not a question of "right" but of the necessities of our common development. In other words, the idea of "Justice" is a purely utilitarian invention upheld in the interests of Life or Progress. The immediate result of such a line of argument is to empty the individual himself of all personal worth; he exists for "our collective growth," or some such vague purpose. He has no imperative claims; he is in reality the tool of the social aggregate, to be flung aside when he ceases to be of use. This is the first

[1] *First and Last Things*, pp. 196 ff.

time that we have had to note in Mr. Wells a fundamental scepticism as to the worth of the individual; but it arises logically out of the realistic position with regard to conduct. If there is no universal element in the individual, we cannot mete out "right" to him; for there is no element in him whereby we can make a social reckoning. He is like $\sqrt{-1}$ in a mathematical problem, an impossible and imaginary quantity; he may be useful for our general purposes, but in the absence of any imperative, universal, and knowable value, he must remain in the long run unrelated to the whole mass.

In fact, this examination into what Mr. Wells means by the "idea of Good" has shown that for him Goodness is merely the tool of Power. It has no sort of worth or meaning as a goal to be attained by the individual. This Power which our individual goodness subserves may of course be benevolent; but it is difficult to find out anything certain about it. "We move towards Power and Beauty," we are told, that is, towards a fuller and richer manifestation of social life; for all life can be conceived in terms of power and beauty. Goodness, then, is that which promotes a more powerful and beautiful development of the collective life. But how can we be sure as to the value of this Power and Beauty, which it is supposed we are bringing in by our individual efforts? No one has done more than Mr. Wells himself to show that the promotion of either of these things may in itself be unutterably bad. What social value could anyone attach to the mechanical power described so vividly in his scientific romances? [1]

[1] E.g. *The War of the Worlds* and *The War in the Air.*

Or again, in his *When the Sleeper Awakes* he has given us a picture of what the world might come to on the lines of " Power and Beauty." Here immense economic and mechanical power are gathered into the hands of a small aristocracy, great success is attained in art and in all that has to do with pleasure and sense, and these things are made accessible to the whole upper and middle classes. Actual poverty and hunger, and—to a large extent— disease, are eradicated ; but the price paid for these things is an enormous slave population, ground down under a merciless tyranny which cares nothing for human life.   Moreover, the author himself appears to condemn emphatically this imaginary state of things which he has so ably conceived and de- scribed. If we are only seeking for Power and Beauty to which Goodness is subordinated as an instrument, the result might very well be some- thing as revolting and horrible as this.

We are left, then, with a vague picture of masses of individuals striving and straining, with apparently no personal incentive, to move the whole social mass further along its way towards some unknown end. The final result, it is conjectured, must in some way be richer and more harmonious ; though exactly who is to get any satisfaction out of this future harmony is not at all clear.   The whole outlook is vague and impersonal ; and therefore it is necessarily uninspiring for ordinary humanity, which inevitably seeks for ends which are significant for itself.   This general vagueness, which is so wanting in inspiration or direction, is well expressed in the following passage :—" When it comes to this idea of raising human beings, I must confess the only person I feel concerned about raising is H. G. Wells, and that even in his case my energies might be better employed. After all, presently he must die and the world will have done with him. His output for the species is more important than his individual elevation. Moreover, all this talk of raising implies a classification which I doubt—I find it hard to fix any standards that will determine who is above me and who below. Most people are different from me, I perceive, but which among them is better, which worse? . . . When I sit upon the bench . . . and commit some battered reprobate for trial for this lurid offence or that, the doubt drifts into my mind which of us after all is indeed getting nearest to the keen edge of life?"[1]

There it is—a fundamental uncertainty as to the direction which ought to be taken by the individual in seeking the betterment of society or in ordering his own life. Now, as we have already seen, Power and Beauty must use Goodness as the useful implement which is to indicate the direction.[2] But Goodness is a personal quality. So then this direction, whether of society or of the personal life, lies in the hands of the individuals who compose society. The whole issue therefore rests with the individual; and it is just this individual who, in all that Mr. Wells has written, is so hopelessly without directive principle himself. The thing resolves itself into one more vicious circle from which there is no outlet. The direction of social progress is to come through the individual; and the individual, looking vainly round for a synthetic principle, a ruling something, is hopeful that at last he has found what he needs

---

[1] *First and Last Things*, p. 102.   [2] See above, p. 105.

in the duty of serving society. But society is uncertain as to its direction, and waits upon the individual ; and so the latter is flung back once more upon
the mass of contradictory motives within him. We
have seen something of the fluctuation in Mr. Wells'
mind upon such an important matter as the question
of personal discipline. First we are offered the
Samurai Rule of stern asceticism ; then this is flung
aside as an unpractical ideal, dangerously near to a
deliberate refusal of experience for its own sake,
and quite a contrary ideal is suggested, as for
example in the following passage. After decrying
purity as a negative virtue, he says : " There is a
lurking disposition to believe, even among those
who lead the normal type of life, that the abstinent
and chastely celibate are exceptionally healthy,
energetic, immune. The wildest claims are made.
But indeed it is true . . . that man is an omnivor-
ous, versatile, various creature. . . . He responds
to stimulants and recuperates after the exhaustion
of his response. . . ." [1] So we are brought back once
more to the Greek idea of securing pleasure by
freedom from excess, by maintaining a balance :
" We none of us altogether and always keep the
balance or are altogether safe from losing it. We
swing, balancing and adjusting along our path." [2]
Now this is really that old static conception of the
individual which we found in Mr. Shaw's writings,
dressed up in another form. There is no progressive
attainment of increasing stability ; the whole remains
to the end liable to a complete catastrophe by loss
of balance. " We swing, balancing "—that is the
whole weakness of this type of individual. He is

[1] *First and Last Things*, p. 183.   [2] *Ibid.*, p. 185.

like a pendulum, and there is no possibility of his ever being anything else.

In Mr. Wells' fiction he has given us a series of vivid pictures of the way in which all this sort of (iv.) The Failure thing works itself out in practice. Two of Experience. main impressions are left upon the mind after their perusal. First there is the uncontrollable character of that turbulent, swaying individuality, which this writer has confessed to be such a hard problem to him. It goes about seeking balance and finding none, just because it is balance which it seeks and nothing higher. Obedient to the self-made rule of evading none of the experiences of life that come its way, it finds itself entangled in a hopeless mesh of insoluble problems; it seeks life and finds only a series of dismal illusions.[1]

Then, secondly, following upon this disillusionment and hopeless perplexity, there settles down a deep despair. The individual who sets out so gallantly, and with such high hopes of bending life to his own purposes or of bettering the social order, drifts at last into a dour fatalism. "These things had to be,"—that is the refrain to which we are always brought back. The whole social order towers up in these vivid pictures as something which overwhelms the individual; it is too stupid to let itself be bettered; and there is no inspiring hope to warrant the individual in going on with his disinterested career of meaningless benevolence. Thus the social order can have little meaning for the individual. These two ultimate centres of interest cannot be reconciled; they are like two circles, each fast closed up in itself, whose centres cannot coincide; or even like two wild

[1] See especially *Tono-Bungay* and *The New Machiavelli*.

beasts, each blindly groping to suck the life-blood
of the other, though all unwillingly.   The individual
must seek a balance for his own life ; and it is more
than probable that the result will prove to be anti-
social, especially when there is more swing than
balance.   In all the works of this writer one cannot
find so much as an approach to a solution of the
question, How is the volcanic self-seeking of the
individual to be reduced sufficiently to order, not
only to set him at peace in himself, but also to
make him a handy instrument for the furthering of
the constructive state of Mr. Wells' dreams ?[1]   And
if anything still less of an answer is given to that
other question, equally important : What is the
value of a social order which habitually plays the
tyrant towards its individual unit, which lures him
on to seek far-reaching interests for the self, and
then hurls him from his pedestal remorselessly ;
which makes a slavish tool of him, and leaves him
battered at the last ?[2]

" It is a note of crumbling and confusion, of
change and seemingly aimless swelling, of a bub-
bling up and medley of futile loves and sorrows."[3]
Such is the impression left upon this writer by his
survey of the social chaos.   When, therefore, we are
told that, "through the confusion sounds another note.
Through the confusion something drives, something
that is at once human achievement and the most
inhuman of all existing things " . . . that " we make
and pass . . . we are all things that make and pass,
striving upon a hidden mission out to the open

---

[1] *E.g.* see *The New Machiavelli* and *The Passionate Friends.*
[2] *E.g.* see *Tono-Bungay.*
[3] *Ibid.*, Macmillan's edition, p. 382.

sea "[1] . . . the words do not carry conviction.   They
fail to do so just because the achievement is so inhuman, just because we pass after making,—just
because the mission *is* a hidden one, and the open
sea may prove to be a horrible grave to which we
have drifted without any lasting achievement.

[1] *Tono-Bungay*, Macmillan's edition, pp. 382, 383.

CHAPTER IV

ETHICAL FOUNDATIONS

WE have now examined four different attempts of
recent years to found human conduct upon pure
Résumé. naturalism. If the criticisms offered
have been in any degree just, those who
think that the Natural Man provides a sufficient
basis for conduct might well pause to consider the
significance of the complete failure of these different
writers to provide any satisfactory or coherent system.
We have seen how in every case the attempt to
confine the lines of human conduct within the sphere
of the purely natural has been found impossible to
maintain. Nietzsche and Mr. Bernard Shaw subordinate the present to the future, which at once
creates the necessity for moral discipline. This is
felt to be a difficulty ; and, to avoid progress by
morality, they have put forward breeding and
nobility of blood ; but breeding, as a substitute for
morality, destroys that very necessity for conscious
individual struggle which their whole systems require.
The subordination of the present to the future has
always a moral colouring ; to avoid this, Davidson
rejects race-progress, as an end to be sought, but
finds himself obliged to plead for it in argument
against profligacy. Mr. Wells acknowledges an
internal discord in human nature, and declares the

inner life of man to be a disorganised muddle, thus overthrowing the self-contained simplicity of Mr. Shaw's supermen. In these two, again, natural instinct and subjective morality have both alike proved themselves incapable of making the individual strong enough to be a dynamic power for the social ends which they both desire. Our examination, then, of this group of writers makes two things clear : first, that the vicious circle of self-contained nature fails to give man harmony and progress ; and secondly, that systems of conduct based upon pure nature, though they may start optimistically, are fundamentally fatalistic, and are bound to end in pessimism.

In view of these conclusions, this chapter will begin with the assumption, first that a morality is necessary, and secondly that it cannot

(i.) What is the Basis of Morality?

be wholly subjective, as Mr. Wells would make it ; that is to say, it cannot be simply the eclectic creation of the individual, formed pragmatically to suit his own estimate of his needs. We have seen that the individual by himself is not sufficiently stable or constant to mark out for himself a course which is unerringly right, in the sense of ministering to the collective social development. If the basis of morality is not to be found in the individual as such, it must be sought in some universal sanction ; and, as a matter of fact, history seems to show that religion in some form has always provided the supreme universal sanction of morality. For, speaking broadly, we see in religion the universal element in man seeking contact with the universal outside itself. Let us therefore at this point make this further assumption, that if a morality is necessary which is not wholly subjective and individualistic, it must be founded upon religion.

But there remains still one question to be decided as to the basis of morality. Can we now say that this religious morality comes to us as something wholly objective ? Can we call it a Moral Law coming down upon us with authority ? Are we justified in concluding, from the ethical failure of the Natural Man, that morality must really be something revealed to us as the expression of the Will of God ? Before we pass on to Christian morality, an answer to this question must be found ; for Christian ethical ideals have always been upheld by the Church on the basis of an answer in the affirmative. The whole attitude of men and women towards moral questions will, if the Church has been right in this, resolve itself into a choice between obedience to a moral law grounded upon revealed religion on the one hand, and a self-made subjective morality founded on Naturalism on the other. Of these two the latter will be open to all the inconsistencies and possibilities of failure revealed in the preceding chapters. There will be no other alternative to this choice, if the Church has understood correctly the ethical foundations which necessarily lie at the root of the Gospel scheme of conduct. The whole of this idea, however, of a Christian moral law objectively revealed and standing in contrast to the subjective schemes of Naturalism has been challenged by a recent writer. Mr. H. S. Chamberlain, in his *Foundations of the Nineteenth Century*,[1] has laboured

[1] English translation by John Lees (John Lane, The Bodley Head).

to prove that the whole conception of a revealed moral law, external to ourselves and claiming our obedience, is foreign to Christianity. If the contentions of his book were correct, Christian morality would be a natural growth ; and, short of returning to the purely individualistic point of view found so wanting in practical working, we should be obliged to find some middle position. We should have to say that morality is based upon the universal element in human nature as opposed to the individual. We might even allow an important place to religion as the exercise of this universal element ; but we should not be able to include in our scheme any intervention or help from a higher Power than that which man may find in himself. If this position were a true one, the Gospel would be only one more attempt on the part of man to find for himself within his own limitations an answer to the riddle of conduct. It is with the conviction that such a conclusion is wrong that the present writer has entered upon this argument. Let us, therefore, in this chapter examine the positions taken up by Mr. Chamberlain. His book is an attempt to provide a naturalistic basis for conduct without rejecting the Christian ideals. To this end he finds it necessary to graft the Christian religion, as it were, on to the Natural Man without the interpolation of objective moral law. Before seeking in a supernatural Christianity the alternative to Naturalism, this possibility of a naturalistic basis for Christian ideals must be examined. If it be found that Mr. Chamberlain has avoided the pitfalls discovered in the preceding chapters, it will then be necessary to contemplate the possibility of a *via media*, a re-

conciliation of Nature and Morality by some other
method than that of subjecting the former to
authoritative law. If, on the other hand, all the
old landmarks of inconsistency, helplessness, and
fatalism reappear, it will be safe to conclude that
Mr. Chamberlain has failed in his attempt.   It
will then be necessary to seek elsewhere, in supernatural religion, the requisite starting point for
conduct.

The key to the proper understanding of Mr.
Chamberlain's astonishing twelve hundred pages is
(ii.) Human   to be found in his view of human nature;
Nature and Sin. for this will be found to underlie every
detail of his argument.   It explains his attitude to
law and his peculiar views about religion and
redemption.   Now, there is no essential difference
between his conception of human nature and that
of Mr. Wells, the nearest to him of the group
already examined.   As, however, he associates
himself with Christianity, one must speak in the
language of Christian theology and say that his
view of human nature is Pelagian ; and this, despite
the fact that in his treatment of the actual controversy he professes to side with St. Augustine
against Pelagius.[1]   His whole position is based
upon the idea that man is a self-contained entity
and that the Natural Man has the solution of
the problem of conduct within himself.   There
are only two possible views about this question of
human nature.   One is that stated above, which we
have found to lie at the root of all the extreme
naturalistic conceptions of life.   The other is the
Christian view, expounded by St. Paul, that man

[1] *Foundations of the Nineteenth Century*, vol. ii. p. 39.

is made up of "flesh" and "spirit," two opposing principles which wage perpetual war upon one another, and must always continue to do so until either one or the other is wholly subjected. Closely bound up with this question of human nature is the question of sin. Without the Christian conception of sin, the Pauline view of a dual human nature would be Manichean; it would involve the idea that man has been created as spirit encompassed by evil flesh. But the Pauline doctrine of the Fall makes the entrance of the evil principle into human life the fault of man, whereby the Divine plan of creation, in which flesh and spirit are both good, was overthrown. Now, Mr. Chamberlain dislikes the whole of this side of St. Paul's teaching. He holds it to be a bit of alien Judaistic materialism, which has remained in the apostle and spoilt the purity and simplicity of his theology.[1] He sneers at his chronological arrangement of a creation, an "accidental fall," and its punishment. St. Paul accepts the view set forth by the Genesis writers that man was in the Divine creative plan free from moral corruption, but that by the action of his own will in historical fact he fell from the Divine plan and became something fundamentally different, something disordered and diseased. This Pauline view of man, sin, and the Fall is not merely at the heart of the Genesis story; it is also the basis of the whole view of life put forward everywhere in the Old Testament. It is in the best sense anti-natural; that is to say, it regards human nature, as it is now, as a corruption and a failure, something vitiated, "the natural man" which "understandeth not the

[1] *Foundations of the Nineteenth Century*, vol. ii. pp. 62–65.

things of the Spirit." This is the only possible
justification for a dispensation of law such as we find
in the Old Testament; it is to be regarded, not as
an end in itself, but as ever tending towards and
preparing the way for a higher dispensation of
redemption and grace.

If one examines Mr. Chamberlain's view of sin,
one sees how totally he disagrees with all this,
and how as a consequence the dispensation of the
Old Testament becomes entirely meaningless and
repulsive to him. The following passage is a good
example of his views on this question :—" Sin and
original sin are synonyms. *It is a question of an
unavoidable condition of all life.* Our conception of
sinfulness is the first step towards the recognition of
a transcendental connection of things. . . . Paul
goes to the root of the matter by calling sin itself
a 'law'—a law of the flesh, or, as we should say
to-day, *an empirical law of nature.*" [1] The words
which I have placed in italics show clearly that
Mr. Chamberlain regards sin as a fundamental and
original condition of human nature, a law of nature,
for which, therefore, man himself cannot be held responsible. St. Paul, however, in the phrase quoted
above, calls it a law of the *flesh* ; and by the flesh he
always means human nature as weakened and vitiated
by the Fall. It is significant that Mr. Chamberlain,
at the beginning of the above quotation, identifies
actual sin and original sin. He makes sin a part
of our original endowment. On the other hand, the
Pauline view is that each soul is born into the world
weakened by the disease of " original sin," and therefore liable to sin ; actual sin itself, however, is in

[1] *Foundations of the Nineteenth Century*, vol. ii. p. 35.

each of us something for which we are directly responsible.

But now let us go further into this question of the nature of sin. Mr. Chamberlain compares his own view to that of an Indian thinker who "'searches eagerly for his sin' and finds it *not in his will but in his condition.*" [1] Thus the whole idea of a responsible will is ruled out from this sphere, and we are left with sin as a condition of nature, for which we cannot be called to account. Now, in the Christian view of the matter, derived from the Old Testament, and everywhere assumed in the New Testament, there are two important features of actual sin as distinct from original sin. They are, first the deliberate rebellion of the will against God, by the transgression of His law ; and secondly the resultant state or condition which follows the first transgression and remains in the individual as a disease, preying upon him and becoming the actual cause of further transgressions. Moreover, this state of things is not stationary ; either it must be cured by the process of redemption, or else the transgressions multiply, the burden of the flesh grows heavier, and the disease destroys the whole moral and spiritual life.

Of these two features in the Christian doctrine of sin, Mr. Chamberlain rejects the former *in toto.* He says : "It is only when we view sin as a condition, not as the transgression of a law, that we can arrive at the two conceptions of redemption and grace." [2] The second idea, that of a condition, he retains ; but he so waters it down that, instead of

---

[1] *Foundations of the Nineteenth Century*, vol. ii. p. 35 ; the italics are mine.

[2] *Ibid.*, vol. ii. p. 36.

the thought of a malignant spreading disease, we
are left with a mere state of imperfection due to
the fact that Nature has not done her work quite
perfectly. We are imperfect, but we may become
better by the help of Christian morality; that is the
essence of it. Thus the sinner is made a passive,
involuntary subject of sin; while all its horrors and
the degradation attaching to it vanish. The use
of the Fall story at all to convey such a view is
really ludicrous. Mr. Chamberlain himself calls
it the myth of degeneration;[1] but what meaning
is left in this central idea of degeneration, this
fall downwards, if after all it was only intended to
symbolize a state of imperfection which has always
been part of man, and which is an "empirical law
of nature"? The effect of this diluted doctrine of
sin upon the idea of human nature follows inevitably. The whole thing is laid bare unmistakably in
Mr. Chamberlain's treatment of Origen's comments
on the Fall. He quotes the following remarks of
Origen from his book on Prayer (c. xxix.) :[2]—"We
cannot help observing that the credulity and inconstancy of Eve did not begin at the moment when
she disregarded the word of God and listened to
the serpent; they were manifestly present before,
and the serpent came to her, because in its cunning
it had already noticed her weakness." Here it is
to be noticed that Origen has two things in his
mind : first, the possibility of sinning which is inherent in human nature, even when in the unfallen
state, on account of the free-will imparted to it by
divine constitution ; and secondly, the fact that the

[1] *Foundations of the Nineteenth Century*, vol. ii. p. 36.
[2] *Ibid.*, p. 89.

actual taking of the apple was only the consummation of the sin. For transgression began the
moment credulity and inconstancy secured a lodg-
ment, the one in her mind and the other in her
will. What existed in her before the temptation he calls "her weakness," that is, an inherent
openness to temptation, and liability to fall; but
this is not sin, it is not even the state of original
sin. Original sin does not mean the addition of
new elements to human nature, but a twist, in the
direction of sin, given to those elements in human
nature which already exist; these in any case form
the materials upon which temptation is able to fasten
itself. What Origen means, then, is this. Human
nature is conceived in the allegory as neither sinful
nor perfected in strength of character before the
Fall; but simply as innocent, untested, and therefore easily to be moulded either the one way or the
other. Unfallen human nature is thus pictured as
possessing all natural human weaknesses; such are
not in themselves evil, but they supply the materials
over which evil may easily gain a hold. Of these
natural weaknesses Origen singles out two as conspicuous in Eve's case, namely, "credulity and
inconstancy." Now it may be admitted that this
phrase in the English translation of Mr. Chamberlain's quotation suggests very distinctly some moral
defect as existing in Eve before her temptation.
Justice, however, is not done to Origen's words by
this rendering. The exact wording of the original
is : ἰστέον, ὅτι τὸ Εὔας εὐεξαπάτητον, καὶ τὸ σαθρὸν τοῦ
λογισμοῦ αὐτῆς . . . ὑπέστη.[1] The natural rendering
of τὸ εὐεξαπάτητον is "liability to be easily deceived,"

---

[1] Origen, *De Oratione*, c. xxix. Lommatzsch's edition, p. 267.

which suggests a not uncommon weakness, but not
however any *moral* defect. Again, τὸ σαθρὸν τοῦ
λογισμοῦ means "the perishability of the reasoning
power." The idea conveyed seems to be that her
human mind was fallible and liable to be overborne
by the exceptional cunning of the serpent. Thus a
door was open at which "credulity and inconstancy"
might easily enter ; but there is nothing in the
language of Origen to suggest any *moral* obliquity
previous to "the Fall."

We are not, however, mainly concerned with
Origen's beliefs, but with Mr. Chamberlain's view of
human nature and sin. He makes the following
comment on the remarks of Origen :—"With this
one sentence the myth is once more awakened into
life. And with the myth nature steps into its rights.
*That which may be called sin, as soon as we aim at
something higher, belongs to us*, as Paul had already
said 'by nature.' We no longer stand opposed to
all nature as something strange, something that has
been born higher but has fallen lower. We rather
belong to nature, and we cast back upon it the light
of grace that fell into our human heart. By carrying on the Pauline thought Origenes has liberated
science. . . ."[1] But the Pauline thought is something entirely different from what Mr. Chamberlain
would make it. St. Paul's phrase "by nature"[2] refers
to the natural man which understandeth not the things
of the spirit, because it is too utterly foreign to the
spirit. What Mr. Chamberlain, on the other hand,
means is that the old doctrine of sin, which is written
large across both Testaments and all Christian the-

[1] *Foundations of the Nineteenth Century*, ii. p. 89. The italics
are my own.   [2] Ephesians ii. 3.

ology, is a horrible nightmare. He dislikes the doctrine because it involves the idea that sinful man is in the truest sense *un*natural, that his life is alienated from God's plan of nature, in which man was to be the crown of all the rest and in harmony with it. Mr. Chamberlain would have it that sin makes no difference. It is itself a part of the whole scheme; and when man leaves it for something better, he is not returning from a bypath which leads astray, but only ascending a little higher on the path, leaving the lower and less perfect stage behind. But all the stages of progress from imperfection to perfection are alike natural and in harmony with the scheme of nature. This is why the view has been expressed that Mr. Chamberlain is a Pelagian.[1] In this theory of sin, the will remains complete, uncontaminated and unweakened, however much sin there may be. With a whole and unperverted will, therefore, man may forge for himself a way to perfection; for what is to stop him? He is advancing in the true line of nature.

This view of human nature and sin is the key to Mr. Chamberlain's intense dislike for the whole idea (iii.) The of law in the sphere of morals. A man's Moral Law. view of the nature of morality depends upon his view of religion, from which morality proceeds; and his view of religion in turn must

---

[1] It has been suggested to me that it would be more correct to call this writer a follower of Marcion than of Pelagius. It is quite true that, taken as a whole, his system bears more points of resemblance to Marcion's than to any other, especially his antipathy to the Old Testament, and his treatment of St. Paul. But for the present argument the thing upon which all else hinges is the view which is taken about human nature in relation to conduct; and in this matter Pelagius is the classic champion of that point of view to which Mr. Chamberlain adheres.

proceed from his conception of human nature. All turns upon that, as has already been said. Now one may gain a fairly clear idea of Mr. Chamberlain's view of religion from his book. He conceives religion to be just what the Greeks made it [1]—man making himself at home in the cosmos by inventing mythologies to bring him near to God and to bridge the gulf between. He says : "What constitutes the essence of religion if not the bridging over of this gulf? All else is philosophy or morals. We are consequently justified in calling the mythology of Greece a religion, for by furnishing conceptions it brings us nearer the Divine." [2] Undoubtedly it is essentially a mark of religion that it should bring us nearer the Divine. Mr. Chamberlain would have us believe that it can do this without a moral law, and also that this religion, which is to bring us near to God, can be manufactured by man himself to suit his own needs. [3] Now all this is in harmony with his view of human nature. Man is in the true line of the natural, and has never deviated from it. His will is sure and reliable. In seeking out religion he is performing a task well within his competence, for it is simply the "natural" seeking contact with the world of phenomena, and striving to understand its significance. Or, to put it another way in Mr. Chamberlain's own words, religion is this "tendency, this state of mind, this instinct, to seek the core of nature in the heart." [4] So then "the religious man appears consciously as a Creator" of religion : "he toils unremittingly at the noble Sisyphus work of

[1] This is well set forth in a small book by G. Lowes Dickinson, *The Greek View of Life*.
[2] *Foundations of the Nineteenth Century*, vol. i. p. 471.
[3] *Ibid.*, vol. i. pp. 214–216.   [4] *Ibid.*, vol. i. p. 216.

giving visible shape to the invisible." Religion thus becomes a man-made thing based upon the instincts of a truly balanced human nature. Not only " the core of nature" but religion and morality also are sought for in "the heart of man."

It follows naturally that, when this writer turns to the Old Testament idea of law, he finds in it something only fettering to the free instincts of man— instincts which can be trusted to guide him aright. Judaism is anathema on account of its conceptions of sin and the fear of God, the transcendent Creator Whose will is revealed in a stern law of righteousness. All these things seem to separate man from God and thus to bring in deism with its gulf between heaven and earth. Even the prophets he criticises on the ground that through them Israel "first received the revelation of the gulf between God and man, and now this gulf yawned threateningly, and not the slightest attempt was made to bridge it over."[1] It is assumed that human nature can of itself bridge the gulf. Now the only possible justification for a moral law lies in the catholic doctrine of sin as a rebellion of will and a consequent state of disease and enfeeblement. When this point of view is assumed, the idea of man being brought near to God by a "natural" religion like Hellenism becomes impossible. He is only brought near, by natural mythologies, to his own tainted views of the world and of life. He is still within the vicious circle of nature, which has shown itself upon examination to be so incapable of supporting him. Belief in such natural religion is a shallow optimism which has in itself no power of permanence. Man thinks himself

[1] *Foundations of the Nineteenth Century*, vol. i. p. 471.

naturally near to God only because he has no
proper sense of sin and scarcely any moral sense.
Mr. Chamberlain is obliged to admit that neither
Hellenism nor Brahminism have touched the will;
in each case only the imagination and the mind
have been reached.[1]   As we shall see later, he has
acknowledged that the problem of the will was not
solved by any religion until Christ came and dealt
with it successfully.   This is why he is obliged to
take the line that religion has nothing to do with
morals.[2]   But the will is the centre of the whole
problem of conduct, the most difficult problem which
man has to solve, as we saw in the last chapter.
What, then, is the use of religion, if it does not
touch this question ?   Is it in that case worth so
much attention as Mr. Chamberlain has bestowed
upon it ?   The religion of Israel, however, did most
emphatically attack this problem ; and it found
the human will just what the failure of all naturalistic schemes of conduct has led one to expect it
would find—a basis for morals insufficient in itself.
Now the people of Israel did not attribute this state
of things to an inherent necessity of imperfection
by nature, as Mr. Chamberlain does—for this idea
is absolutely fatalistic and paralyzing to moral effort.
They traced it to a deviation in the past, which
can be put right.   Yet clearly man cannot put it
right by himself; for he is incapacitated.   So, then,
God must intervene and provide him with a moral
standard, by which his perverted will may direct
its way afresh.   This standard of morals must be
divinely given to ensure that it is a true guide to
conduct ; it is also necessary that it should have

[1] *Op. cit.*, vol. ii. p. 41.   [2] *Ibid.*, vol. i. p. 215.

authority over conscience as a law which commands obedience. It must govern the will besides offering it guidance; man must retrace his steps out of sin by way of a stern and toilsome moral discipline. Moreover, if the Christian view of human nature and sin is once postulated, there is no force in the complaint that the religion of Israel set a gulf between man and God. It was the only possible way of advance; the gulf was there already, as the result of sin. Two things, then, had to be done; first to convince man that the gulf was there by showing him the moral requirements of God, and secondly to bridge it by means of Divine Grace. The first of these two was the work of the Old Testament and the Law; the second was accomplished by Christ, and could only be so accomplished after the preliminary dispensation. Thus, whilst the dispensation of law did not solve the problem of the will, it shed a flood of light upon that problem from all sides and prepared the ground for its solution. One may say that in Mr. Chamberlain's view religion is a matter of shallow optimism, built upon the insecure basis of the Natural Man, and covering only the partial grounds of imagination and intellect; whereas it is the function of religion to appeal to and to uplift the whole personality. In the Catholic view, on the other hand, the Old Testament provides a preliminary basis of pessimism,[1] in which

---

[1] It is quite true, however, that this fact did not become fully apparent until St. Paul treated the matter from the more adequate standpoint of Christianity, and showed for all time that "the strength of sin is the Law." Yet St. Paul only revealed the significance of materials which were already latent in the pages of the Old Testament. The psalmists and prophets came face to face with the fact of sin as it is, and their experience demanded a gospel of redemption.

the facts of human nature are taken into account and dealt with as completely as a preparatory stage of religion could deal with them. Upon this preliminary basis of truthfulness to the darker realities of human nature our Lord was able to found His enduring optimism. First the disease was disclosed, and then the remedy was provided.

It is necessary now to examine two objections raised by Mr. Chamberlain against the idea of a Moral Law, objective and authoritative, coming to us from a personal and transcendent God. The first of these is that the Mosaic law was an *external* thing superimposed upon man, and therefore wholly artificial and alien to his life. He says: "Its moral commandments do not grow with inherent necessity out of the depths of the human heart, they are 'laws,' which were promulgated under definite conditions, and which can be repealed at any time."[1] He constantly speaks of the law under the aspect of numberless separate commands, which bewildered the mind and stifled the free growth of religion in the heart. Ezra and Nehemiah, by imposing it, finally killed religion and then mummified it; "by art of magic they had transformed warm blood into cold metal, and of this they had forged a vice for the soul . . . they had tied the arteries of spontaneous feeling . . . of the instinctive creative activity. . . ."[2] In all this denunciation of the law as external and artificial, Mr. Chamberlain exhibits great similarity to Mr. Shaw, who dislikes "morality" on the ground that it stifles the instincts.[3] We have seen how the latter

The Law objected to as (*a*) External.

---

[1] *Foundations of the Nineteenth Century*, vol. i. p. 229.
[2] Vol. i. pp. 473, 477.   [3] See above, Chapter III. 1. (iii.).

speaks of existing moral customs and ideas as artificial and alien, pernicious to the best interests of life, because they are moral. By this similarity between the two writers one may see where this tendency of thought in Mr. Chamberlain must lead. Early in this chapter it was said that, if he were right in his idea of the true ethical foundations, he would assuredly have escaped the pitfalls and inconsistencies into which other writers whom we have examined have fallen. Mr. Shaw founds conduct upon instinct because conduct is for him a subjective matter for each individual to decide; its basis is the isolated ego. Mr. Chamberlain's acceptance of Christian ideals might have led one to expect that he based morality upon religion, and therefore upon the common universal element in man, which would at least be a surer basis than pure individualism. We have seen, however, that in his view morality cannot be founded upon religion, for we are told that they have nothing to do with one another. As a matter of fact, however, in his account of Christianity he quietly assumes that the whole purpose of the religion of Christ was moral, in that it concentrated upon the will, as the instrument of conduct. This by the way; but even if Mr. Chamberlain had consistently maintained a religious basis for morality, it would not have improved matters much. We have seen that religion is in his view a thing of purely human device, born of human instincts, fashioned by man entirely according to his own fancies, and that therefore we have no guarantee that it expresses the universal in man. Yet if it does not do that it can supply no sure basis for social conduct.[1]

[1] See above, pp. 104, 105.

9

Thus, whichever way we turn, Mr. Chamberlain appears to have no better foundations than either Mr. Shaw or Mr. Wells. His whole scheme proceeds from "the heart of man"—a very vague and uncertain factor upon which to rely.

But let us return to the objection against law, on the ground that it is external. It will not be necessary to repeat all that has been said already about the delusion of thinking that a moral code must be artificial and formally imposed from without.[1] Morality, it is necessary to remember, can become as instinctive as instinct, if a man is going the right way about it; doubtless it did become so to vast numbers of pious Jews. The existence of Pharisees and legalists amongst them proves nothing to the contrary; whereas the 119th Psalm would have been an impossible production in a society on which law exercised the crushing effect described by Mr. Chamberlain. On the other hand, just because the moral law, where accepted, is always becoming increasingly a part of the man's inner life, there is ever something beyond instinct, which we may call the sense of duty. This is the advance guard of the moral life, the perception that there is more yet to be appropriated, and that by discipline of the will, before it too can become instinctive.

But behind this idea that the law is artificial and external lies the thought that it is arbitrary. "They are laws which were promulgated under definite conditions on fixed days, and which can be repealed at any time."[2] The only meaning which this sentence can convey

The Law objected to as (*b*) Arbitrary.

---

[1] See above, pp. 73 ff.
[2] *Foundations of the Nineteenth Century*, vol. i. p. 229.

is that the God Who gave the moral law is an arbitrary, capricious Person. If such be the case, then the law, though it may or may not change, is in essence arbitrary, because it is the expression of an arbitrary and all-dominating will; to obey it, therefore, is to be in a state of slavery and fear. In the introductory chapter it was said that, "if the fact of sin be true and the moral law a necessity, *we must pass behind it* and fall back upon a supreme righteous Personality, a moral Governor, whose authority we can accept as we cannot that of mere law in itself."[1] The three things hang together. If human nature be conceived of as perverted and weakened by sin, it must seek for a directing and regulating power outside itself. In its weakness and uncertainty, it must trust itself to that power absolutely, and obey it. There must, then, be law; and human nature finding itself so situated will gladly accept such a law. But it accepts the law, not for itself, but as the expression of a living Mind and Will behind, which is believed to be righteous and unchanging in its requirements. If a man believes himself to be a fallen sinner, the commands of a Righteous God are not arbitrary to him, but rather furnish his one hope of recovering the right path. He does not want his conduct to proceed from " the heart of man"; for he believes it to be "deceitful above all things and desperately wicked."

On the other hand, with Mr. Chamberlain's view of human nature as a reliable and stable foundation for conduct, the whole idea of God seems really unnecessary; and the imposition of His law upon the uncorrupted heart of man comes like an imper-

[1] See above, p. 20.

tinence.   From the same point of view the whole
of Israel's conception of their national history, as
ruled and directed by the Providence of God, naturally seems to be slavish and narrow.   Though we
put children to school, Mr. Chamberlain will not
allow that the human race could need any moral
discipline to lead it to Christ in its childhood.   In
his argument from the character of Jehovah, as he
conceives it to be depicted in the Old Testament, he
builds upon statements which are mutually contradictory.   At one time Jehovah is said to be grossly
partial to His chosen people, promising them bribes
to love Him, and from motives of favouritism
destroying all other nations.[1]   At another time we
are bidden to contrast the Heavenly Father of
Christ's teaching with the hard, stern taskmaster
who, by the mouth of the Deuteronomist, inculcated
a slavish fear.[2]   It is of course quite easy along
these lines to prove that the God of Israel is
"arbitrary."   If it is presupposed that all moral
discipline is arbitrary, then Jehovah comes under the
same charge, for He treats His people as children
who need both encouragement and chastening.
But when Mr. Chamberlain writes in this way, the
real thought at the back of his mind is that the whole
idea of a free Personal God, ruling the universe in
wisdom by His Will, is impossible.   To him the
universe is "mechanical" and governed by necessity.
He says: " He who mechanically interprets empirical
nature as perceived by the senses has an ideal religion
or none at all. . . . The Jew knew no mechanism of
any kind : from Creation out of nothing to his dreams

---

[1] *Foundations of the Nineteenth Century*, vol. i. pp. 392, 427, 453.
[2] *Ibid.*, vol. i. pp. 223, 240, 453.

of a Messianic future everything is in his case freely
ruling, all - powerful arbitrariness. . . . Consistent
mechanism, on the other hand, . . . is compatible
only with a purely ideal, *i.e.* transcendent religion,
such as Jesus Christ had taught : the kingdom of
God is within you." [1]

In these last words he means by "transcendent"
something entirely free from manifest connection
with the phenomenal world (such a connection, for
example, as is involved in a historical religion). In
other words, by a transcendent ideal religion he
means one which is wholly bound up in internal
spiritual experience transcending outward phenomena. This distinction is important, as will be seen
when we come to consider the sense in which he
interprets the final words of the above sentence,
quoted from our Lord—" The kingdom of God is
within you."

In Mr. Chamberlain's view the world of phenomena
has been finally proved to be absolutely mechanical ;
and therefore religion must be confined to the inner
experience of the soul. It has no place in history.
Consequently there is no place either for the idea of
a moral Creator governing the universe. [2] But this
is not all. He traces the Jewish belief in a Divine
Creator and Ruler to their exaggerated development of will and their strong belief in human free-
will. Accordingly he throws overboard, not only
divine, but also human free-will in the following
emphatic words : " Freedom of will implies nothing
less than 'ever-repeated acts of creation'; carefully
considered it will be clear that this supposition (as

---

[1] *Foundations of the Nineteenth Century*, vol. ii. p. 291.
[2] *Ibid.*, vol. i. p. 240.

soon as it has to do with the world of phenomena) contradicts not merely all physical science, but also all metaphysics, and means a negation of every transcendent religion. Here cognition and will stand in strict opposition."[1] Thus the poor will of man is shut up within his inner nature and its experiences, and is permitted no power of acting upon its phenomenal environment. Truly this is the apotheosis of fatalism, and the entombment alike of all religion and morals! Mr. Chamberlain, however, points with approval to the prevalence of the idea of Necessity amongst the Aryan races, as a mark of genuine religion; as, for example, when he writes thus of the fatalism of Homer: "Morality is in a way a personal affair, man is lord of his own heart, but not of his destiny;[2] there is no Providence that protects, punishes, and rewards. The gods themselves are in fact not free; Zeus himself must yield to fate."[3]

Thus far one seems driven to the following conclusions. Mr. Chamberlain can find no place in his scheme of life for any personal responsibility either for sin or for moral conduct. Man is not under the rule of a Personal Righteous God; there is no such thing as Divine Providence. Four-fifths of the life of man is bound down under the iron necessity of a mechanical world, including all that has anything to do with his outward conduct. Man cannot get rid of sin, for it is irretrievably a part of his own nature. He is avowedly upon the wheel of fate at every point, except that he still

[1] *Foundations of the Nineteenth Century*, vol. i. p. 241.

[2] This sounds like—"One can do as one likes without being responsible for the consequences."

[3] *Op. cit.*, vol. i. p. 239.

possesses a small circle of inner soul experiences, in which an "ideal" religion may flourish. Such are the results of throwing over the Christian conceptions of human nature and sin, God, providence, and the moral law.

We must now turn to Mr. Chamberlain's treatment of our Lord's Gospel of conduct, in order to discover whether it is possible to find a place in his scheme for any religion or morality worthy of the name at all; or whether here also, as elsewhere, fatalism does not bear him down.

Mr. Chamberlain speaks of Christianity as a religion of redemption and grace, and of our (iv.) Moral Lord as the Saviour. Also, he warmly Culture: approves what he calls the "cycle of (a) Redemption and Grace. myths" dealing with redemption, on the ground that they are anti-Judaic and Aryan. He applauds St. Augustine too for upholding the conception of grace against Pelagius. He says: "The kernel of the Christian religion . . . is the conception of a redemption of man."[1] But these sentiments are emptied of all meaning when one comes to look at his view of religion as a whole. His doctrine of human nature and sin, as has already been pointed out, leaves no place for any work of grace. Since he has changed the meaning of sin from "degeneration" to "imperfection," there can be no place for a recovery. What meaning can one give to the word "redemption," when we have been told that sin is a necessary part of our nature, a state from which we cannot escape? And what is to be thought of the word "grace" when used in this connection? Let us

[1] *Foundations of the Nineteenth Century*, vol. ii. p. 31.

hear his own definition of the meaning of these phrases:—"The idea of redemption—or let us rather say the mythical conception of redemption —embraces two others: that of a present imperfection, and of a possible perfection by some non-empirical, that is, in a certain sense supernatural or transcendental process: the one is symbolised by the myth of degeneration, the other by that of a gracious help bestowed by a Higher Being."[1] The more one considers this statement, the more firmly is one convinced that it strips the whole phraseology of redemption of every shred of meaning. Redemption is said to mean that we are not yet perfect, but that we may become perfect by some process, the experience of which we cannot analyse or understand. The process by which we progress is not to be reduced to the phraseology of mechanical science; that is all that grace amounts to. It should be noticed that Mr. Chamberlain only allows that these things are "symbolised by myths." The weak point, however, is that the symbol conveys an idea which is entirely different from the reality. "Degeneration" is not "imperfection," and "gracious help bestowed by a Higher Being" is emphatically not the same as possible perfection by a process which we cannot analyse. For the process may come from within ourselves, and in this case it is simply folly to say that it can be symbolized by any idea of gracious help. The truth is, if the above quotation means anything at all, it means that redemption can be reduced to the dimensions of the word "progress," understood to mean progress in perfection, which we can effect for ourselves, though

[1] *Foundations of the Nineteenth Century*, vol. ii. p. 32.

we do not know enough to say how it actually takes place. In this way Mr. Chamberlain is able to say that the ideas of redemption and grace are common to all Aryans. A sense of imperfection, failure, and a disordered world, a need of help from the gods, the pains of remorse, the thought of pursuing furies, these things are doubtless familiar features of Greek tragedy; but in what sense can they be compared to the biblical ideas of redemption and grace? Did they provide any platform upon which a higher optimism might be directly built? Indeed was it not in spite of these things that the cheerful tempera- ment of the Greeks persisted in asserting itself? They were in no sense redeemed from the evil to the good, but they accepted the two things together upon the same plane. In the case of the Indians Mr. Chamberlain admits that the idea of a degenera- tion is not clearly formulated; that is to say, they have no sense of the failure of life, of a "present imperfection": "On the other hand, grace is the radiant sun of Indian faith."[1] Or to put it in his own phraseology, though they have no clear sense of imperfection, they do believe in the possibility of perfection by some non-empirical process. A little further on Mr. Chamberlain makes clear what he means by this Indian belief in grace; and at the same time, whilst he puts the Christian conception of grace on a level with it, he shows unmistakably that in neither case is it really grace of which he is speaking at all. It is the same here as in the case of Hellenism, referred to above, where the note of tragedy has no claim to be identified with a doctrine of redemption from sin. This is what he says of

[1] *Op. cit.*, vol. ii. pp. 32, 33.

the Indian and Christian ideas of grace : "What gift is it that this metaphysical myth lets us 'receive by grace'?   According to the Indo-Eranians knowledge, according to the European Christians faith ; both guaranteeing a regeneration, that is, awakening man to the consciousness of a different connection of things.   I quote again the words of Christ, . . . 'The kingdom of God is within you.' This is a discernment or a faith obtained by divine grace. Redemption by knowledge, redemption by faith : two views which are not so very different as people have thought : the Indian and Buddha put the emphasis on the intellect, the Græco-Teuton, taught by Jesus Christ, upon the will : two interpretations of the same inner experience."[1]   Yet he acknowledges the former to be negative and the latter positive.   But whatever distinction he makes between the two, Mr. Chamberlain would have us believe that grace is a poetical name for a process of redemption *by our own faculties*.   If it were true that Christian redemption were by faith alone, then indeed our religion would be no better than the Brahmin's ; for whether it be intellect or will which is exercised, the whole process would come from ourselves alone.   But this is not the teaching of St. Paul, whom Mr. Chamberlain frequently quotes to his own convenience.   He says : "By grace have ye been saved through faith."[2] Faith is here the instrument of grace ; whereas Mr. Chamberlain makes grace an expression for the mere exercise of faith autonomously.   Thus, following the lead of more orthodox Protestants before him, he preaches salvation through works under the guise of faith.   Enough has, perhaps, been said to

[1] *Op. cit.*, vol. ii. pp. 40, 41.   [2] Ephesians ii. 8.

show that Mr. Chamberlain's view of redemption and grace is of a piece with his ideas about human nature and sin, religion and morality. It is all based, from beginning to end, upon the unaided will of man.

Let us now turn to his summary of the Gospel teaching, and see how he grafts it on to this stem. (*b*) Treatment He takes the keynote of our Lord's of the Will. teaching to be "the regeneration of the human will," and rightly so. But the idea of re-generation or re-birth to a new spiritual life has always meant for Christians a supreme work of God, wrought by Him upon the heart and will of man. It is a work which man has not, and never can have, any power of accomplishing for himself on account of the diseased state of his will. Mr. Chamberlain correctly speaks of it as "a conversion of the direc-tion of life,"[1] quoting St. Matthew xviii. 3. Again he says: "The one thing which concerns Him is the inner and spiritual conversion,"[2] and "it is not merely self-control . . . but that conversion of the will, that entry into the hidden Kingdom of God, that being born again, which makes up the sum of Christ's example, demands a complete con-version of the feelings. This, in fact, is the new thing."[3] This is undoubtedly the very essence of the Gospel; but what possible connection can it have with the view of human life unfolded by this writer? How can a will which has suffered no degeneration or misdirection, which sin has left un-touched by any contaminating influence, which is only imperfect, though rightly orientated in the

---

[1] *Foundations of the Nineteenth Century*, vol. i. p. 188.
[2] *Ibid.*, p. 192.   [3] *Ibid.*, vol. i. p. 195.

direction marked out by nature—how can such a
will require conversion? Strengthening perhaps;
but re-direction would involve a flat denial of every
single thing Mr. Chamberlain has said elsewhere
about the nature of the will and its relation to sin
and to religion.   If it is so self-contained and
sufficient that by its exercise man can be redeemed,[1]
how can it possibly require to be re-born?

If "regeneration" and "conversion" meant to
Mr. Chamberlain what they mean to the ordinary
Christian, one half of his system would be completely contradictory to the other; but as a matter
of fact what he means is something different, as
he has made abundantly clear. He compares the
work of our Lord for man to our modern discovery
of electricity. As man has discovered hidden in
the world a power already there, which he now
knows how to use, "so Christ *pointed to a hidden
power*[2] in the unfathomed and unfathomable depths
of the human heart, a power capable of completely
transforming man, capable of making a sorrow-
trodden wretch mighty and blessed. The lightning
had hitherto been only a destroyer; the power
which it taught us to discover is now the servant
of peaceful work and comfort. In like manner the
human will, from the beginning of time the seed
of all the misfortune and misery that descended
upon the human race, was henceforth to minister
to the new birth of this race, to the rise of a new
human species."[3] The language used here, and
especially the simile of lightning employed, make
the writer's meaning perfectly clear. The work of

---

[1] See above, p. 138.   [2] The italics are my own.
[3] *Foundations of the Nineteenth Century*, vol. i. p. 196.

Christ for man was to discover for him a hidden power in his will. The power was already there; our Lord merely brought it to light and showed man by example how it might be used. This is not a "conversion"; to use such a word is entirely misleading. The only change here conceived of is in the nature of a development. What was implicit all along becomes explicit; its use is understood for the first time, but nothing new is added. So the writer goes on to describe the fruits of this so-called "conversion" of the will exactly as though they proceeded from the development of some faculty, though it happens to be a moral faculty, and not an æsthetic or intellectual one. "What Greece did for the intellect, Christ did for the moral life; man had not a moral culture till He gave it. I should rather say the possibility of a moral culture; for the motive power of culture is that inner creative process; the voluntary masterful conversion of the will, and this very motive power was with rare exceptions quite overlooked."[1] The last word in this passage shows once more that the power referred to is conceived as being there before; it might have been discovered by anybody. The use of the word "culture" also is significant. It conveys the idea of something acquired entirely by the exercise of the human faculties. So again a little later, speaking of the introduction of Christianity, he says: "Now and now only did life become truly tragical. This was brought about *by man's own free act in rising against his animal nature*. As Homer had created gods such as he wished them, so now man rebelled against the moral tyranny of

[1] *Op. cit.*, vol. i. p. 197.

nature and created a sublime morality such as he desired."[1] Thus Christ is only a giant amongst heroes. He only saw and pointed out that which belonged to all. The Gospel is thought of, not as a redemption of the weak and sinful, but as a discovery of the inherent greatness and self-sufficiency of man. The Sermon on the Mount becomes merely a proclamation of what the human will is capable of attaining by its own unaided greatness. The new Adam has appeared, but he is not the Head of a new race saved and reborn out of the old. He is only the usher who points the way to a fresh development of human power; there is no breach with the past, no intervention of God.

It is extraordinary that anyone with Mr. Chamberlain's appreciation of our Lord and His teaching (c) Incompatibility with New Testament teaching. could have blundered so far from the truth. His description of that teaching contains passages full of glowing appreciation; his seizure of the central idea of will-conversion is admirable, and his description of its significance for conduct is impressive. It would indeed have been profoundly true, if only he could have seen that the basis of this new will-power lies wholly in God and not in man. But indeed he must have found it hard to fit Christianity into his view of life. He is obliged to admit that our Lord accepted certain fundamental Jewish ideas;—as though, whilst he holds them to be anathema in the Old Testament, they could become true in the New Testament. The " Heavenly Father " of the

[1] *Foundations of the Nineteenth Century*, vol. i. p. 198. The italics are my own.

Gospel forgives sins and gives daily bread in answer to our prayers. But on Mr. Chamberlain's showing there is no such thing as transgression of the law of God by the human will, and therefore forgiveness is meaningless and impossible; whilst he holds that the Jews are base and selfish materialists for seeking their daily bread from Jehovah. So too the Law, which he will have nothing of, was not, as he suggests, acquiesced in with indifference by our Lord and repudiated altogether by St. Paul. It was actually referred to with emphatic approval by both. "I came not to destroy the law but to fulfil." "Not one tittle of the law shall fail." "The scribes and Pharisees sit on Moses' seat: all things therefore whatsoever they bid you, these do and keep." "The law is holy, and the commandment holy and just and good." "The law is spiritual."[1] These sayings do not agree well with Mr. Chamberlain's theory. He has, moreover, himself pointed out the revolutionary character of Christ's teaching, and shown how completely it transforms all ordinary values. Can he really have believed that this could issue from a normal development of the human will from imperfection towards some higher stage? In this connection it should be noticed that, while his rejection of the ascetic traits in the Gospel is in complete harmony with his Pelagianism, it is in violent contradiction to his recognition of the revolutionary character of our Lord's teaching. "The life of Jesus," he says, "is an open declaration of war, not against the forms of civilisation, culture, and religion, which He found around . . . but certainly against the inner spirit of mankind, against the

[1] St. Matthew v. 17, 18; xxiii. 2, 3. Romans vii. 12, 14.

motives which underlie their actions, against the
goal which they set for themselves in the future
life and in the present."[1]   One sets this beside
such a sentence as the following: " The Buddhist
steering for death may be satisfied with poverty,
chastity, and obedience; he who chooses life has
other things to think of."[2]   These "other things,"
as we have just seen, include the task of revolu-
tionising the spirit of mankind, and this revolution
is to be effected by the will of man, unaided and
undisciplined, and without any alteration of its
direction.   We shall consider the value of asceticism
in a later chapter; for the present, one may here
observe how the rejection of objective moral law
involves also the rejection of all moral discipline.
The human will is thus supposed to need neither
superior guidance, rule, nor discipline; naked and
alone it must embark on a crusade against "the
inner spirit of mankind."   But "the inner spirit of
mankind" must surely reside in the will, and therefore the will must needs fight against itself, nature
against nature.   The whole conflict goes on within
the "circle of nature"; and thus we are brought
back to the method which, as we have seen in the
case of other writers, proves such a complete
failure.

Before concluding this criticism of an attempt to
base the Christian ethic upon the Natural Man, it
(*d*) Fatalistic is necessary to refer to one or two
Tendencies. features of Mr. Chamberlain's system
which seem to be subversive both of religion and
of morality.

[1] *Foundations of the Nineteenth Century*, vol. i. p. 193.
[2] *Ibid.*, p. 192.

First, let us notice his intense dislike for the Christian doctrine of rewards and punishments. His objections are similar to those usually put forward on this subject : "Ecclesiastical Christianity rests on fear and hope, on the one side eternal reward, on the other eternal punishment." He speaks of the "fundamental difference between a religion which addresses itself to the purely selfish emotions of the heart, *i.e.* to fear and desire, and a religion which, like that of Brahma, regards the renunciation of the enjoyment of all reward here and in the other world as the first step towards initiation into true piety."[1] He goes on to say that such a religion of rewards and punishments is inconsistent with the whole idea of redemption. It is obviously impossible to enter at length into the catholic doctrine upon this subject in the present work. Moreover, for our immediate purpose it is sufficient to point out that it is so firmly rooted in all the accounts of our Lord's teaching that it is impossible to get rid of it. Mr. Chamberlain, however, finds it convenient to pass that by ; and thus he affords one more clear proof of the incompatibility of his system with that of the New Testament. It is not hard to see why he dislikes this particular doctrine. It is inconsistent, not with redemptive religion, but with a naturalistic view of redemption, which rejects the idea of a moral law. We have seen elsewhere how Mr. Chamberlain eliminates the responsibility of the individual for his sins.[2] The individual is autono-

(1) Elimination of Rewards and Punishments.

---

[1] *Op. cit.*, vol. ii. p. 47, with the footnote; *cf.* vol. ii. pp. 414–417.
[2] pp. 116–123 ff.

mous; he is answerable to no higher power, and therefore rewards and punishments are alike impossible. Yet as a matter of fact Mr. Chamberlain does not get away from these ideas. He speaks with approval of the Indian doctrine of transmigration of souls; and in his description of it he shows that he quite understands its only possible significance, for he quotes with approval Origen's views on the subject: " The spirits of men are regarded as being created from eternity; according to their conduct they rise or sink, until finally all without exception are transfigured, even the demons." To this he adds the remark: " In such a system, it is plain that neither the individual life itself, nor the promise of reward and the threat of punishment, has anything in common with the Judæo-Christian religion." [1]   But what are we to call this belief that "according to their conduct they rise or sink"? It is simply the doctrine of rewards and punishments in a fresh setting. Indeed, the only difference is that in the Christian scheme the individual personality is treated with greater respect, being regarded as responsible for its own actions. On the other hand, according to the theory of transmigration of souls the individual may have the " reward " of being merged in a final transfiguration; but his personality is not preserved as having any value in itself. In short, this dislike for rewards and punishments is fatalistic; it is all in harmony with the repudiation of a ruling Providence and of the reality of moral evil. The extent to which all this undermines religion may be gathered from such a passage as the following:—" Almost all genuine humanists, when they

[1] *Op. cit.*, vol. ii. pp. 48, 49.

have the necessary courage, devote much thought to the already discussed central problem of all ethics, and are all without exception of the opinion . . . that a virtue which aims at reward is no virtue; that to regard fear and hope as moral motives is childish and worthy only of the uneducated mob; that the idea of immortality should be considered from a purely philosophical standpoint and has nothing to do with the theory of morals . . ."[1] Now for Christians morality has always been a means to an end; and the end is holiness, blessedness, a state of perfect communion with God. A belief in immortality is vital to this; for without it conduct has no religious aim at all, and religion has no practical bearing upon this life. Thus morality, secularized and destitute of any eternal import, becomes a mere culture of this world, fundamentally opposed to that Christian Gospel which Mr. Chamberlain professes to embrace.

Moreover, by making morality non-religious and disinterested he falls back into the purely naturalistic (2) Race Culture. groove, and has to seek elsewhere for an incentive to moral effort. He does not succeed in eliminating the need for moral incentives; and since he will not have those provided by the Gospel, it is not to be wondered at that he finds the needed stimulus in something very earthly and material.[2] We have seen, how, one by one, each

---

[1] *Op. cit.*, vol. ii. p. 429.
[2] It must not be concluded that the present writer believes all the moral incentives of the Christian to lie in the hope of *future* reward. This is very far from being the case, as will be gathered from Chapters V. and VII. The present aim is to show the failure of " disinterested morality," which scornfully rejects *all* idea of " incentives " to virtue as such.

of the writers examined hitherto has made his own attempt at solving this problem of the end and aim towards which man should be setting his face. Some have sought it in happiness for the individual or for society as a whole ; others in the advancement of the race to greater individual or social power, or in the birth of a new race through the development of a new science of breeding. It has remained for Mr. Chamberlain to treat Christianity as the "moral culture" suitable to one particular section of humanity, the Anglo-Saxon and Teutonic, and as the ripe fruit to be looked for from successful breeding of race. Anyone who reads his treatment of this question of race-breeding in the light of the criticisms here made upon his religious and moral ideas will see at once their close connection.[1] Throughout this chapter at one point after another it has been maintained that this writer bases all conduct upon a power inherent in the unaided human will, conceived as self-sufficient and autonomous ; and that at the same time he destroys all idea of personal responsibility for right and wrong action. It follows that the real problem of importance in history is neither a religious nor a moral one ; the question is, rather, how to produce by natural means such vigorous specimens of the human race as will possess the necessary vitality of will to achieve a high moral culture. Fortunately for his own sake, Mr. Chamberlain does not, like Mr. Shaw, attempt to solve this problem of breeding ; he considers it to be solved already in his noble Teutons, the nations of Germany, Britain, and North America. Having reached the conclusion that the Teutonic race has the necessary physi-

[1] See especially vol. i. chapters iv.–vi. of his book.

cal basis for a high moral culture, he considers it sufficient to point out that our Lord, Himself akin to the Teutons by blood—for so it is seriously contended,—has shown the moral possibilities of a strong and efficient will such as these happy Teutons possess. By this means "moral culture" is confined to those who are alone capable of it by blood; and for those who are in this fortunate position the incentive to high and noble conduct is that such conduct brings further glory to their race, and fresh proof of their pure blood. As for the unfortunate races of "the Chaos," those of mongrel blood, they must perforce remain content with their slavish religion and their bad moral traditions. Thus conduct is in fact made to depend upon purely physical considerations, as it is by Mr. Shaw and also by Nietzsche. For Mr. Chamberlain the Teuton occupies very much the same position as the superman does in these other systems. All through, in fact, in spite of his appreciation of our Lord's ethical teaching, he betrays his affinity with the group of writers examined in Chapters II. and III. Both the features last alluded to—namely, a disinterested non-religious morality, and the basing of conduct upon breeding —have appeared in slightly different guise in those writers. They are the only possible result of attempting to build conduct upon purely natural foundations. They involve the elimination of all free-will, all significance for the individual as such, and therefore all justification for attaching any value to the Christian or social view of life; for that view is based upon the supremely important place given by our Lord to each individual soul. Thus Mr. Chamberlain's attempt to accept the Christian view of conduct, without the objective moral law, must be pronounced a failure. At every point his system falls back on to that same plane of nature which, as has already been shown, is an impossible basis for any ethical system except the most extreme of all; and this, if consistently practised, would destroy its adherents.

Human nature is disordered and weakened and requires a new direction. It requires a law, higher (v.) Transition than itself, and coming from a super-to Part II. natural source, to furnish guidance to it in unravelling the tangle of life. But *law by itself is not enough*. That is the truth of all the criticisms of morality and law which we have encountered in this discussion. Law by itself would be tyranny; that is the truth of all that has been said in depreciation of " duty "—a note which several writers have struck recently.[1] And, if duty were all, they would be right; as they would if duty had to be met by the Natural Man whose failure we have traced. But that is not so. Christianity stands for the conviction that a way has been provided whereby man may be lifted out of the purely natural sphere, and may receive power to obey the moral law with ever-increasing conformity to its inner spirit. In this chapter it has been argued that one must either recognize the necessity of this supernatural basis for conduct, or else move back to some extreme form of individualism. It appears that a position such as that taken up by Mr. Chamberlain will be seen increasingly to be impossible. Men

[1] *E.g.* Mr. H. W. Garrod, *The Religion of All Good Men*, p. 155; *cf.* Mr. Shaw's treatment of the subject in his plays and prefaces.

will not be deceived into accepting the idea of a genial Hellenic Christianity which can be practised instinctively without the discipline of duty. There are those who expressly declare their dislike for the Christian way of life because of its stern, ascetic devotion to duty; Hellenism is preferred because it seems to stand for all that is bright and harmonious.[1] Mr. Garrod, in his *Religion of All Good Men*, has declared war on Christian morality on the ground that it is "a kind of misology," something anti-natural; only he does not agree that Hellenism is an adequate substitute. He sees that the Natural Man cannot of himself solve the problem by mere "æsthetic contemplation," and assumption of a beautiful harmony which does not exist. "Hellenism," he says, "is superior to Christianity in and so far as it is more natural. But what we want, if we are to live good and effective lives, is something that shall have the naturalness of Hellenism and yet at the same time a deeper earnestness, a character more vigorous and robust."[2] He thinks this is to be found in "the morality of the North," the original natural virtues of the races of Northern Europe. He goes on to reject the idea of "doing one's duty" on the ground that it is cold and insufficient; for duty he would substitute the "Gothic" virtue of honour. This plea for "honour" in place of "duty" is closely similar to Mr. Shaw's preference of instinct to duty. It is a plea for live conduct as against mere convention, for behaviour corresponding to the soul's inner life rather than to external standards. Attention is

---

[1] *E.g.* Mr. G. Lowes Dickinson in his *Religion : a Criticism and a Forecast*, pp. 70, 71.

[2] *The Religion of All Good Men*, pp. 143, 152, 153, 161.

drawn to it here because Mr. Garrod's treatment of "duty" forms part of his criticism of the Christian ethic. It provides one more example of a widespread idea that the Christian ideal of conduct must be gloomy and uninspiring because it is based upon moral rule and law, and not on natural instinct and feeling. Morality starting from authoritative rules which come into conflict with natural desires is supposed to be inevitably a pessimistic and forbidding thing.[1] Christianity is regarded as ending in law and the sense of sin. But these are in fact only the starting-point of the Christian, parts of the foundation upon which the superstructure is built. The true method by which Christianity moulds conduct will be set forth in what follows.

[1] See Prof. Karl Pearson, *The Ethic of Free Thought*, pp. 317–325 (1st edition). *Cf.* G. B. Shaw and H. G. Wells, *passim.*

Part II.—THE CHRISTIAN ETHIC

CHAPTER V

THE OTHERWORLDLY PRINCIPLE

So far the purpose of this discussion has been to show that in the search for the foundations of conduct one is driven from the natural to the supernatural. This is not to be construed as meaning that the natural order is in itself bad, but rather that it is imperfect and incomplete. It contains within itself certain possibilities of moral achievement which it is unable to realize. "The children are come to the birth, and there is not strength to bring forth." That is the tragedy of the situation. This imperfection takes the form of a kind of over-luxuriousness; there is a want of restraint and balance, an impression of vagueness and discursiveness. The appearance of the Natural Man is like a plant unable to bear the weight of its own wild growth, trailing upon the ground, and needing something strong and stable to support it. There is an abundance of sap, but not of the right sort. An endeavour has been made to show that the objective moral law is like the wall upon which this trailing plant must be trained to climb. If there is an inherent weakness somewhere within it, it cannot provide for itself a support and a direction for its

(i.) Résumé.

153

growth. That must come from an independent
source. But even so the whole difficulty has not
been covered. Rather the weakness has only now
been revealed ; since by the law comes the knowledge of sin. Some superior vitality must enter the
plant, in order that it may be able to climb to the
heights now required of it. This need is met by
the supernatural Gospel of Christ.

George Tyrrell has reminded us that it is essential,
in all that bears upon conduct, to remember that
man is so constituted that he must live his life in
two worlds, which he calls the world of phenomena
and the world of reality ; and by the latter he means
that invisible sphere of the self to which the will
holds the key.[1] Some such conception appears to be
absolutely necessary. Whether we call the invisible
world " the world of reality " or not, we must at least
hold that the whole significance of man's inner life
belongs to that world. Moreover, whilst there is no
ground for doubting their reality, the phenomena
of the earthly and visible sphere have no sort of
ultimate meaning or value for man, except in so
far as he can correlate them to that invisible world,
whence for him supreme reality springs. From this
point of view all the failure of the Natural Man
which has been traced in Part I. is seen to be due
to the attempt on the part of man—not perhaps to
rest in the world of phenomena, as though it alone
were valid, but at least—to find in that world the
centre of gravity for human life ; whereas the real
and proper centre of the will-activities is elsewhere.
Now the Christian interpretation of life is based
upon this assumption of a transcendental and super-

[1] *Lex Orandi*, ch. ii.

natural centre of gravity, from which the will-activity must proceed.   The truth of this assumption has been confirmed by the fact that the attempt to base Christian conduct on the opposite presuppositions is seen to break down (chapter iv.). Mr. Chamberlain, however, appears to stand alone in his attempt.   For the most part modern objections to the Christian ideals are based expressly upon the ground that they are absolutely bound up with a supernatural or, as some prefer to call it, an anti-natural view of life.   In other words, the Christian way of life is seen to be the complete antithesis of all other ways ; and it is so because it claims to be based upon a real entrance of Divine grace into the heart of man, which lifts him on to an altogether different plane.   From that plane the whole of life in all its relationships is viewed with different eyes.   Nothing but good can come from the recognition of this great gulf fixed.   The Christian has everything to gain, and nothing to lose, when attempted compromises are given up, and this supernatural and universal claim is frankly acknowledged and examined.

It is this which gives value to some recent criticism of Christianity by Mr. H. W. Garrod in the earlier (ii.) Mr. H. W. part of his *The Religion of All Good* Garrod's Essay: *Men* (Essay I., "Christ the Forerunner"). *Christ the Forerunner.* With the help of his criticisms it is possible to go at once to the very heart of our Lord's standpoint in matters of conduct.   Reference was made just now to the great gulf fixed between the Christian and all other views of life.   This writer makes us see this gulf with remarkable clearness by his treatment of the Apocalyptic element in our

Lord's teaching. We may set aside here his peculiar idea that our Lord believed Himself to be only a Forerunner of the real " Son of Man." Such a question lies outside the limits of a discussion about the ethical ideals of Christianity ; and the elimination of this point does not seem to affect the general bearing of the essay. With this limitation, therefore, let us now briefly survey his argument.

John the Baptist came as a prophet, preaching the Messianic doctrine of a Kingdom to come ; but, unlike most of the prophets, he made it perfectly clear that that Kingdom was on the point of being inaugurated. He emphasized this sense of immediacy by instituting his baptism of repentance for sins. The Kingdom of God, which was at hand, was in fact none other than the end of the world ; it was depicted as the consummation of the wrath of God, and it would come as a fire to burn up the ungodly. Under the sense of this approaching end the ordinary affairs of life sank into insignificance in John's eyes. He gave advice upon questions of conduct, which it would be impossible for any to follow if they wished to provide for a normal future. This was John's purpose ; he desired to show that the ordinary rules of life were no longer of any use. Only one thing was important—to prepare for the approaching catastrophe. Christ was a disciple of John the Baptist who on the whole held the same views as His master. The only difference is that the approaching end of the world was viewed by Him, as time went on, less as a coming of wrath and judgment to the ungodly, and more frequently as a coming of peace and rest to those who under-

stood and were prepared. Mr. Garrod considers
that our Lord developed John's central idea in this
and other ways ; amongst these developments was a
distinction made between two comings of the Son of
Man, the first being described by Mr. Garrod as
apocalyptic, and the second as *eschatological*.[1] Our
Lord therefore spoke of the end of the world in two
senses. First there would come the end of the
present order, though *not* of terrestrial existence.
The Son of Man would reign upon earth in the new
order of life ; and then finally there would come
a more remote *eschatological* end of the world,
when the scene would be shifted from this earthly
plane altogether. The point of importance for our
present purpose is that the era ushered in by the first,
or *apocalyptic*, coming of the Son of Man is conceived by Mr. Garrod as being one in which all the
relationships of life are so entirely changed that
existing standards of value will be of no account
whatever. Accordingly our Lord addressed His
ethical teaching to men who accepted His prediction
of the immediate approach of the apocalyptic end ;
and the ideal of conduct set forth in the Gospels
must be appraised in the light of these circumstances which gave rise to it. With these views
as his starting-point, Mr. Garrod does not find it
hard to point out their significance. The Christian
ideals of conduct were first set forth by One who
believed the existing order of things to be at the
point of dissolution to men who accepted that
supposition as true. For Christ and His disciples,
therefore, His teaching had a tremendous meaning.

[1] *The Religion of All Good Men*, Appendix A, p. 114; *cf.*
p. 20 note.

For us, who know that the world did not come to an end and that it has not yet done so in the manner expected, such teaching, in so far as it hinges round this apocalyptic idea, has no meaning whatever ; it must be discarded.   Mr. Garrod does not think that all our Lord's teaching would be ruled out as impracticable on these lines, but that most of it would be ; and that all the more arresting and revolutionary elements would thus be eliminated.   He believes, however, that in spite of all this Christ and His words are still significant for us ; as also are the messages of St. John Baptist and St. Paul, which are so closely bound up with those words of Christ in the New Testament.   In the concluding words of the essay he sums up what he believes to be the truth which remains to us of our Lord's teaching :— "The year [of the End] is ever upon us daily . . . the end of all things is ever staring us in the face. John was right, Jesus was right, S. Paul was right, when each proclaimed the immediate coming of the Kingdom of God.   It comes daily, when Satan (that is, Sin and Ignorance . . .) is cast down . . . when 'men of a savage temper' are diverted from their wrath by the soft answer of good sense.   It comes daily to all who, without losing interest in life, or the healthy sense of the world, *yet feel that all their actions look to an end that is not on earth.* . . . For that which sent John to the dungeon, Christ to the Cross, Paul to the block, each filled with the faith of the instant coming of the Lord, was nothing else than this—the sense, which should be in each one of us, of a perfection ever about to be attained, a joy and peace ever about to be realised.   He who has not this sense of the ideal may, as truly as he that

lacks ' charity,' be counted dead before God."[1]   The
words placed in italics are of special interest because
they seem to show that the writer is prepared to
accept the Christian conception of two worlds, the
one phenomenal and the other spiritual ; and of
these the spiritual world is at least regarded as the
magnetic centre towards which all actions ought to
be directed.   In other parts of this book, however,
the writer makes it perfectly clear that he does not
accept the spiritual world as in any sense the *starting-
point* from which the human will should be stirred and
empowered for its activities.[2]   There would thus be
two centres of gravity, the natural and the spiritual ;
and all conduct would find its original inspiration and
power wholly in the former, whilst its aim and purpose
would have reference wholly to the latter.   Such a conception would no doubt seem feasible to Mr. Garrod,
because he believes that we should hold to an ideal
of co-operation between flesh and spirit, instead of
accepting the antagonism found everywhere in the
teaching of St. Paul.[3]   If he admits the conception
of two worlds, as the words quoted above suggest,
they are not separated, as Christians hold, apart
from Divine grace ; but, rather, they are like circles
intersecting.   The centres may be distinct, but we
may pass easily from one to the other by natural
processes.   This seems to bring us back to the
naturalistic conception of human nature, in which
there is no dualism,—a conception similar to that of
Mr. Chamberlain, when he speaks of the moral life
as being in the heart of man and proceeding from

---

[1] *The Religion of All Good Men*, pp. 111, 112.   The italics are
my own.

[2] *E.g.* pp. 152, 153, 161.   [3] *Ibid.*, p. 101.

his own will.   For Mr. Garrod therefore the words "The Kingdom of God is at hand" have much the same significance as for the author of *Foundations of the Nineteenth Century*; only the latter prefers the alternative phrase, "The Kingdom of God is within you."   In both cases the apprehension of the Kingdom by the individual is conceived as "natural" and autonomous.   The difference of phraseology, however, is characteristic of a difference in outlook.   Mr. Garrod sees the catastrophic aspect of the Gospel, the other regards it as an inward secret of harmonious development ; both views are adequately recognized in that of the catholic tradition.

At this point in the inquiry one may well feel that the very heart of the whole problem before us has been reached.   Naturalism has failed at every point.   The necessity of fulfilling a moral standard lies upon man ; and that standard must be exacting in its demands, because it is in some sense not of him, but over against and above him.   Then there is set before us this other picture of a Kingdom of God, "a perfection ever about to be attained, a joy and peace ever about to be realized."   Can we enter it of ourselves?   Mr. Chamberlain replies, "Yes, emphatically, for by an effort of will you may find it in your own heart"; Mr. Garrod, more doubtfully and with many qualifications, would say, "Yes, but not as Christ and His immediate followers did." Many of the ideals which our Lord placed within the bounds of that Kingdom are, we are told, impossible; as, for example, universal love, humility, and meekness under all circumstances.[1]   Now these

(iii.) The Otherworldly Principle : (a) The Christian Experience.

---

[1] *The Religion of All Good Men*, p. 74.

are just those virtues most characteristic of our Lord Himself and of those saints who have seemed to come closest to Him in sympathy and character. Moreover, they have practised these things, and have been able to do so (for thus they all bear witness) just in so far as they have known Him not as an example merely, nor even as a Personality which has become impressed upon their imagination, but as a living Person. They bear witness that He has actually communicated His personal Presence to them, creating a spiritual atmosphere in which His life has mingled with theirs as a cordial in the blood, setting on fire their inmost souls with high conceptions and aspirations, and bracing them with power to accomplish in due course that to which they have aspired. All this has been the common experience of the saints, and, in a lesser measure, of all who are Christians in more than name. Yet it is just this element of experience which Mr. Garrod rules out from that measure of Christianity which he is prepared to accept.

"This unique and potent personality," he says, referring to our Lord, "we cannot too intently contemplate. I say *personality* advisedly and not person. The *Person* of Christ has passed for ever from the earth. . . . They are foolish Galileans, who think to-day to recall it. . . . We can never know Christ as the Middle Ages, with their vigour of faith and defect of history, thought to know Him. He can never be to us a person, a friend. . . . We cannot, as we fain would, lavish on His Person the devotion of intimacy."[1] Also in a note he speaks of "this unknowable thing—the Person of Christ."

[1] *The Religion of All Good Men*, p. 70.

Now it is words such as these which are the proper key to this writer's view of the Christian way of life as something transitory and unpracticable, as the overstrained ideals of a visionary. The whole of this essay ("Christ the Forerunner") gives the impression of an external survey, which misses the mark. For the Christian rule of conduct must always remain, as it were, written in a cypher, unless one has found the key to it ; and that is contained in the experience of the Person of Christ. All such criticisms as those which we are now considering fall flat upon the ear of the Christian who has this experience. Indeed, they must do so from the very nature of things. His experience of personal relationship to a living Christ is—speaking in the strictest sense—the most real and objective fact of which he has any consciousness, if perhaps we except the consciousness of his own existence. There are times, too, when even this latter reality seems merged in the former : " I live, yet not I, but Christ liveth in me." It is this absolute certainty which justifies him in taking up, in the first instance, a Tertullianist attitude. In the light of this one supreme experience every word uttered by our Lord, however strange and abrupt it may seem, has its necessary place in the rule of Christian conduct. Without this one supreme experience of the personal touch of Christ upon the soul, the whole New Testament becomes a meaningless enigma ; and it is only the force of tradition which has obscured this fact from the eyes of many in the past. But this is not to plead for obscurantism. Having said this much, one may now go on to give in some detail the interpretation of those points which Mr. Garrod has raised.

First then it appears that this writer has described the external features of our Lord's teaching very clearly, with, however, one important exception.[1] The Kingdom of God, or of Heaven, is undoubtedly the core of His positive message ; and it is conceived in terms which bring us at once into an atmosphere of immediacy and intense crisis. Mr. Garrod seems to be quite right in holding that the coming of the Kingdom is pictured by our Lord in two ways, which, as he says, may be conveniently described respectively as apocalyptic and eschatological. The coming is both immediate and remote ; it involves urgency which brooks no delay, yet patience also which will try a man's powers of endurance. The latter conception—that of a remote consummation, which is none the less certain—could hardly strike anyone as disruptive of ordinary moral motives. Rather do the rewards and punishments associated with it seem to be natural incentives which human nature requires.[2] But what of the other coming, that which is apocalyptic and immediate ? Is it true, as Mr. Garrod asserts, that this ushers in a dispensation in which all things are entirely different ? May this arrival of the Kingdom of God be described without qualification as the end of the world, so long as by "world" we understand not "mundus" but "societas hominum"?[3] Yes, indeed it may. Christianity brought a disruption quite as complete

(b) The Disruptive Element in the Gospel.

---

[1] The chief passages on the subject in his book are pp. 15–20, 60–65, with Appendix A, pp. 113, 114. The important exception is discussed below, pp. 164 ff.

[2] I have already discussed the question of disinterested virtue ; see above, pp. 145–147.

[3] See above, *The Religion of All Good Men*, p. 114.

and universal as any which Mr. Garrod has pictured. He has pointed to a fact which, while fundamentally true, is ever in danger of being obscured and forgotten. It is perhaps the most characteristic feature of the Kingdom, in so far as we are allowed to know it, that *it is disruptive*, the entering in of a new creation and a new "societas hominum." "Old things are passed away, behold all things are become new."

But by this disruptiveness of the Kingdom our Lord meant something very different from what (*c*) Disruptive, Mr. Garrod has depicted. This writer but wishes us to believe that the prevailing not Negative. thought in the Gospel is a negative one. He rightly sees that our Lord asks a man to surrender everything, including life itself, if need be; but the conclusions which he draws from this are not justifiable. This negative action is neither to be considered as an end in itself, nor is it of such a character as to contradict purely neutral conditions of existence which belong to the natural life on earth. By "neutral conditions of existence" such institutions as marriage are meant—things good in themselves and necessary to the existence of society. On this point Mr. Garrod says : "How utter and complete Christ figures to himself this disruption Marriage and we see in such sayings as, ' In the King- the Kingdom. dom of Heaven they neither marry nor are given in marriage.' A kingdom in which we are to be ' as the angels ' may fairly be spoken of as an ' end of the world,' *from my point of view*, which is merely that the teaching of Christ is inapplicable to ordinary human society or to any society other than a supernatural one." [1] He is referring of course to

[1] *Op. cit.*, p. 114.

our Lord's answer to the Sadducees' question about
the Resurrection. It is perhaps the only incident in
our Lord's teaching which Mr. Garrod has entirely
misread and misquoted. None of the Gospels use the
phrase, " In the Kingdom of Heaven they neither
marry nor are given in marriage." In all three
cases it is made perfectly clear that the period when
marriage will cease *will follow the Resurrection.*[1]
St. Mark says, " When they rise from the dead, they
neither marry, etc."; in St. Matthew the words are,
" In the resurrection they neither, etc."; whilst St.
Luke declares that it is " those who are accounted
worthy to attain to that age, and the resurrection
from the dead" who neither marry nor are given in
marriage. Our Lord was replying to the question,
" In the resurrection, whose wife shall she be?"
The particular answer He gave, confining His attention to the change in human relationships *after*
the Resurrection, was necessary in order to meet the
denial which lay behind the question of the Sadducees. For they were the worldly and sceptical party,
who disliked the idea of a Resurrection, just because
they had no wish for a totally new order of things.
The Resurrection, both to them and to our Lord,
meant the entrance upon a heavenly and not an
earthly life. This is made remarkably clear by
St. Luke, who uses the two phrases, "this age" and
"that age." In the former marriage is a normal
feature of society; in the latter, which is associated
with the Resurrection from the dead, marriage will
cease to be. Now when the word αἰών or its ad-
jective is used in this way, it is always with a view
to bringing out the contrast between the earthly

[1] St. Matt. xxii. 30, St. Mark xii. 25, St. Luke xx. 34–36.

dispensation and that which Mr. Garrod himself recognizes as a supra-terrestrial existence ushered in by a remote "eschatological" coming.

As to this last-mentioned opinion of Mr. Garrod, one may refer to the fact that he quotes St. Mark x. 29 and 30 in proof that our Lord believed in this more remote coming as well as in that which he calls apocalyptic.[1] In this connection he points out that ἐν τῷ καιρῷ τούτῳ refers to a terrestrial period of existence, whereas ζωὴν αἰώνιον, "in the age to come," has reference to a Kingdom "elsewhere" than "on our present earth" and subsequent to the first period. Thus Mr. Garrod has placed the stage when we shall be "as the angels" into the pre-eschatological or terrestrial period of the Kingdom, whereas the Gospels represent our Lord as placing it in the final or supra-terrestrial period.   He is wrong, therefore, in thinking that our Lord pictured the immediate coming of the Kingdom as contradicting fundamentally necessary conditions of terrestrial existence.   The most startling argument he has put forward to prove that this was so, namely, that marriage was to be abolished, has been found to be based upon a misreading of all the Synoptic Gospels. The other arguments used in order to prove that the morality of the Kingdom is unsuitable to the normal life of earthly society will be dealt with presently.

We must now return to the more general charge that the injunctions of our Lord are almost wholly of a negative character, and indeed, in so far as they have reference to the coming of the Kingdom, wholly so.[2]   He allows, it is true, that some parts

[1] *The Religion of All Good Men*, p. 114.
[2] I refer to such passages as pp. 61–63 of Mr. Garrod's book.

of our Lord's teaching are sound and practical, but he thinks that these are accidental and that they cannot be harmonized with the central ideas.[1]   The main trend is negative.   The case is put concisely in such words as these :—" He did not wish to give men 'something to live by' but something wherewith to face the day of the Son of Man.   The question He tried to answer was not πῶς βιωτέον; but πῶς ἀθανατιστέον;[2]   He thought that the way to God was very far away from men, or perhaps away with men from the ordinary conditions of human society."[3]   Once again : "The cardinal thing is the getting rid of one's riches, *the losing of one's life*; the giving to the poor is only the means to this end which is readiest and most obvious."[4]   These two passages taken together show that Mr. Garrod does not quite put the teaching of our Lord by the side of that of Buddha.   It was not, he would say, a will-to-die for the sake of death, but a will-to-die to the whole cycle of ordinary human interests for the sake of attaining a certain visionary ideal, which was really a delusion and therefore not worth the sacrifice.   Philosophers have sometimes taken to weighing up the losses and gains of life with a view to justifying philosophic pessimism or its opposite. Mr. Garrod has similarly sought to weigh up the losses and gains in the Christian scheme.   His conclusion is that our Lord Himself was justified, because He believed in His own apocalyptic vision ; but that to all who have followed His

[1] *The Religion of All Good Men*, p. 72.
[2] *I.e.* not "how must one live?" but "how must one become immortal?"
[3] *Ibid.*, p. 71.   [4] *Ibid.*, p. 63.

immediate disciples the way of Christ *must* be negative, because the vision proved to be a complete mistake.

If Mr. Garrod had read his Church history as seriously as he has read the Gospels, he might

The Witness perhaps have seen that the one proof History. vides a key to the other. As he rightly says, the expectation of a Messianic coming of the Son of Man in the clouds immediately after the Ascension was disappointed. We see the process of disillusionment in the New Testament itself; and very soon the Church had to face the ordinary problems of life without taking into account any such supernatural conclusion of her anxieties and difficulties. But the important thing to notice is that the spirit inspired by our Lord's apocalyptic teaching, and so well described by Mr. Garrod, *did not disappear*. It continued to manifest itself persistently for century after century in a great variety of different ways, and is still doing so.

The persecutions which took place during the early centuries of Christianity under the Roman Empire supply a series of striking illustrations in this connection. It might, on Mr. Garrod's assumption, be supposed that men like St. Stephen and St. James the Apostle suffered martyrdom in the hope that they would somehow find a place in the Messianic Kingdom which might be set up on earth at any moment. But after the first generation this was no longer possible. On Mr. Garrod's own showing, the one source of inspiration to our Lord and His first disciples was the immediate coming of the End; this one source of inspiration (and in this too we are following Mr. Garrod's own argu-

ment) had been withdrawn by the time of the
Emperor Domitian.[1] How was it, then, that the
Christian martyrs went so joyfully to their death
for two hundred years and more from that time
onwards ? The command to endure death itself if
necessary was still there, but the inspiring motive
had long since been proved false. Yet they acted
exactly as the Apostles and their contemporaries
had done. It might be replied that these later
generations still relied upon the deliverance to be
afforded by a coming of the Son of Man ; but that
in their case it was the eschatological, or remote,
consummation towards which they looked. But
do men in fact ever find a remote consummation
sufficiently vivid and engrossing, in moments of crisis
and mortal agony, to make them not only endure
persecution and death, but endure these things with
calm and joyful expectation ? Such a hope of remote deliverance would undoubtedly explain the
many cases of apostasy during these persecutions ;
those who had no more than this external hope
gave way. But nothing of this sort is sufficient
to explain the phenomenon of martyrdom joyfully
embraced. This spirit, inspired in the primitive
Christians by our Lord's apocalyptic teaching, has
perpetually appeared and reappeared in a pre-
eminent degree in the course of history. In this
connection one may point to the whole story of
monasticism. Some would interpret that movement
as an incursion of oriental nihilism into western
religion. That point of view will be considered
elsewhere.[2] But we have seen that Mr. Garrod

[1] See *The Religion of All Good Men*, p. 55.
[2] See Chapters VI. and VIII.

does not discover in the earliest disciples a Buddhist desire for death for its own sake, but always as the gateway to the Kingdom of Heaven ; nor apparently does he find the will-to-die in the later ages of Christianity.   Where then would he place monasticism ?   It cannot be said of the monks that they were inspired to enter the cloister by the thought of the remoter coming of Christ ; such a statement would be even less in accordance with the probabilities of the case than the similar supposition already considered with respect to the martyrs. For in the case of the latter death might perhaps be supposed to destroy the burden of the intervening period ; though even then it is hardly conceivable that a remote and external object of hope would have made them face death calmly.   In the case of the monks, however, if Mr. Garrod's view of the Gospel were right, we should have to explain the incredible spectacle of thousands of men and women, entirely robbed of the hope of an immediate coming of Christ, yet embracing most literally the evangelical counsels of poverty, celibacy, and obedience, with all the severe discipline involved in them. Again, the same problem is raised by the appearance of the friars as well as the missionaries of all ages. It would be difficult for Mr. Garrod to explain what inspired St. Francis of Assisi, Raymond Lully, St. Ignatius Loyola, St. Francis Xavier and David Livingstone.   All these and many others of modern times have closely followed the Gospel precepts ; yet according to this writer the only incentive provided for them had proved a delusion long centuries before, not to outsiders only, but also to the whole Church.

The principle which produced such examples of heroism and sacrifice as these was something much (d) The Posi- more positive and personal than the pro-tive Principle. spect of an external coming of a Kingdom, whether immediate or remote, could ever have been. Mr. Garrod has, in fact, himself hinted at the true explanation, though only to rule it out as no longer one which we can take into account. "We can never know Christ as the Middle Ages, with their vigour of faith and defect of history, thought to know Him. He can never be to us a person, a friend."[1] It was undoubtedly this vigour of faith in Christ as a Friend which inspired martyrs, monks, and missionaries. All that long line of disciples would have agreed upon this point. In fact, the real incentive of Christian conduct has always been both positive and present; for it is the experience of Christ entering into and abiding in the soul. Mr. Garrod himself points out the value of a phrase used by St. Paul to describe this experience.[2] "St. Paul," he says, "speaks of the 'life hidden with Christ in God,' and that phrase, perhaps, expresses better than anything else the secret of the peace which is to be had in the religion of Christ." But what meaning can we attach to such a phrase, and to many others like it in St. Paul, if the idea of a personal intercourse with our Lord is removed? Take away this central thought from St. Paul's writings— all that is summed up in that terse phrase $\dot{\epsilon}\nu\ X\rho\iota\sigma\tau\hat{\omega}$ —and what would be left? Now it is just this central conception which St. Paul everywhere and always declared to be the only remedy for that conflict of flesh and spirit which he felt so acutely.

[1] *The Religion of All Good Men*, p. 70. [2] *Ibid.*, p. 76.

The remedy for the disorder of the natural man
was not to be sought in any co-operation of such
ill-assorted elements,[1] but in passing right out of
all this into another sphere, another world of which
Christ is the centre.   This passing from one sphere
to another, from the natural to the spiritual, meant
for St. Paul *a disruptive change in the centre of gravity*.
If a man became ἐν Χριστῷ, he could no longer be
ἐν σαρκί;[2] he could only have one centre of gravity,
and it must be either the spiritual or the natural.

This is the real significance of all that disruptiveness which Mr. Garrod has so rightly pointed out
in the Gospel teaching.   This is the
meaning of that immediate apocalyptic
Coming of the Son of Man.   It is
a mystical experience which takes place in the
Christian soul.   One may even trace within the
pages of the New Testament the stages by which
the primitive Church passed from the apocalyptic
framework to the kernel of truth which lay beneath
it.   When she discovered this she found it to be
identical with her own innermost experience.

The Coming not External but Mystical.

It was necessary that our Lord should use the
imagery of His place and time, the ideas of the
Kingdom and the Coming.   That imagery is still
the only possible way in which the human faculties
can think and speak of the remoter consummation.
But it was also the only material ready to hand by
which our Lord could convey a vivid impression
of the revolution in religious experience which was
to follow the accomplishment of His sacrifice.   At
first the early disciples followed Him with no understanding of all this; their conception of the King-

---

[1] *Cf.* p. 159 above.   [2] Romans viii. 1-9.

dom was based upon popular ideas of the day : all
was outward and material.   But it is probable that
in most cases the attractive force was, not the
preaching of the Kingdom, but the Person of the
Lord ; though with Judas and possibly with Simon
the Zealot it may have been otherwise.   St. John the
Baptist had preached the Coming Kingdom, but they
left him for One who at first delivered exactly the
same message.   The impression left upon us by the
Gospels is that the Apostles forsook all to follow a
Person, rather than because a particular treatment
of the Messianic hope appealed to them.   To the
last they were unable to connect our Lord and His
character with the conceptions of the Kingdom to
which they still clung.   Only—when He said, " The
Kingdom of God is at hand," they were persuaded
that here was One who would presently point them
to something which would satisfy their souls' cravings.
In Mr. Garrod's opinion the Apostles at once grasped
the central thought, πῶς ἀθανατιστέον ; and, understanding this, were able to embrace the whole
revolutionary scheme of conduct set before them.
But the one thing written plain in the Gospel
narrative is that they had no conception whatever
of a Kingdom beyond the earthly limits, " a Kingdom of this world."   After Pentecost, when the
great experience came to them of Christ living in
fellowship with their souls, they still held by the
side of this experience, and, for a time, unrelated to
it, the hope of an immediate return of the Messiah
upon the clouds to inaugurate the real Kingdom.
We see the transition stage in St. Paul's Epistles to
the Thessalonians. Then gradually there dawned
the vision which brought a calmer outlook into the

unknown.   The apocalyptic imagery was pushed forward into the distant future.   They now began to see that between this distant future and the present would intervene a long period of earthly activity, during which the great Universal Church would extend her boundaries, and would come into conflict with world-powers.[1]   At length the author of the Fourth Gospel silently completed the transformation.   To him the apocalyptic and immediate coming of the Son of Man is identical with the mystical experience into which the Church passed at Pentecost.   He does not deny the more remote consummation ;[2] but his immediate interest is in the present experience of an interior Coming of the Son of Man into the heart of every disciple.   It was of this inner experience that our Lord spoke when He said, "Ye shall not have gone through the cities of Israel until the Son of Man be come."

To summarize results, then, one must say that the Gospel is disruptive.   It means the setting up of a spiritual order of existence in place of that which is merely natural.   The transition, however, from the natural plane to the spiritual is not by effort of the man's self, which is incapacitated for the task, but by a Coming of the Son of Man.   This Coming is not external but mystical ; and it becomes the Christian's experience of fellowship with Christ.   In the case of the Apostles the Kingdom of this Coming was preached to them before they had received the experience ; consequently the whole imagery of the Kingdom was largely incomprehensible to them as a vehicle of

Summary.

---

[1] See the later Epistles of St. Paul and the Apocalypse of St. John.

[2] It seems to be recognised in chapter v. 28, 29.

truth. It was counteracted by their own prejudices until the experience came at Pentecost. *Then*, however, in the light of the experience they looked back and gradually came to understand the meaning of that Kingdom to which they now held the key. Thus the foundation of Christian conduct is not the vague hope of an external catastrophe, which did not happen, but an interior certainty of experience in which the glorified and ever-present Christ is the supreme reality. The whole New Testament rings with this one idea. Whether in the apocalyptic imagery of the Synoptic Gospels or in the mystical language of St. Paul and St. John, it is the same supreme experience, which is first proclaimed as imminent, and which is afterwards apprehended as an abiding fact. This, then, is the experience—we cannot of ourselves pass into the other world which our Lord has revealed; but He has come to us. He has passed into, and abides in, the whole Christian Society; and thus tabernacling passes continually by sacramental channels into the individual soul. By virtue of that Personal Coming He uproots us from the natural plane of experience, and replants us upon a supernatural plane in the spiritual world. We are in Christ seated with Him in the heavenly places in the otherworldly sphere, and there henceforth must be our centre of gravity.

"The Kingdom of God," then, "is within us" if we have been incorporated into Christ; the centre of gravity is fixed henceforth, for it is the Christ-self of the other world in us. Yet this is only one half of the truth. Thus far there appears only a preliminary uprooting, followed by a state of

(iv.) The Transvaluation of Values.
(*a*) The Spiritual Ascent.

harmony and completion. The Kingdom of God has come; and yet it is equally true to say that it has not come. "He that endureth to the end, the same shall be saved." "In your patience possess ye your souls." We are still in the two worlds, the phenomenal and the spiritual, and a progress is still necessary from the one to the other. One supreme change has been effected; the centre of gravity has been shifted from the phenomenal to the spiritual. Nevertheless, for us the spiritual is still in a certain sense within the phenomenal; and we have to reach the spiritual harmony, towards which our soul now gravitates, by a pathway, in itself by no means easy, which traverses the outer world of nature and sense. We have to live in a world of sense with our sense-windows opening upon it. The Power which enables us to move along lines of spiritual activity proceeds wholly from that other-worldly centre where our life is hid with Christ in God; but this Power has to be exercised in the phenomenal world upon the natural plane. The spiritual activity which has begun to stir and move in us can only realize itself by completing a circuit. It proceeds from the "Christ-in-us" of the other world, and is as yet only potentially part of us. It must pass to its realization through contact with the phenomenal world; thence it will return — human as well as divine, because our humanity belongs naturally to the phenomenal world, as well as spiritually to the Christ-world. Even so did our Lord pass from the Father into the world, and then, through the mediation of His Human Nature, return from the world unto the Father.

This is why the Kingdom of God is not only "within us" but also "at hand." At every moment

The Sacramental Principle. of our life we may pass up into the otherworldly sphere, but always along the same pathway, through the phenomenal world. Always there is just before us a manifestation of the Kingdom ready to hand; only always it is veiled by the phenomena of the earthly life. These phenomena are not to be regarded as hindrances and obstructions —in the manner of oriental pessimists, and, in a lesser degree, of all puritans—but rather as means whereby we may enter sacramentally into the Presence of God. Yet the puritan recoil from the full use of the natural order serves the truth well, if it reminds us that our relation to that natural order must always be guarded and sacramental rather than absolute and instinctive. In the Divine plan the natural is not bad, but good; and this goodness remains in a certain sense completely unaffected in spite of the general disorder wrought by the entrance of sin. We must hold fast to this goodness of the natural. Whilst, however, the thing itself remains unchangeably good in its own being as the creation of God, it is true to say that *our use of it* is affected by the incursion of sin in suchwise that, while itself good, the thing presents itself to us as *neutral in relation to the moral order*. It has still its own inherent goodness just as the moral order has also; but the goodness of each is of its own kind, the one natural and the other moral. Now human nature is such that it was intended to be the meeting-ground of the two. Here the goodness of the moral order was to be built upon the goodness of the natural order; the two creations were to be bound together by the human link. The

12

effect of sin's entrance was to destroy the natural binding power of this link. Man cannot pass freely from the natural to the moral and spiritual. In his person these two now stand unrelated. Thus it comes about that that which is good upon its own plane presents itself as neutral upon a higher plane, and may thus furnish a basis for either good or evil in the moral sphere. Not then instinctively, but sacramentally and in this way alone, can we, whilst using the natural order, redeem it, extract from it its true worth and significance, and make it the gateway to heaven. Our Lord realized to the full this sacramental value of the natural order in the moral sphere. That is why so many have been able to find in His teaching so passionate an apprehension of the natural that they can see nothing else.[1]

Thus far the Gospel may be held to include all that is best in natural religion ; for it counts all the natural order to be the antechamber to the throne of God. This is the truth emphasized by the Alexandrine school in the Primitive Church. But this is not all. Christianity has in it an element which makes it something more than the crown and consummation of all the natural religions ; and this "something" is to be seen clearly in its attitude towards sin. The central faculty, whereby man relates himself to both the natural and the spiritual worlds, is his will. It is therefore the one connecting link, whereby the spiritual power of the other world must pass upon its circuit through the earthly sphere and become

The Disruptive Element and the Sinful Will.

[1] See, for example, Harnack's *What is Christianity?* and Mr. Chamberlain's book.

part of the inmost life of the soul. But it is just here, in the will, that the disease of sin is situated. That is why the Natural Man is powerless to bridge the gulf between the natural and the spiritual. The gulf, however, is bridged for him by the redemptive power of Christ, and the whole man is planted afresh in the spiritual sphere. His will has now, by this replanting, received a fresh orientation towards a new centre of attraction possessing a magnetic power to hold it; it has therefore become a serviceable instrument for the activities of the spiritual world. For the regenerate will, drawing its energies from the other world, and always directing itself towards the realization of otherworldly values, is able to appropriate to itself sacramentally the whole range of earthly phenomena, whatever their surface worth may seem, whether beautiful or commonplace, pleasant or painful. From these it draws material to feed its own otherworldly energy and to bear it back richer in spiritual quality into the heavenly places in Christ. Now this spiritual activity of the will acting upon the phenomenal world can be achieved only whilst the will keeps its direction true and its centre of gravity in the other world. The least disturbance of this spiritual mechanism nullifies the will's power of dealing with the phenomenal world. To this end the will must remain truly free; it must be able to pass through the earthly order of things without becoming entangled in it. The phenomenal must be the veil through which the will passes into the spiritual. The will must not find in the former an end for it to rest in; for if it does, the circuit of will-activity is broken in its course, the centre of gravity becomes shifted from heaven to earth, and the whole life of the man sinks on to the natural plane once more. Now even the regenerate will, centred as it is in God, is weakened and bruised by the effects of past sin upon it. The whole life of the man—now spiritual because it is centred in God—was once natural, lying helpless upon the plane of nature. It is these two distinct states which St. Paul described as "the Spiritual Man" and "the Natural Man." Now the Natural Man is not neutral towards the moral order in the sense in which nature as a whole may be said to be neutral. As we have already seen, the whole natural order is good, including human nature; but the unredeemed human personality has by sin become estranged from the true use of the natural. Even the Spiritual Man, therefore, approaches the natural order in the first instance as a neutral thing which must be recovered and made once more a realized good in relation to himself. The Natural Man, however, though he may not know it, cannot even approach the natural order as something neutral. He is not even, strictly speaking, a part of nature, in the sense of the divinely ordered plan of the world; he is rather a denaturalized growth, at home indeed on the natural plane as we know it, though not truly at home in nature. For in the Natural Man there is the sin-stricken will, not only unrelated to the spiritual world, but in active opposition to its influences. But when a human will which is in opposition to the forces of the spiritual world comes in contact with the neutral order of the phenomenal world, it must necessarily misuse that order. In such circumstances the will treats the phenomenal world unsacramentally as material for satisfying its own isolated and mis-chosen ends, rather than the universal God-ward purposes of the spiritual world. For the will which is weakened by past sin, though its activity be now rooted in God through Christ, still has in it something which responds only too readily to the magnetic attraction of the earlier centre of gravity in the phenomenal world. It is like a comet, which, in its passage round the sun, has to pass danger-ously near to another celestial body which may divert it from its path. By the power of the other world it has to steer its course through innumer-able manifestations of that earthly magnetism which once held it entirely. Thus it is that as we pass through life the fleshly tendency to rest satisfied with the earthly plane is insistent. We sink to-wards it imperceptibly; and a catastrophic re-direction of the will upward is therefore constantly necessary to prevent its becoming, before we are aware of it, wholly immersed once again in the natural order.

At this point it becomes clear that the proper use of the phenomenal world is a serious and delicate problem for the Christian. All true mani-festations of the natural order are to be the means of his sacramental entry into the other world; and yet he knows by experience that an overweight of the earthly phenomena will inevitably prove to be more than he can use sacramentally. The earthly veil will become so thick and gross and tightly drawn that he will be unable to pass through it into the beyond of the other world; the clouds will hide the light instead of reflecting its brightness. When such a thing happens he knows that at that instant the natural order has ceased to be sacramental for him, and has become instead a hindrance and a snare. He must then, whilst using the phenomenal world, sit loosely to it ; he must not let its influences gather upon him too thickly. He must be sparing and watchful in his use of it, holding to a certain simplicity, which will raise the sacramental value of the smallest thing in it to its fullest power. His use of the phenomenal world must be after the manner of St. Francis, who found in a piece of dry bread, a stream of water, and a seat of stone the material for grateful joy.

But, once more, the ground of this watchfulness in using the natural order is the fact that there are two (*b*) The Direc- distinct standards of value whereby such tive Values. a use of the natural order may be judged. These two standards correspond to the two possible centres of gravity, the natural and the spiritual. The Christian, by his incorporation into the other world and by the alteration of his centre of gravity, has become pledged to the otherworldly standards of conduct. Thus there has already been potentially effected in him a transvaluation of values. He has the mind of Christ. The Spirit of Christ in him re-directs, first his imagination and reason, and then his will, towards those otherworldly standards of value which were realized personally by our Lord in His Incarnate life on earth, and which now form the supreme law of the Christian life also. His will must always be directed towards the realization of these otherworldly values throughout his use of the phenomenal order. Moreover, he must habitually pass judgment upon the phenomenal order in the light of the otherworldly standards of value, lest he abuse that order instead of using it, lest his will swerve from its path into the morass of earthly values.

For in this self-direction towards the otherworldly values the Christian finds himself at variance with a whole range of earthly valuations. These were valid for him when his centre of gravity was in the natural order, and they are still valid for "the world," that is, for all who are living on the natural plane, and know little or nothing of the otherworldly values. On this natural plane of the world there is no real objective standard of values possessing final authority. On the contrary, there is a continual process of subjective valuation going on; for the world's values are earthly, and depend upon passing dispositions of the phenomenal order. There is also in the sin-tainted will of the Christian a constant tendency to accept these worldly valuations; an involuntary echo of them is liable to make itself felt in his heart. In the direction, therefore, of his will towards the otherworldly standards, he comes on the one hand continually into conflict with this natural attraction in himself towards the subjective earthly values; while on the other hand he finds himself at cross-purposes with the general acceptance of these earthly values by others around him. There must, then, be a great antagonism ever present in his life as long as he remains in the phenomenal world. He must be ready at any moment to withdraw himself from the use of things upon which he finds he is putting a false value. At all costs he must retain the otherworldly direction of his will. He must be willing to renounce any-thing or everything in the phenomenal world which endangers his hold upon the otherworldly values. This is the meaning of all that stern and abrupt renunciation of earthly things which Mr. Garrod has pointed out in our Lord's teaching ;—a renunciation which extends not only to everything hostile to the otherworldly values in the Christian's own personal life, but to everything of the same kind in the world around him.

What, then, are these supreme otherworldly values towards which the will is always to be directed? They are summed up in the one word, Love— Love in its threefold activity, towards God, towards the Christ-self, and towards the Neighbour. In all earthly standards of valuation one of these three pivot-points is omitted, namely, the first. In the case of these earthly standards, therefore, the valua- tions are subjective and start from the self—not the Christ-self but the natural self. We have seen how in this subjective method of valuation the starting- point must necessarily be, not any universal element in the man, but the individual ego, the natural self, which finds itself in opposition to the social order.[1] The reason for that inevitable deadlock now becomes apparent. These two can be reconciled only by virtue of their subordination to the third pivot-point, namely, God ; for in Him alone is the key to the meaning both of ourselves and of the social world to which we belong.

God is the spring and source of the Christian's life.

(1) God.   By incorporation into the other world, the whole activity of the man's personal life has become rooted in God through Christ, so that it both proceeds from God and returns to Him.

[1] See Chapter III. II.

It proceeds from God ; for from God there flows into
him the power to exercise Faith ; and this in turn
passes into Hope and Love.   By Faith, Hope, and
Love the whole personal life of the man opens
towards God ; and, expressing itself through worship and work, it flows back into the otherworldly
sphere of which God is the centre.   In that sphere in
Christ, the man beholds, at first partially, but with
ever-increasing clearness, the Holiness and Love of
God ; and thereby a flood of light is in turn cast
upon those two other pivot-points, the Self and the
Neighbour.   In God he comes to know the supreme
value of himself, the otherworldly self hidden in
Christ, and also the value of his brother's self,
seeing that this also belongs, at least potentially,
to the otherworldly sphere.   Thus the supreme
reality of the otherworldly experience is Love.
God is Love ; and His Being flows out to the
individual soul, and awakens a response of love in
him towards God.   To the man who experiences it
this interchange of love reveals the supreme value
of a loving personality and of the reciprocal relationship of love between personalities.   He sees
that to be more loving is to be fuller and richer in
personal life ; for the essence of love is a free interchange of appreciation between persons, and in this
interchange each gives the whole of his personality
to the other.   In the course of this inquiry we have
found again and again a tendency to undervalue
the worth of the individual unit of humanity ;
but since society is composed of individuals, its
meaning is entirely lost if the individual ceases
to be of value in himself.   The personal worth,
therefore, both of the Self and of the Neighbour

must be realized if the individual and society are to have any meaning for one another. It is this realization of personal worth which the otherworldly love-values alone can secure and develop to its full extent. For there, in the otherworldly sphere, all the apparent antinomies of earth find their reconciliation. In the life which is hid with Christ in God the man finds that the only self in him which is of worth is the Christ-self, not the antagonistic natural self; and he finds, too, that the same is true of every other individual, either actually or potentially. In Christ, therefore, the earthly antinomies of self and other disappear. The interests of the self are identical with the interests of society; and the preservation and growth of the Christ-self in the personal life is a social process just as much as an individual process. The individual in the otherworldly sphere is completely social; and society, in turn, exists only for the realization of the fulness of all its members. Indeed, the growth of every Christ-self to perfection would mean the fulness of social as well as of personal life. When considered in this light, all those parts of our Lord's teaching which seem to be abrupt and revolutionary are seen to be absolutely essential. They group themselves round the two values, Self and Neighbour, as seen in their otherworldly relationship to God and to one another. In dealing with misapprehensions such as those of Mr. Garrod with regard to the social worth of our Lord's teaching, enough will have been said with respect to the first of the three pivot-points of the otherworldly sphere, if it is seen that in their relationship to God the other two find their value and their natural reconciliation.

Next, then, in order to reach the perfection of the otherworldly life, the Christian finds that he must develop to the uttermost the Christ-self within him. This is his one supreme asset; and its development will come through the direction of the whole life Godward in all its use of the phenomenal world. Self-sacrifice and renunciation of every kind are inspired and directed solely by the needs of this higher self. The Christian seeks nothing but life in the form of an ever-increasing spiritual efficiency and a growing apprehension of the otherworldly values. This means that he must always be prepared to cast away relentlessly anything and everything which he finds to be actually hindering the growth of the Christ-self in him. Such an idea had never been heard of before; and it was clean contrary to all the natural instincts, habits, and conventions of the world into which our Lord came. It had been the prevailing rule both amongst the Jews and in the Græco-Roman world to merge the individual in the society. A man's religion was as a matter of course that of his father and mother, his home and nationality; conscience was largely governed by convention and common custom. All this was inevitable when all were upon the same natural plane. With the introduction of the other-worldly values into the personal life of the individual all was changed. Our Lord, then, was obliged to emphasize the ultimate issues in the strongest possible terms; for to have done anything else would have been to obscure those issues. The wealth of society lies in the character of the individuals who compose it. If all had attained the perfection of the higher self, all the problems of society would be solved; for

(2) The Self.

the antinomy of individual and social would in that case have disappeared.   There is no greater obstacle to the welfare of society as a whole than the impossibility which has been discovered of reconciling the individual and social principles on the natural plane.   To remove this antinomy, even in one individual, would be a step towards the betterment of society ; and this can be done only by the development of the Christ-self towards the realization of the otherworldly values of love to God and Neighbour. Corresponding to this tremendous task there must necessarily be great sacrifices.   The higher self belongs to the individual, and only in the second place to society.   A man's soul must not be in the keeping of parents or wife or children or friends. If any of these should unhappily be found to be in opposition to his true development, he must reckon his duty to the Christ-self to outweigh all other considerations.   The spiritual benefit thus obtained will react socially upon society, though for the moment it may seem to produce disturbance and disruption.   The perfection of the Christ-self in each individual is of more importance to society than his possession of riches, wife or children, health, or even of physical life itself.   Again, the principle contained in the words, " If thy hand cause thee to stumble, cut it off," [1] is one which is taken for granted daily in our hospitals.   The man whose limb has become diseased consents to have it amputated rather than that his whole body should become infected with corruption.   To save a comrade in danger of accident, a brave man will risk the loss of his own limbs.   If through cowardice he holds back, he may

[1] St. Mark ix. 43.

save his body from mutilation ; but he will have taken a step towards the destruction of his truest self. Nothing which belongs to the natural order in man's life must be counted of worth when the interests of his whole personality are at stake.

The same principle holds good in the relations of the Self to the Neighbour. Society lives, not by (3) The means of, but in spite of, the conflict of Neighbour. natural powers and forces which is ever active upon the earthly plane. Only when it in some measure transcends that natural conflict, can society be said to exist; and this can only be by means of ideals drawn from the atmosphere of the other world. In the light of those ideals personal life is seen to be the most precious thing which society possesses. Conduct, therefore, is most social when it promotes the recognition of these personal values, and when it is based upon reverence for the Christ-self in one's neighbour. Men are won over from individual-ism to social conduct when they meet with this rever-ence for the Christ-value in themselves; for it must be reverenced, even when it is as yet only potential.

Herein lies the whole significance of our Lord's treatment of social relationships. It is only when we have grasped the method of the otherworldly principle that we can begin to understand the teach-ing of the Sermon on the Mount. It is not, then, to be wondered at that such writers as Mr. Garrod should find in it an outlook impossible to reconcile with their own interpretation of life. Mr. Garrod summarizes his estimate of the Gospel teaching in these words : " There is no one who does not know that these precepts, literally pursued, mean, in any age, the dissolution of what is called society : and so we approve them with our lips, but not with our lives. But they were meant to govern, they did govern, the *lives* of those to whom they were addressed. What are blows, coats, money, to men before whose eyes floats ever the vision of the end of the world and the day of the Son of Man?"[1] In such words as these a challenge is offered to the whole range of Christian conduct, as something— not merely too remote and out of the way for the ordinary man, but—directly opposed to civilization and the best welfare of society. It may be well, then, to try and come a little closer to the meaning of these two types of life, which are thus depicted as mutually destructive systems.

First, then, what is the outstanding feature of that type of character which is set before us in the Sermon The Personal on the Mount? The reply to such a Method of Love. question can hardly be doubtful. It is that the whole emphasis is laid upon the possession of certain fundamental dispositions of the heart and will by the individual. The whole atmosphere is one which is intensely personal; interest centres in the supremacy of the three love-values (of God, Self, and Neighbour) over each individual soul. If the motives and dispositions of the heart or will are such that love reigns over it on these three sides, then it is assumed that the resulting conduct will be true. This is made particularly clear with regard to love of the Neighbour, and the social relationships which flow out of it—the point with which we are now especially concerned. In this matter of right con-

[1] *The Religion of All Good Men*, p. 65. He is referring especially to the teaching in St. Matthew v., which comes to a climax in the commands to "turn the other cheek" and to forgive enemies.

duct towards one's neighbour the one thing needful is that there should be *an otherworldly relationship of persons*. The whole of our Lord's teaching about neighbour-love is concerned with the personal relationship of individuals. Nothing else really seems to have had any importance in this connection ; for He knew that all the wider and more complex relationships of society hinged round this one. Such wider relationships are relative and to some extent changing and accidental ; but the problems of personal relationship between individuals are unchanging and absolutely determinative, for upon them, in the last resort, the whole structure of society rests. Thus it will be true to say that, whilst society and all its problems seethed around Him on every side, our Lord was content to be immersed in the problems of the other world. From His high vantage-ground He re-laid the foundations of human personality in the otherworldly sphere. With unerring insight He calmly marked out the nature of the dispositions and relationships between individuals which can be generated only upon that higher plane of life, but whose presence in society is absolutely necessary to its highest welfare.

But meanwhile, what is the nature of this "society" which we are considering, and in what way exactly will the generating of personal relationships of the otherworldly kind solve its problems?

In the course of this discussion, reference has frequently been made to two planes of conduct, as The Plane of they have been called—the natural Natural Rights. and the spiritual. In these lie the two centres of gravity from which opposing types of conduct proceed. But human society as we know it can hardly be said to exist on either of these two planes entirely. If it were wholly governed by the tendencies of the natural plane, it would be a world such as Nietzsche dreamed of, with monstrous individualism dominant everywhere. If, on the other hand, it were wholly spiritual, the Kingdom of God would already have come. It is necessary, therefore, to assist the imagination by picturing society as existing upon a kind of middle plane, which may conveniently be called the Plane of Natural Rights. It is easy to understand the existence of this middle plane of conduct in a civilization which is nominally Christian; for here both the natural and the otherworldly influences are continually active. Here too society as a whole appears to belong wholly neither to the one nor the other. Its character is mixed, neither all good nor all bad, and a certain standard of moral obligation prevails. But in reality this mixed character of society goes much further back and is not a mark of Christian civilizations only. From the earliest times the same phenomenon appears. Society exists by virtue of the recognition of certain "natural rights" belonging to groups, to families, and, in the last resort, to individuals. This fact, indeed, bears witness to the divine origin of man, to the image of God which lies behind all the ravages of sin. Here is a basis of good, founded on natural social instinct and moral sense and implanted in the human race from the beginning. Now this plane of natural rights upon which all human society is built is not a thing to be despised; its limitations, however, must be made clear. All that is best in man as he exists upon the plane of nature works upward towards this other plane, upon which mutual recognition of rights begins to appear. But when it is reached from the natural side, it is found to be a flat surface, the end of a development, from which no further social advance is possible. Upon that surface all kinds of skilful combinations may be effected, but it remains without the promise of progress to perfection. Its combinations are static. In them the individual is of necessity treated simply as an institutional unit, tending to be a mere pawn possessing attributes called "rights"; for in such recognition of these "rights" as is possible upon this middle plane there is always something wanting to the adequate appreciation of living personality. The explanation is that, whilst nature can disclose the existence of the rights of personality, only love can reveal their significance and raise them to their full power. By means of love, then, the plane of natural rights, so full of promise as it is, can be uplifted and transfigured. Natural rights indeed are like so many finger-posts all pointing upwards to that otherworldly sphere where alone they receive adequate recognition.

For when the influence of the otherworldly principle is entirely absent from the middle plane of right, the principle of the lower self is still so dominant that individual rights are magnified in every direction. Under such circumstances they become so clamorous and their growth becomes so deeply debased that they strain all the bonds of society to the utmost. The respective rights, therefore, of the individual and of society (that is, of the mass of other individuals over against whom each single individual finds himself) are perpetually liable to clash. An exaggeration of rights in any one

13

direction always works serious harm in other direc-
tions.   In the problem of rights lie at once all the
hopes and all the perils of society.   For the sense
of right is in itself wholly good ; it is in reality a
sense of the value of the self, of the preciousness
of personal dignity and liberty.   Yet there are a
hundred ways in which this sense of right may
become dangerous.   In the old pagan society we
see some of these perilous developments and the
havoc which they wrought.   In the old aristocracies
rights were the prerogative of the favoured few.
A selfish tyranny of the few over the many was
hardly questioned ; whole masses of individuals
never roused themselves to ask whether they had
any rights at all.   In our modern civilization, on
the other hand, while the old tyranny of the few
still holds sway under more subtle and perhaps more
malignant forms, the many are no longer in passive
submission ; all ranks and classes are becoming
increasingly conscious of the possession of rights.
Moreover, Nietzsche and others have quite truly
pointed out that this is directly due to the influence
of Christianity.   The otherworldly love-values have
been leavening society long enough to have brought
some sense of personal dignity within the consciousness of most men.   But here a new peril manifests
itself, one so real that Nietzsche has accused Christianity of inoculating society with mortal disease.
In reality the true growth of a sense of rights will
bring no danger to society ; but if a movement,
which received its original incentive from the otherworldly plane, loses its contact with the other world
and becomes a debased and perverted growth centred
in this world, then indeed disease has set in.   For

on the middle plane a general growth of the consciousness of rights cannot come to fruition unless the sense of personal right is charged with an otherworldly significance.   An otherworldly sense of personal worth is to be identified with the love of the Christ-self; and this, as we have seen, is one of the three pivot-points round which all conduct must move. In the otherworldly sphere all rights are harmonized ; whereas on the natural plane they become hardened and stiffened until a conflict of rights is the inevitable result.   For that which has been called, for convenience, the middle plane of right is in reality only the upper surface of the natural plane.   It is that part of the natural plane which is most directly capable of providing a foothold for the activities of the other world—activities which, indeed, furnish the one hope of a redemption and completion of the whole structure of the natural order.   This conflict of rights, then, once aroused, must, if deprived of the otherworldly influence, become more and more intense, until it occasions the dissolution of society. In such circumstances all the machinery of society may be multiplied to an unlimited extent, without having the smallest power of checking the downward tendency.   Legislation, law courts, police, force and persuasion alike, will be powerless to stem the growing tide of individualism, which, lying hidden under the name of "rights," will eventually swallow up the good of the rights altogether.

Now natural rights in themselves have to do with Love and the the phenomenal circumstances of the Plane of Rights. individual life as lived in society ; and as long as the individual is moving from the natural centre of gravity his personality is wrapped up in this welter of natural rights. These rights are good because they are the assertion of phenomenal needs, the satisfaction of which provides the normal and divinely appointed basis of spiritual personality and the starting-point of its activities. But the goodness of the natural right is here seen to be not the highest good, but only the normal groundwork of the highest good. The individual may, therefore, spoil in his pursuit of them, if they become for him in the process the highest instead of a relative good. Yet the unrelieved plane of rights allows him no other alternative than this very engrossment in a relative good which will inevitably prove his destruction. Now the otherworldly principle lifts the individual into a position in which he is made independent of phenomenal circumstances. Natural rights then become subordinate to the otherworldly love-values. The individual accepts the rights, it is true, as a good gift from God, and as furnishing the normal rule for his life in society; but he does not regard them as a "prize to be clutched at." He experiences an independence of them which is due to the fact that the central fortress of his personality is found to be situated—not in them but—in the Christ-self of the otherworldly sphere. He therefore uses them, and yet all the while stands above them and detached from them. He does not, however, despise them, but rather sees their full worth both for himself and for others, constituting as they do the conditions under which the development of personality is in general attained. Now, just because he has this sense of the universal value of rights, he is very jealous for the rights of others, when he sees them imperilled. But whilst the rights of others will be his first care, he will regard his own rights in a very different light. The more he is inspired by the consciousness of the otherworldly love-values, the more loath will he be to champion his own natural rights ; for to do so always involves some risk of entanglement in the phenomenal order from which those rights proceed. To cling tightly to these things, even though it may be entirely justified on the plane of right, may work disaster in the otherworldly sphere. The supreme interest of the Christian must be the perfection of the Christ-self both in himself and in his neighbour. If, then, the championing of personal rights on the lower plane were to detach the man's allegiance from the Christ-self and re-establish the natural self in its old sway even for a moment, he would instantly have lost his power of fulfilling the otherworldly neighbour-love. But that is the basis of all social relationships, which only the supremacy of the Christ-self can ensure. Thus in the pursuit of a relative good he would have ruined for the time being the whole of the otherworldly relationship in which he stood towards his neighbour.

The otherworldly principle, however, will always constrain a man to be jealous for the rights of others, especially of those who are under disadvantage, such as the weak, the poor, and the oppressed. For here the Christ-self in the man, being free from dependency upon the phenomenal order, and therefore unentangled by over-engrossment in personal rights, is unfettered by the distractions and the cramping power of self-interest. It can, therefore, concentrate attention and interest

upon the needs of the Neighbour.   Moreover, this
method of love, whereby the tension of conflicting
claims is relieved and growing harmony is introduced,
has a power of communicating itself from one individual to another by a mysterious personal influence
which eludes definition.   It is this live and growing
character of love which constitutes its superiority
over the plane of rights.   The fault of these latter
lies not in their *being* rights, but in their static and
isolated character.   Their defect is that they have
no power to bind individuals together, but rather a
tendency to separate them; that they add weight and
complexity, rather than life.   They are, in fact, like
a fence set round a man; whereas what is wanted
is something to increase his vitality and his power of
dealing with circumstances.

What then is the attitude of the otherworldly
principle towards that great mass of customs, institutions, and practices of mixed or
doubtful character which exist in society
from time to time?   What are we to
think of slavery and war, property, capitalism, law
courts, and the like?   It has already been pointed
out that the activities of the other world always
work along the most personal lines, making their
first concern the setting up of right personal relationships.   Consequently the method of the otherworldly
principle is to mould persons first and institutions
afterwards.   Society makes the institutions; and the
character of society is composed out of the individual character of its personal units.   The character
of institutions therefore depends upon the prevailing
character of personal relationships.   Institutions,
then, are not *directly* attacked by the otherworldly

Love and
Social Insti-
tutions.

influences.   But as the love-values come to possess
the wills of men, personal relationships are transformed.   In this way some institutions, which are
wholly bad and have no natural good in them that
might be transformed into an otherworldly good,
are brought to an end simply because they cannot
exist in the otherworldly atmosphere.   Other institutions which are of mixed character often offer a
longer resistance, just because of the degree of
good which undoubtedly exists in them.   Yet even
in their case, those elements in them which cannot
be turned to sacramental purposes by the otherworldly principle must in the long run be purged
out.   Otherwise the corporate Christian consciousness must inevitably, in so far as it is true to itself,
be ranged in opposition ; or at least it must dissoci-
ate itself from the use of them.

There are of course some institutions whose
existence is inevitable upon the plane of rights, but
which witness to the present imperfec-

The Use of
Force and Non-
resistance.

tion of society, and of whose dissolution
the otherworldly activities provide a perpetual promise.   Into such a group would fall war
and the whole administration of justice, law, and
order ;—in fact, all action whereby force is used in
defence of social rights.   Now we have seen already
that the Gospel distinctly discourages the use of
force by the individual, when his own personal
rights are attacked.   Nothing can be clearer than
this fact that love does not stand upon its rights.
The highest personal ideal is without doubt that a
man should refrain not only from all use of force
for purely personal ends, but also from the assertion
of legal rights, in so far as they affect himself alone.

In a perfect society there would be no occasion either for the use of force or for the assertion of legal right. It follows that, the more men are dominated by the otherworldly ideals, the more such things will drop into the background. The injunction to "turn the other cheek"—that is, to exercise passive love rather than to assert rights—has probably a far wider application than the majority of even good Christians realize. Force has the mark of earthliness about it. Genuine love will not rely upon the police to keep it in perpetual security and comfort. It has better weapons than force and a higher goal than earthly security. But when we turn to the *corporate* use of force for social ends, as in the case of a war which has a righteous purpose behind it, or when the individual exercises force from no private motive whatever but wholly in defence of the rights of others, the whole matter appears in another light. We cannot repudiate our membership in society. In many things the present imperfection of society casts its shadow upon us all just because we are members one of another. The use of force belongs to the plane of right, and not to the plane of love. But society exists on the plane of right; and since we are members of it, we cannot shirk the fact that we are involved socially in the imperfections of the plane of right. That plane is indeed manifestly inferior in the light of the otherworldly ideals; but love must not on that account ignore its existence. It must rather come down into the world and strive to redeem and transform the whole order of natural rights by purging it of all that proceeds from the selfishness of the Natural Man. In this way will all natural institutions be

moulded afresh and become increasingly fitted to be
the sacramental means through which the love-values
may be made effectual in society.

Enough has perhaps been said to show the place
of non-resistance in Christian conduct. Just one
The Method of thing more must be added upon this
Love illustrated subject. The patience and meekness
—Meekness. which love exercises under evil treatment is not to be mistaken either for mere sullen
and stoical resignation or for cowardice and want
of spirit. At the very moment when the other
is acting anti-socially towards him the Christian
who is dominated by the otherworldly principles
will direct all the energies of his will towards the
furthering of the Christ-self which exists potentially
in the offender. His meekness will be a generous
longsuffering, cheerful, calm, and kindly. Under the
surface-passivity there will be a glowing activity
of love reaching after the Christ-self in the other.
This generous activity of love in the midst of
patient endurance flashes forth in those words of
our Lord, " Turn to him also the other cheek . . .
let him have thy cloak also." This Christian meekness, for all its appearance of passivity, is seen to
be in reality love actively using earthly circumstances of adversity, humiliation, and suffering as
sacramental means to the realization of the otherworldly values.

In illustration of the method of the otherworldly
principle let us now pass to the consideration of one
Liberality. or two examples of what is sometimes
called Active Love, that is, love under
circumstances where the initiative rests largely or
entirely with itself. Let us take the case of Christian

Liberality.   This virtue has perhaps been mis-used and misunderstood more than any other, because it has not been kept within the sphere of the otherworldly principle.   In St. Matt. v. 42 we read: "Give to him that asketh of thee, and from him that will borrow of thee turn not away." Mr. Garrod has pointed out that the misguided philanthropy of a promiscuous almsgiving is not inculcated by our Lord's words about giving to the poor;[1] and he has referred to "passages where Christ even seems to discountenance" such giving.   He alludes of course to the saying, "The poor ye have always with you; but me ye have not always," spoken in defence of Mary of Bethany, when she lavished upon Him money which "might have been given to the poor."   Now the point of this saying was not that to give to the poor was unim-portant, but that to show love to Himself was even more important.   In other words, there is some-thing more important than mere almsgiving, which, if necessary, it must overrule.   This "something" is the supreme otherworldly value of love to God in Christ, which, as we have seen, includes the two values, love to the Christ-self and to the Neighbour. The Christian virtue of Liberality will, therefore, if it is true to itself, be a realization of the otherworldly value of love to the Christ-self in the Neighbour. For otherwise it will be out of harmony with that love which we owe to our Lord.   "Give to him that asketh of thee"—yes, but give him the best. Give him something which, whatever its outward and phenomenal form may be (food, shelter, friend-ship, advice), will be a sacramental means through

---

[1] *The Religion of All Good Men*, pp. 62, 63.

which he will be brought to realize the otherworldly values, the Love of God for him and the value of the higher self in him.   It was not according to our Lord's method of working to alter existing institutions or to devise schemes of philanthropy.   All such things grow with the growth of experience in a Christian society ; but they can only grow out of the spirit of giving.   What is sometimes called "charity" is often only a useless and demoralizing act—not governed by the otherworldly values.   It is dictated either by the desire to appear generous, or by a too easily satisfied conscience, which seeks to rid itself of responsibility with the least possible trouble.

One word must be said here about another form which active love takes, namely, Pity or Mercy towards the weak and suffering.   This appears to be what is meant by Mr. Garrod in his brief allusion to "fostering the feebles" as he calls it.[1]   The fashion of decrying Pity was set by Nietzsche, who pursued this virtue with remorseless animosity through all his works.   Pity seemed to him to indicate nothing but morbid sentimentality and sheer weakness of character.   His argument was somewhat as follows :—A weak character likes someone to sympathize with him in his sufferings ; but such sympathy is bad for him because it promotes a sense of dependence upon the other, whereas he should be self-contained and self-reliant.   Again, a weak person who comes in contact with suffering sees one who is in a condition like his own, crushed in spirit, and unable to face hardship.   His own poor-spiritedness finds kinship in that of the sufferer. He therefore enjoys showing pity, because such

Pity.

[1] *The Religion of All Good Men*, p. 61, note.

action ministers to his own softness as well as to that of the other.—Now it is natural that, when looked at from the point of view of earthly valuations, the self-abandonment of the otherworldly love should seem to be a mere dissipation induced by foolish sentiment. In reality, however, this self-abandonment is not a sign of weakness, but of strength. It fulfils that condition of true nobility which Nietzsche described when he wrote, "Squandering is typical of genuine goodness."[1] Christian pity for the weak and suffering is not the attraction of emotional flabbiness and morbidity towards those who are of a similar temperament. On the contrary, it is the overflow of superabundant vitality, which is only possible where there is a calmness and strength of soul, due to the inner harmony of a life rooted in the other world. Pity is a mark of the man who possesses αὐταρκεία ;—not the self-contentment of the Natural Man, but the spiritual certainty and confidence of the Christ-self. With his own deepest needs satisfied by the Love of God, the man finds his life becoming so rich that he must discover an outlet for the pent-up energy which is now within him. To revert to a simile used in an earlier chapter, he is like the lake into which a pure stream of water has begun to flow in rich abundance ; an outlet must be found to relieve the pressure, and only so can the stream give its full value to the lake. Thus Christian sympathy, mercy, and pity are the active energies of the Christ-self seeking to find an adequate object upon which to lavish its superabundance.

The definition of Pity reached in the last sentence

[1] *The Will to Power*, by F. Nietzsche, § 935 (English trans. by A. M. Ludovici, vol. ii. ; T. N. Foulis).

would apply equally well to all forms of active
Christian love.   But Pity has further characteristics
peculiar to itself.   So far from being an inferior
form of love, Pity is rather the highest possible
form which love can take on earth ; because it is,
in fact, the form taken by the supreme exhibition
of the Love of God in the Incarnation.   Christian
love is a going out of the Christ-self in us towards
the Christ-self in another,—a desire for union with
it, the strongest of all social principles.   Christian
Pity is this same love in action, when the Christ-
self of the other is in difficulty or distress of some
kind.   When a soul has been baffled in its growth,
or when some rending or breaking in its phenomenal
world has for the time being crushed the normal
channels of its sacramental self-expression ; when a
man's life has been thrown into sudden disorder and
is for the time under a sense of disablement, then
Pity can work.   Now, in the Incarnation the Pity
of God was seen dealing with the universal disorder
of human life, physical, mental, and spiritual, due
throughout its entire range to the disruption and
disablement wrought by sin.   Christian Pity likewise seeks to deal with some manifestation or other
of this disorder.   It endeavours first to apprehend
the disorder and then to assist the Christ-self of the
other to set it right.   The activities of Pity must
therefore cover a very wide area, nothing less than
the whole of human life ; it must address itself both
to moral evil and to mental and physical suffering
and weakness.   It must necessarily be the complete
and universal motive for altruistic conduct in a
disordered society.   Now Christian Pity always
directs itself primarily towards the otherworldly

value, the Christ-self in the neighbour; but it does
not for that reason neglect physical and mental
disorder.   A concern for these too is involved in
the sacramental, that is, the distinctively Christian,
view of life.   For the Christian is the only kind of
person who can really love both worlds, the phenomenal and the spiritual, to the full.   He appreciates
the full worth of the phenomenal world because it is
the means whereby the spiritual world expresses
itself.   He loves the Christ-self in another and
desires his spiritual good; but for that very reason he
desires the whole phemonenal order to be helpful to
that other, that is, to be the means of the fullest and
freest expression of the otherworldly value in him.
Christian Pity will therefore be active over the
whole field of human life.   For in the first place it
will seek, in any moral or spiritual crisis or trial, to
apprehend the needs of the one in difficulty, and
by sympathy to assist actively the growth of the
Christ-self in him as he passes through his trouble.
Secondly, when any physical or mental disorder has
disturbed the normal phenomena of the natural world
through which the Christ-self of the other has been
accustomed to express itself, and has set up a new
set of phenomena, Christian Pity will seek to enter
sympathetically into the difficulties of the situation.
It will lead the stricken individual to relate the
new set of phenomena to the other world, that they
may become a new means to the self-expression of
the Christ-self in him.   But further, Pity will come
down, if need be, from the spiritual to the earthly
plane, and will enter sympathetically into purely
physical disorder or material loss; and that not in
any artificial way, as though physical suffering did

not really matter.   For body and mind are to the Christian inseparable from the higher life of the spirit, because they are the means of its sacramental self-expression.   Everything in the natural order which becomes a means to the self-expression of the spiritual order is thereby caught up into the other world and endowed with the highest spiritual value. Moreover, so long as its sacramental use continues it cannot be separated from the otherworldly values, but remains transfigured.   The *Communicatio Idio-matum* applies not only to the Incarnation and its perpetuation in the Holy Eucharist, but also to the whole of human life, as brought within the sphere of the Incarnation.   Just as the Humanity of our Lord is divine and the consecrated Host is the Body of Christ, so also the frail disfigured body of a poor stricken invalid possesses, for the Christian, the supreme otherworldly value of the Christ-self.   He sees in it the sacramental means whereby that higher self is manifested in the earthly sphere.

Thus the otherworldly principle of the Christian outlook gives to the whole field of human life and conduct, both individually and socially, a worth and a significance for which the natural order in and by itself could never provide a basis.   Christianity, by supplying a supernatural foundation for conduct, empowers it to be truly natural.

CHAPTER VI

THE ASCETIC PRINCIPLE

In the last chapter an attempt was made to show something of the basis upon which Christian conduct (i.) Intro- rests, and the aims towards which it ductory. directs its energies. Let us now consider more closely the method by which Christian character is built up. For this purpose it will be necessary to inquire into the significance of that revolutionary and "anti-natural" attitude which belongs to Christianity and to which exception is taken by so many.

In the title of this chapter the method by which Christian character is built up has been called the Ascetic Principle. This is not to be taken to mean something entirely distinct and separate from that which, in the last chapter, was called the Otherworldly Principle. The two things might quite as well be spoken of as two aspects of one principle; but, for the sake of clearness, it is convenient to treat them separately. The starting-point and the objective of Christian conduct lie in the other world; from the point of view, therefore, of the supernatural significance of Christian conduct its method may be called the Otherworldly Principle. But from the point of view of the actual process itself, seen in the light of its antagonism to sin, this same method may be called the Ascetic Principle. It is from this point of view, then, that it will now be regarded; and our task is to consider some of the objections which have been urged against Christian ideals on the ground of a supposed hostility to the whole natural order of life.

The etymology of the word "asceticism" suggests at once its fundamental idea. In classical phraseology the words ἀσκέω, ἄσκησις were used to express the idea of athletic exercise or training; the ἀσκητής was an ἀθλητής. In patristic literature the Christian hermit was an ἀσκητής, because the object of his life was considered to be a positive one, namely, that of training his soul by spiritual exercises, as the athlete trained his body by physical exercises. Asceticism is the steep mountainous path by which the Christian seeks to reach the otherworldly heights; it is the method whereby he attains his ideals, a method which is therefore of necessity strenuous and exacting. Something has already been indicated as to the reasons which make this asceticism necessary in a discussion of the otherworldly principle in relation to the sinful will.[1] The purpose of the ascetic method is to train and develop the faculties in such a way that they become serviceable instruments of the otherworldly principle. Especially is it intended to brace the whole personality against the weakening effects of the sinful taint and the lingering attraction of the natural centre of gravity, so that it may acquire an ever-increasing habit of using the phenomenal

[1] pp. 178–182.

14

world sacramentally, as a means and not as an end. Viewed, then, as a means of training the faculties to serve the highest ends, the ascetic principle is seen to be supported by countless analogies from the ordinary affairs of life. It is simply the highest example of that specialization which is a fundamental principle of human life. The athlete voluntarily cuts himself off from certain bodily indulgences which are in themselves innocent, but which hinder him from attaining that special bodily condition which he has in view. The scholar denies himself many pursuits, good and useful in themselves, in order that his mind may be the more free to concentrate upon the special interests which he has chosen. The successful business man is simply a specialist who has trained his whole personality to master certain principles. Such principles make him efficient in his particular sphere of activity; but in order to master them he has had to make constant renunciations. Everywhere in human conduct the same method is adopted; and *no one ever dreams of questioning its value, except when the method is employed in relation to ideals which lie outside the natural order of experience.* Moreover, the same principle may be said to run right through the natural order. What meaning has the whole theory of adaptation and selection in nature, if it is not that particular organisms survive by turning limitations to account? For every action of environment upon organism involves a limitation; and thus through limitation in one direction the organism specializes in another direction, and a higher manifestation of life is the result.

The hostility of Nietzsche to Christian asceticism is a most remarkable example of that unreasonable prejudice to which reference has just been made in the italicized sentence. For his own system was really ascetic at bottom. The general trend of his message was that life is a serious thing, and that the progress of the race is to be achieved at the cost of great individual sacrifices. The superman is to come through the sacrifice of slaves; the race as a whole is to achieve a certain ideal by carefully not following the line of least resistance, by turning away from mere softness and pleasure. All this is essentially ascetic. " I teach you to become hard," cries Zarathustra; and so too in a very different sense did our Lord speak. Yet because Christian asceticism aims at attaining ideals which belong to a sphere outside the natural order of experience, the method itself is discounted. The difference between the hardness which Zarathustra inculcates and that which our Lord requires, appears on the surface to be simply this, that in the former case a man is to be hard towards his neighbour, whilst the Christian is to be hard towards himself. Nietzsche seized upon this point as the basis of his criticism. Christian asceticism seemed to him to be mere self-torture,—poor and degrading, because serving no worthy purpose. The otherworldly values were beyond the range of his observation; he could not see the real motives of the Christian nor their justification in experience. He therefore used his imaginative powers to invent a large number of physical and psychological reasons for conduct which was otherwise inexplicable. The following is a good example of an attempt to find

(ii.) The Ascetic Principle as Will to Power.

a psychological explanation :— " The ascetic and martyr . . . experiences the utmost satisfaction, because he inflicts on himself, as a result of his desire for distinction, that pain which his opposite, the barbarian . . ., inflicts upon those others, upon whom and before whom he wishes to distinguish himself." [1] Or, again, this :—" The mightiest men have hitherto always bowed reverently before the saint as the enigma of self-subjugation. . . . They divined in him . . . the superior force which wished to test itself by such a subjugation ; the strength of will, in which they recognized their own strength and love of power, and knew how to honour it. . . . It was the 'Will to Power' which obliged them to halt before the saint." [2] The ascetic principle then is, according to Nietzsche, something active, "a desire for distinction," a will to power testing itself by self-subjugation. So far there is no necessary condemnation of the principle. It is something positive at work. It is indeed, according to his later phraseology, a manifestation of the universal Will to Power which is at work throughout the entire range of life. But this Will to Power works itself out in the bad elements of life, as well as in the good. In the *Genealogy of Morals* we learn the real significance of the ascetic principle according to Nietzsche. It is the Will to Power manifesting itself under conditions of degeneration and decay. It is the will of the weak sufferer seeking to subjugate his depression by a drugging, stifling,

Nietzsche's Objections. (a) Suppression of Vitality.

---

[1] *The Dawn of Day*, by F. Nietzsche (English trans. by J. M. Kennedy, p. 114 ; T. N. Foulis).

[2] *Beyond Good and Evil* (English trans. by Miss Helen Zimmern, § 51, p. 70).

numbing process ending in annihilation of life.[1]
He says :—" Precisely *this* is meant by the ascetic
ideal that something *was* lacking, that an immense
gap yawned round man. He was unable to justify,
explain, be-yea himself, he *suffered* from the problem of his significance. He suffered also in other
respects ; he was in the main a *sickly* animal.
Not suffering itself, however, constituted his problem, but the lack of the answer to the cry of
the question : *Wherefore* suffer? Man *Wills* to
suffer ; he even seeks for suffering, provided that
he is shown *a significance*, a *therefore* of suffering. . . . *And the ascetic ideal offered to mankind
a significance* . . . man was saved thereby ; he
had *a significance* . . . *will itself was saved*. . . ."
And what is it that is willed by the ascetic? "*A
Will-to-Nothing*, a horror of life, an insurrection
against the most fundamental presuppositions of
life ; nevertheless it is and remains a *will*! And
to say once more at the end what I have said at
the outset : rather would man will *the Nothing*, than
not Will. . . ."[2] Asceticism, then, is a device of
the Will to Power for annihilating the unfit. By
the invention of such ideas as guilt and sin the
ascetic priest has rendered weaklings harmless ; for
he has taught them to turn their resentful feelings
(due to their sufferings) against themselves instead
of against others.[3] Now the whole of this theory

---

[1] But see above, Chapter II. (iv.), pp. 54, 55.
[2] *The Genealogy of Morals*, iii. § 28. The italics are Nietzsche's
throughout.
[3] *Ibid.*, iii. §§ 15, 16. At the same time it must be acknowledged that elsewhere Nietzsche speaks of a revolt of the "slaves"
against "the nobles." Apparently asceticism appeared to him
to be the will to power in the throes of a deadly disease, tending

of a Will-to-Nothing is built up upon the following presuppositions : (1) there is no spiritual world; (2) religion and the whole psychology of religious experience can be explained away as delusions due to physiological weakness and depression ; (3) all restraint and economy in the use of the natural world is bad, *when it is due to ideas denied under* (1) *and* (2). Nietzsche's own philosophy required a certain asceticism of its own, as has already been said; what else can be the significance of his repudiation of utilitarian motives for conduct ? Yet he rejects this method, wherever it appears in relation to ideals ruled out by himself. That is why he calls modern science and philosophy ascetic, because they seek to discover Truth.[1] His real objection is after all, not to the ascetic method, but to the ideals which inspire it. He saw only one will to power, that of the Natural Man ; whereas in reality there is another which is greater, the will to power of the spiritual world, whose existence he denied. In the light of his experience of the otherworldly values the Christian knows love as the highest power; and thus Christian asceticism is seen to be the will to power of love striving to realize itself in spite of the difficulties introduced by sin. The Christian knows that love is the most intensely vital thing of all. But he knows also that sin is a drug which has found an entrance into human life and has infected the whole of the "natural" side of human personality, constituting it "the flesh." By putting, then, a strict restraint and rule upon his use

to extinction. Yet "it is and remains a *will*," liable to spasms of self-assertion. (See above, pp. 54, 55.)

[1] *Op. cit.*, §§ 24–26.

of the phenomenal order, he does not merely practise withdrawal and negation through absence of the power of enjoying that from which he withdraws. The will to power of the Natural Man can only find ends for itself in the natural order. Now the Christian knows only too well his fatal powers of assimilating himself to the natural order and enjoying its purely natural ends. On the other hand, his experience of the other-worldly values tells him that they are infinitely better as ends. Accordingly he allies his whole personality to the higher will to power of love, which braces him to discipline his use of the phenomenal world.

The ascetic principle seeks, then, not to suppress the man's vitality but to quicken and direct it ; for (*b*) Equality before God— " Levelling down." the supreme motive of all true Christian asceticism is to bring the Christ-self to its full development. Nietzsche constantly attacked Christianity on the ground that its doctrine of "the equality of all before God" is destructive of all individuality. He conceived it as levelling all men down to the value of the most worthless, so that only the lowest common denominator is to be taken into consideration. It is as though Christian equality were obtained by an emasculating process, like the common residuum of undenominational religion. With a view to stifling all individuality, Christianity, it is supposed, has sought to replace freedom of action by a deadening mechanicalism. In the third essay of the *Genealogy of Morals*, already quoted, we read of "machinal activity and all its appurtenances . . . a certain permission of, nay training to 'impersonality,' to

self-forgetting, to *incuria sui.* . . ."[1] Here again
the misunderstanding is due to complete ignorance
of the otherworldly values. " Equality before God "
is not the dull uniformity which Nietzsche supposed
it to be. Nor is it an external end towards which
everything in humanity must be artificially forced.
It is indeed not the end at all but the starting-point—
one of the central axioms which the otherworldly
experience reveals. Nietzsche could hardly have
condemned this genuine equality if he had known
it. What he recoiled from was a certain supposed
standard of equality which degraded all alike.
Exactly the reverse of this is the truth. To the
Christian all souls are equal before God, because he
discerns in all alike eternal possibilities of greatness.
It is an equality not of poverty but of riches. In
mathematics infinity is treated as a quantity which
reduces all fixed and limited quantities to insignificance. In the same way, in the presence of the
eternal worth of an individual soul, the limited gifts
and powers which distinguish one personality from
another are, though precious, of no account for
purposes of comparison. They belong to the phenomenal order in themselves ; and their worth lies
solely in their intimate connection with the otherworldly value of the soul. Sacramentally they are
raised to being of the highest importance, as means
whereby the Christ-self may express itself. If used
sacramentally they become transfigured ; and their
worth then passes up permanently into the sphere of
the Christ-self. There they become jewels in the
diadem of that moral perfection which the individual
soul will at length attain.

[1] *A Genealogy of Morals*, iii. § 18.

But are we justified in pressing this idea of
"equality" and making it so all-important? Will
not the effect be to minimize that element of diversity
which is the salt of human fellowship? What of
the principle of election, so firmly rooted in religious
history? Have not some individuals a larger part
to play in the Divine plan of the world than others?
Now this apparent conflict of equality with diversity
ceases to be a difficulty when we remember that
the two things belong to entirely different planes,
and must be measured in different scales. It is
here that our illustration from mathematics fails us.
The difference between infinity and any fixed number
is immense; yet both belong to the same order of
things and can be compared by a common scale of
measurement. Four is nearer to infinity than three,
and these can all be arranged together in the order
of their relative value : infinity, four, three. But this
is not possible when we are dealing with values which
belong to two entirely different planes. The worth
of a soul is an otherworldly value, nothing less than
a potentiality of the fulness of the Christ-life. Moreover, the values of the otherworldly sphere are not
relative but absolute, inasmuch as they furnish complete and final ends for human conduct. All the
diversities of life, on the other hand, belong to the
natural order ; and, in so far as they are not to be
traced to sin, they are good. On the natural plane
there is an immense variety of gifts and powers in
human society ; and corresponding with these a like
variety of vocations. These furnish a right and
proper differentiation between personalities, and
make possible that social unity which grows out
of individual diversities. These natural diversities,

however, all centre round units of personality.
Thus they can only bring their full contribution to
the social unity, which they are intended to serve,
when they are seen to have a sacramental value by
virtue of their connection with human personality.
Seeing, then, that the worth of personality lies in
the otherworldly sphere, it is clear that the realized
sacramental worth of the whole range of natural
diversities depends upon the degree in which the
otherworldly value of individual souls is recognized.
The value, then, of the natural diversities of gift and
function can begin to be truly realized only after the
preliminary recognition of the value of the individual
personalities.   This is a value which is different in
kind from the other sort, and far more fundamental
in character.   Now in the sphere of otherworldly
personal values the substantial worth of each unit is
the same, even though their functional powers may
vary greatly in quality and capacity.   All the personal units are equal and alike in their fundamental
capacity for giving and receiving otherworldly love.
So then, weighed in the scale of *moral* potentiality
they are equal ; and the moral standard of valuation
is infinitely the highest and the most important.
Moreover, each personal unit is a centre round
which the otherworldly activities gather, and from
which they pass to the sacramental appropriation
of the natural gifts and powers.   Thus personal
units are the only points of connection between the
two worlds, as far as human conduct is concerned.
To each and all of them must be given that equal
recognition of otherworldly value which is their due.
In this way only can we ensure the full liberation of
their God-given powers, whereby the rich varieties

of natural function and endowment attaching to them may be sacramentalized and redeemed.

Thus the equality of souls before God is to the Christian the platform from which all can ascend the steepest heights. The worth of each soul is indeed so great that all false and destructive individualism must give place before it. In seeking this consummation, the ascetic principle does not train the individual to "impersonality," as Nietzsche supposed. It leads him, rather, through a simplifying process such as that of which Mr. Wells has seen the value.[1] Now the whole trend and aim of this process is to raise the individual to a higher level of personality by constraining him to clear away the obstructions of false individualism. To those who are ignorant of the otherworldly values Christian conduct must of necessity appear strange and unaccountable. It appears to depreciate the value of the phenomenal order, because it treats it as a means instead of an end; when, however, the real ends are seen, all appears natural. That "self-forgetting" and "incuria sui" which Nietzsche thought to be mere vacuity and nothingness, rendering all activity "machinal,"[2] is in reality the sign of the spiritual will to power. It is the "squandering" of the "noble," conscious of spiritual wealth. He who has found a priceless treasure can afford to sell all, that he may possess it. To realize the Christ-self he gladly forgets the clamour of the lower ego. He is no longer over-careful about his worldly circumstances, nor as to the exact arrangement of the phenomenal order around him. His most real self is independent of these things. In all his activity

[1] See Chapter III. II. (ii.).   [2] See above, p. 215.

he seeks to turn everything that belongs to the earthly order into a means towards higher ends. By so doing he finds that his interest in these things grows not less but greater; just as the cloud is most beautiful, not in itself, but when it is lighted up by the setting sun. Thus was St. Francis passionately at home in nature, because the centre of his life's interests was so entirely beyond nature in the spiritual world. So, as the Christian grows in the other-worldly experience, life becomes for him less and less "machinal," more and more free, personal, and significant in its smallest details. By the ascetic principle a man's whole personality, imagination, reason, and will are trained, tempered, and sharpened to appreciate the otherworldly values, and to deal skilfully with a multiplicity of phenomena for the highest ends.

Through mistaking the ascetic principle for a will to nothing, instead of seeing in it, as is really the (c) Christian case, a will to power, Nietzsche went on Fellowship— "the Herding to treat all the social virtues of Christi-of the Sick." anity as so many signs of weakness, cheap palliatives for a sickly race. His treatment of Christian Pity has already been considered. In his essay on the meaning of asceticism he speaks of such social virtues as being little devices invented to soothe the sickly sufferer as the will to nothing fulfils itself in him. He says :—" A still more highly prized means in the struggle with depression is the ordaining of a little joy. . . . The most frequent form in which joy is thus ordained as a remedy is the joy of *bringing* joy. . . . In the struggle against depression, the *formation* of herds is a decided advance and victory. . . . Prompted by a desire to cast off the sullen depression and impotence, the sick, the sickly, will instinctively strive for gregarious organization."[1]   This idea of the herd, with the corresponding thought that strength lies in selfish isolation, is one of the most familiar in the writings of Nietzsche. It has, however, already been shown, in the preceding chapter, that the social virtues of Christianity are *positive*, being directed entirely towards the realization of the otherworldly love - values. It will be useful now to examine the matter from the standpoint of the ascetic principle. So far from the social virtues being palliatives to make the ascetic process tolerable, they are themselves to be attained only as the hardly-won fruits of that positive spiritual power which the ascetic process accumulates. Nothing could be more unlike mere herding or mob-association than the fellowship which Christians are ever striving to realize.

The truth is that there are two great instincts rooted in human nature, the one individual and the other social. There is the desire to be distinct and separate, and there is the complementary desire of entering into relationship with our fellows. On the natural plane both of these instincts may become entirely degraded. The former may become arrogant selfishness ; whilst the latter may make a man lose his proper independence, drift with the tide of fashion, bow to the passions and prejudices of an excited mob and become a mere shadow or echo of others out of timidity. In every society the number of such camp-followers as these is large ; but if a society were wholly composed of them it

---

[1] *A Genealogy of Morals*, iii. § 18.

would dissolve through universal mutual distrust. Distrust is a dividing factor which isolates individuals from one another and makes them separate and self-centred units. Thus that which degrades people from a fellowship into a mob is that very spirit of isolation and selfish loneliness which Nietzsche considered to be the mark of the true noble. On the other hand, the one force which binds society together is the power of mutual respect. When this mutual respect exists all individuals are treated as of worth in themselves, and thus mutual confidence spreads. The association of a herd is a purely self-centred affair, due to the instinct of self-preservation, which leads the weak individual to seek the protection of numbers. The fellowship inculcated by Christianity is an ideal which runs directly counter to this herd instinct. It requires the individual to exercise his whole personality ascetically with a view to the realization of the otherworldly value of love to the Neighbour. The earthly values centering round the lower self are always ready to hand; and the will may easily and quickly descend and become engrossed in this lower plane. For the realization of the love-values, on the other hand, a continuous ascetic effort has to be made by the Christ-self to assert itself. Thus the social activity of the Christ-self is essentially positive. It adopts an independent attitude towards all which is not in harmony with the otherworldly values. Thus it is that the saints have always been in the truest sense the lonely ones. For in comparison with their realization of love there is so much of the mob in those around them. They reach out in love towards others; but the Christ-self in these latter is undeveloped and overlaid with the false isolation and distrust which marks the mob spirit. The ascetic character, therefore, of all other-worldly activity must in these circumstances be deepened enormously. There is so much that obstructs and distresses love in its attempt to cope with such a situation. This ascetic loneliness is of the essence of the Gospel; the loneliest figure in all history is that of the Man of Sorrows. Yet such loneliness is neither the self-absorbed aloofness of the superman, nor the will to nothing which has no positive end. It is the method by which the Christ-self keeps itself free from all weakening attractions of the flesh within and of the world without, in order that it may be stronger in the power of love and more able to enter by love into fellowship with the Christ-self in others. Thus all Christian social virtues are seen to be the fruits of an otherworldly will to power, won to the larger purposes of love by ascetic subordination of the lower self and its desires. This will to power of love reaches its highest concentration when the ascetic principle has attained absolute control over every individual in the community. In a fellowship of the saints—for those who could behold it understandingly—there would be concentrated greater energies of power than any which this world has ever imagined.

These otherworldly activities maintained by the ascetic principle seemed to Nietzsche to be merely negative distractions and futilities—on that account comparatively innocent. There is, however, another side to the ascetic principle, which from the Christian point of view may truly be called negative; namely, its rela-

(d) The Ascetic Principle in Relation to Sin.

tion to the facts of sin and the sinful condition of the individual. Its method of dealing with these Nietzsche calls "the more interesting, the guilty, means" employed by the ascetic to drug his sense of suffering. Whilst to him asceticism seemed to be essentially self-torture, to the Christian it is essentially the method of self-realization. For the whole penitential experience of the ascetic is negative, always present indeed, but always the preliminary purging which is necessary to liberate the Christ-self for its positive activities. The Christian finds that he must say nay to sin before he can say yea to love. All disciplines such as fasting are means to this negation of sin as a preliminary to a fresh energizing of the higher self towards the love-values. Nietzsche calls this penitential experience "the ascetic ideal in the service of an extravagance of feelings."[1] Christian sorrow for sin must indeed seem extravagant to those who have no Christian experience of love. But it is often a good sign to be thought extravagant; heights and depths go together, and in this case they are better than a monotonous level. An intense horror of sin would be morbid by itself; but, as the counterpart of intense appreciation of that love which sin opposes, it is natural and healthy. Once again it is necessary to assert that this intense activity against moral evil is no mere destructive principle, but the self-assertion of love against that which would destroy it. So far from the penitential experience being one which makes the individual a prey to lunacy and neurosis, as Nietzsche supposed, it has exactly the opposite effect. It leads to peace and interior calm; and this

[1] *A Genealogy of Morals*, iii. § 20.

must have a good effect on both body and mind. The peace of soul which penitence brings renews the soul's vigour and gives it fresh courage to pursue its pathway towards the otherworldly values.

It was necessary to deal separately with Nietzsche's criticisms of the ascetic principle, because his whole standpoint is unique.   Let us now turn to the consideration of some more general criticisms which have been passed upon the Christian view of life. From various sides it has been declared that the whole outlook of genuine Christianity is so revolutionary and so destructive of all that is natural, that it is an impossible one for anyone to entertain who would live wisely and usefully in the world.   Such writers as David Strauss, Professor Karl Pearson, Friedrich Paulsen, and Mr. H. W. Garrod—the earliest of these in the middle of last century, and the last-named quite recently—form a group whose opposition to Christianity takes this general ground.   Like Nietzsche, they dislike especially the strong ascetic note ; but, as we have already seen in the case of Mr. Garrod,[1] they do not, with Nietzsche, brand Christianity as a mere will to nothing.   They see in it rather an intense antagonism to the whole natural order of human life based upon the hope of immortality in the future world.   They believe that Christians are lured on to undervalue this world by a delusion that another world in the future will make up for the worthlessness of the present.   They emphasize the negative character, as they regard it, of the

(iii.) The Ascetic Principle and the Destruction of the Natural Man: (a) Criticisms by other Writers.

[1] See above, p. 167.

Christian way; though they admit in a greater or less degree that its aims are positive. Before passing on to their treatment of Christian asceticism, let us notice their views as to the positive aim of Christianity. In his *Ethic of Freethought* Professor Karl Pearson points out that whilst Christianity agrees with Buddhism in proclaiming "sensuality a delusion," it disagrees with the latter in its treatment of individuality. For Buddhism the permanence of personal existence is another delusion; whereas for the Christian it is the supreme hope dominating his whole conduct. This hope of personal immortality, together with his belief in God, "so far from being delusions for him, are the terms which regulate the whole conduct of his life; they are precisely what induces him to renounce the world of sense."[1] Again: "The Christian admits that by accepting his revelation he reduces this world to a sphere of sorrow and trial . . . yet on the other hand, sure of the after-life, he holds the sacrifice more than justified."[2] Similarly Paulsen wrote: "Christianity is not essentially negative, like pessimism, but positive; the eternal life which is to come and is close at hand overshadows the temporal life."[3] A little further on he actually describes the positive element as something which has a transforming power for the *present*. "It creates a new will which strives after holiness . . . a new feeling of self-reliance . . . a new form of human intercourse . . . a new relation to the earth and its goods: the Christian is the master of all things,

---

[1] *The Ethic of Freethought*, p. 75.
[2] *Ibid.*, p. 78.
[3] *A System of Ethics*, English trans. by F. Thilly, p. 88.

capable of enjoying all innocent pleasures and yet firmly attached to none." This is a very generous estimate, coming from such a quarter; and yet, in spite of such a large appreciation, the writer concludes : " That such a state is not adapted to promote what is called civilization can hardly be doubted : he whose heart is in heaven will not be very apt to make this earthly life rich and beautiful and grand. . . ."[1] We have already seen how close to all this is Mr. Garrod's estimate; but we saw in his case, what is really true of Paulsen also, in spite of his perception of a present transforming power, that in the summing up Christianity is regarded as *primarily* negative. The original ground of this negativity is regarded as interesting for the student of ideas; it is perhaps poetic and beautiful, capable of conveying, as through an allegory, some slight lesson.[2] There is, however, not the least notion that it can really remould the individual into a more social being and a more useful citizen. It is in fact impossible to find any rational meaning in the ascetic principle apart from the otherworldly experience. Even Paulsen's admission that eternal life has a present value for the Christian can hardly mean more than that an intensely vivid expectation has a subjective influence, enabling a man to treat the object hoped for as something already won. Thus the point where this group of writers may be said really to misunderstand Christianity lies in this, that with them the motive for Christian asceticism is conceived of as something wholly

[1] *A System of Ethics*, p. 94.
[2] *E.g.* see the last page of Mr. Garrod's *Christ the Forerunner*, quoted above in Chapter V. p. 158.

belonging to the future.   Yet as a fact the universal
Christian experience is that, whilst the future is a
very real source of inspiration, it is a subordinate
motive compared with what exists already in the
present.   The real basis of Christian conduct is
a constant present experience of mystical union
with Christ, with all the consciousness of peace
and security with which that union already fills
the soul.   Without this present reality the hope
of future glory would be a feeble and uncertain
thing, liable to give way just when it was most
needed.

Nothing is more invigorating to the faith of the
Christian than to read such criticisms of the ascetic
principle as these.   When the really revolutionary
character of the Christian ethic is grasped—as it is
by these writers—it is set aside as unpractical
solely because it is approached from an external
point of view and without the key of the otherworldly experience.   The Christian knows his task
to be gigantic.   It is nothing less than the complete destruction of the natural man—not the natural
order of humanity in itself, but the sinful taint which
is at present rooted in it.   The Christian, however,
is conscious of possessing a key which can unlock
the floodgates of power, and that too a power which
is capable of universal extension throughout human
society.   He knows too that this power from the
other world, in so far as it has already destroyed
the Natural Man in himself, has been doing a wholly
constructive work ; for, with every weakening of the
Natural Man, there is a growth of the Spiritual Man,
the true social unit.   Moreover, he finds that by the
ascetic method of detachment from the natural order

he is becoming daily a more social, because a more spiritual, being—that is, one more capable of realizing the otherworldly values. In the extension, therefore, of the power of the Christian experience to all humanity he sees the possibility of all men becoming truly social. He is not, then, disturbed by the complaint that he is indifferent to the natural order or opposed to it. He knows the worth of the natural order, as even Paulsen admits. He puts a higher value upon that order than any can possibly do who make it an end in itself. It is to him the very body of the spiritual world; and for that very reason he cannot be content until it is made worthy of so high a connection. He wishes to realize the full value of the natural order here and now; but, by reason of the existence of the sinful tendency both in himself and in all mankind, he knows that this cannot be done by short cuts. At every moment he must act in opposition to the Natural Man. It is a crooked instrument, and by its aid he could only misuse the natural order. But, whilst this opposition is permanent, it is also only preliminary. At each stage of the process, after the preliminary movement of antagonism towards the false method, he seizes once more the true instrument, the Spiritual Man; and, thus equipped, he approaches afresh the task of appropriating the worth of the natural order for spiritual ends.

Christian detachment from the natural order is therefore the necessary method of realizing its full worth. It is not a mark of indifference but of interest, strange as this may seem on a surface view. It is no mere attempt to cut oneself adrift from the interests of life, as Prof.

(b) The Charge of Indifference.

Karl Pearson supposes when he writes :—" The lives of Buddhist monks, of Christian ascetics and pietists . . . prove sufficiently that men can render themselves more or less indifferent to the storm of outward sensation. . . . May we not ask with Herder whether man has any right to remove himself into this blessed indifference, whether it must not destroy that sympathy for his fellows which can only arise from like passions?"[1] Similarly Paulsen says :—" A traveller does not take any active interest in the affairs of a foreign country, but bears them as best he can. So the Christians behave with respect to this world . . . they do the work which living in the world imposes upon them, but they have no interest in it."[2] Nothing could be further from the truth than these statements. The atmosphere of Christianity is utterly opposed to this picture of doleful estrangement and mere passivity. When Quietism of this kind has appeared in the Church it has promptly been detected as something false. Christian detachment is not indifference or lack of sympathy. It is rather the breathless attention of the athlete who holds aloof from his task for a space that he may not blunder prematurely into it ; he would first measure the effort required, and then gather up all his energies to achieve it. The Christian believes himself to be incorporated into the other world of the Kingdom of God. Yet, owing to the sinful taint in his nature, the world of moral evil, the kingdom of Satan, still has a hold upon his life. The phenomenal world, where his bodily existence is set, lies midway between these

---

[1] *The Ethic of Freethought*, p. 95.
[2] *A System of Ethics*, p. 88.

two kingdoms of good and evil, and is the scene of the struggle between them. Now it is not true to say that the Christian identifies the phenomenal world with the kingdom of moral evil;[1] he holds that the forces of evil are encamped in that world over against the forces of good. The phenomenal world therefore possesses a mixed character, both good and evil;[2] and the Christian, recognizing this, desires the triumph of the good over the evil, and is intensely interested in the conflict. Christian asceticism is his method of allying himself with the good against the evil, with a view to rescuing the phenomenal world for spiritual purposes. His appreciation of the true worth of the phenomenal world will not allow him to treat its present condition as wholly good, whether as manifested within himself or without. Moreover, by virtue of his detached position, he can sympathize more, and not less, with the struggle of his fellow-men; for he is of like passions with them, and knows the misery of being immersed in the world of phenomena without firm attachment to the kingdom of the good. In this connection it is important to notice one of the principal grounds upon which Paulsen bases his contention that Christianity is unpractical, namely, that the virtues inculcated by our Lord are of a negative character. He says:—"The Gospels nowhere say, Accumulate wealth and save, care for your own and the economic welfare of your family.

---

[1] *The Ethic of Freethought*, p. 75. "The phenomenal world is essentially a world of sin."

[2] *Cf.* H. Martensen, *Christian Ethics* (the General Part), in the English translation by C. Spence (1888). His analysis of the ideas of "evil" and the "world" in the section on "The Highest Good," §§ 49–51, pp. 160–164.

But they do say, Take no thought for your life, what ye shall eat. . . . We nowhere read, Have a care for the development of your natural capacities; train the body . . . the intellect and the senses. . . . But we do read, If one of thy members offend thee, pluck it out. . . ." In a similar manner he refers to the beatitudes and to the evangelical counsels. Enough has probably been said in this chapter and the preceding one to make clear the true significance of those sayings of our Lord which might appear to be merely negative.[1] Let us now confine ourselves to the question raised in the above passage from Paulsen. Why did our Lord say so little in the way of direct instruction about the ordinary activities of human life? Why indeed does He seem to have deliberately avoided such questions? Our Lord's teaching is full of illustrations drawn from the world of nature and the round of earthly toil and industry. When, however, parables and sayings are examined in detail the lesson inculcated is in every case seen to be one whose reference lies wholly in the other world. Thus the parable of the Ten Virgins shows intimate acquaintance with the wedding customs of His time and place. Yet for all that the sole purpose of the parable is not to inculcate industry, thoughtfulness, and carefulness in any form of social activity, but to teach the purely spiritual duty of watching for the Lord's return. Or again in the parable of the labourers hired for the vineyard we have a graphic picture of human toil and the rewards of industry; yet the otherworldly idea once more dominates the situation. The lesson in this

[1] *E.g.* Chapter V. pp. 163–168, 187–189.

case is that spiritual service, whatever its apparent
quality in human eyes, is not to be judged by earthly
standards ; that its reward will not be according to
human merits, but according to a heavenly scale of
valuation. It would be easy to show how entirely
the otherworldly issues possess the field in every
case. Now two points must be noticed in this connection. In the first place, whilst the otherworldliness of all this teaching is unmistakable, it must not
be inferred that its trend is passive and negative.
Balancing the directly negative injunctions, such as,
"If thy hand offend thee, cut it off," we find here a
whole world of positive activity. The watchfulness
inculcated may be for a Coming which seems strange
and out of place ; but it is to be a watchfulness which
is intensely active, attentive, expectant—one that
makes the watcher ready to move forward instantly
to greet the returning Lord. The service inculcated
may be emphatically the minding of heavenly and
not earthly business ; but it is to be a service in
which the man gives his best, and spends all his
powers like a labourer toiling under the hot sun.
The Gospel then is concerned entirely with inculcating the otherworldly spirit ; but it is to be a spirit
which, in its own proper sphere, is intensely active,
alert and full of energy. Secondly, this activity of
the otherworldly conduct, while moving towards the
supernatural ends, does not reach them directly.
It reaches them, as we have already seen, by passing
through the earthly materials, using them as means,
and so transmuting them. Activity which has in
the first place an otherworldly significance cannot
remain suspended as it were aloof from the phenomenal order ; nor is there any trace of such an idea

in our Lord's teaching. On the contrary, it must leave the record of its supernatural energy upon the natural plane as well. Moreover, when it reaches that plane *its influence upon it is found to be not less but more thorough* by virtue of its otherworldly character ; because in such activity the phenomenal order is not an end but a means to that which is divinely constituted as its sole and proper end.[1] Behind Paulsen's criticism here lies the thought that this otherworldly Gospel is a thing suspended in the air above us without anything to connect it with the earthly plane. This is not borne out by our Lord's emphatic statement that He came not to destroy the law but to fulfil it. It was not His method to abolish the existing order of life but to introduce a new element from above which would crown and complete it.

The fact is that the ordinary practical activities of life to which Paulsen refers, such as attention to worldly and family cares, training of body and mind, marriage and citizenship, the attainment of fame and

---

[1] A significant passage in this connection is St Luke xvi. 9–11. In this parable of the unrighteous steward the earthly business of money-making is introduced to inculcate an otherworldly wisdom. But this heavenly wisdom leaves its mark upon mundane affairs ; for it bids us "make to yourselves (*i.e.* in your own interests) friends out of the mammon of unrighteousness (*i.e.* from the use of your wealth)," and by this method we shall qualify for reception into the eternal habitations. And again v. 11 teaches that if the proper use of earthly wealth is neglected, we shall be found unfit at the last to become stewards of the real (that is, the other-worldly) treasure. This passage makes it clear that the acquisition of heavenly wealth by means of heavenly wisdom is not merely analogous, in some sense, to the employment of skill for winning success in the business of this life. By means of the *heavenly* wisdom a right use is to be made of *earthly* wealth ; and this sacramental effect of heavenly wisdom upon our use of the natural plane is to be the test of fitness for otherworldly blessedness. Compare with this what has been said on pp. 190, 191 above.

position—all these are precisely the things in which, before our Lord came, the whole world had been engrossed. It would, indeed, be more correct to say "immersed." For upon the natural plane these things were inevitably made ends in themselves, instead of being used for sacramental purposes. Now our Lord came to lift men on to a higher stage, on which these things would still be actively used, but in a different way. He knew that men's chief danger is, not to be too much of the other world, but to be too much of this world, with the result that the very things they strive after lose their value as soon as they are attained. All this use of the natural order existed already; it was the material upon which our Lord had to work. He took it for granted :—"I came not to destroy the law." The law had prescribed the lines upon which the natural order could be used with the fullest benefit. But the law could not raise men on to that higher plane where, detached from the natural order, men could use it in such a way as to realize its full worth. Our Lord took this also for granted :— "I came . . . to fulfil." Now, therefore, He was about to inaugurate those new conditions under which, by the power of the other world, men could for the first time rejoice in the use of the natural order, without seeing its worth elude their grasp. Of what use then would it have been for Him to have spent His time in teaching men their normal daily occupations, which they already knew by nature? What they needed to learn, the great lesson which as yet they knew not, was *in what spirit* they must approach those earthly tasks and conditions. They needed such teaching as would guide them in preserving the spirit of the other world, and deepening its impression upon their lives; and such is the teaching which our Lord actually gave. Yet even this was subject to the condition, which no mere teaching by itself can effect, that they must first enter upon the experience of actual incorporation into the other world.[1] The mass of mankind are wholly engrossed in providing either the necessities or the luxuries of the bodily life with incalculable loss to their whole personality. What they need is to learn the secret of that spirit, whereby, in seeking after necessities, one may do so with an eye which looks beyond them to otherworldly realities, the possession of which will remove the bitterness of want, the weight of anxiety and the desire for superfluity. The mass of mankind are naturally interested in the cultivation of either body, mind, or æsthetic sense. The danger often is that one or other of these will receive excessive attention, and make a man hoard and hug his culture like a miser to the endless loss of his personality as a whole. What he needs is the power, if necessary, to cut off deliberately from his life that thing in which he delighted, either in part or altogether, in order that he may redress the balance. For if any interest in life cannot be made a means to spiritual realities it will become a blind alley. The man will advance no further in that direction towards possession of the fulness of his personality. The exercise of "the power to cut off" must be understood in the light of the limiting words which follow, "that he may redress the balance." It is no mere mania of destruction which the ascetic

[1] See Chapter V., especially pp. 160–162.

principle inculcates. It is rather that spirit of independence which enables a man to hold the pruning knife in readiness, to be used or not as the other-worldly values direct, but to be used unhesitatingly when spiritual interests require it. The vast mass of mankind are in no danger of relinquishing the sexual instincts, which are part of their natural heritage. The danger lies wholly the other way, either in the direction of sensuality, or in the more subtle and less readily acknowledged peril of making marriage, home, and family love ends in themselves, instead of sacramental means whereby the spiritual ends of society are realized. What men need is to have the vision of a Higher Love kept ever before their eyes, for the sake of which the comforts and consolations of the earthly home may have to be renounced by some, in order that its otherworldly reference may be impressed upon all.[1] Again, the mass of mankind are in no danger of forgetting to seek for earthly position and honour. What they need is the constant reminder that such things are harmful and not helpful to the personality, when they are made mere decorations of selfish pride, instead of being turned into means of wider social influence. The ascetic principle teaches a man both how to abound and how to be in want. It teaches him to use honour and success in the spirit of detachment for social ends; and, again, to turn misfortune, hostility, and disaster into means of deepening this spirit of detachment from the natural order, so that it may always be used with a high and sober purpose.

[1] See Chapter VIII.

But this general attitude of detachment from the natural order is only as it were a safeguard and a pre-

(c) The Exter- paration—the wearing of one's armour
mination of the in readiness for the more serious business
Natural Man. of the real fight.   For the ascetic prin-
ciple passes quickly, according to the demands of circumstance, from a quiet detachment into a hard and even fierce antagonism.   The group of writers whom we are now considering regard Christianity as "anti-natural."   In this they are right in so far as they mean by such a phrase that Christianity is, and always must be, in violent revolt against the *status quo* of human nature.[1]   In the words of one writer, "Until the sensuous world has been renounced, until the 'flesh' with all its impulses and desires has been crucified, there can be no entry into the higher life."[2]   These writers, however, do not merely charge Christianity with being "anti-natural" in the sense which has just been defined. Paulsen, for example, quotes the words of 1 St. John ii. 15, 16: "Love not the world, neither the things that are in the world.   If any man love the world, the love of the Father is not in him.   For all that is in the world, the lust of the flesh, and the lust of the eyes, and the pride of life, is not of the Father but is of the world."   Upon this he makes the following comment: "So the Apostle John . . . debarring not merely coarse sensuous pleasure, but also æsthetical pleasure (the lust of the eyes) and everything that makes life glorious and grand (ἀλαζονεία τοῦ βίου) in the eyes of the children of this

---

[1] *E.g.* H. W. Garrod, *The Religion of All Good Men*, p. 152 ; K. Pearson, *The Ethic of Freethought*, p. 75.
[2] Pearson, *ibid*.

world."[1]   Now by this comment we are intended
to understand that Christianity sets itself in opposition to the goodness of the natural order after the
manner of Buddhism.   The logical result of this
attitude would be that we must neither eat, sleep,
marry, nor enjoy any form of pleasure, because all
are utterly sinful.[2]   But such a view is based upon a
complete misunderstanding of the phraseology of the
New Testament.   In the passage from 1 St. John
quoted by Paulsen the things condemned are not
the *use* of the flesh or of the eyes or of life, but the
lust of the flesh, the *lust* of the eyes, and the *vain-
glory* of life.   It is in each case not the gratification
of natural instinct as such which is condemned, but
the sinful method of gratifying such instincts.   It
is not nature which Christianity opposes, but the
Natural Man's perverted use of nature.   Ἐπιθυμία in
this passage, as almost always in the New Testament, means desire for that which is forbidden;
that is, desire which, by failing to rise above
the sensuous, passes into an unsacramental use.
Desire begins to be used unsacramentally when it
is exercised in such a way that the indulgence of
sense is allowed to dominate and crush spiritual
activities.   To such spiritual activities desire was
divinely intended to give sacramental expression.
This is effected only when the spiritual activities
dominate and use desire wholly for their higher
purposes.

But, it may be urged, does not this Christian view
of ἐπιθυμία necessarily involve the giving up of some-

[1]   *A System of Ethics*, English translation, p. 75.
[2]   *Cf.* H. W. Garrod's attempt to prove that our Lord abolished
marriage, pp. 164 ff. above.

thing which is one of the real goods of life? Does not ἐπιθυμία, whether good or evil, hold in its keeping a warmth and richness of passion which is so intensely human that to rule it out as forbidden fruit must leave human nature cold, negative, and uninspiring? Is not all this attempt to be "independent" of the natural plane based upon delusion, a shrinking back from life's fulness upon unjustifiable grounds? Can the Christian ever fill the vacuum created by the removal of ἐπιθυμία? Let us look once more at the words of 1 St. John ii. The key to their interpretation really lies in verse 17, which Paulsen does not quote in his criticism of the passage. The verse runs as follows: "And the world passeth away, and the lust thereof: but he that doeth the will of God abideth for ever." As we are here given the grounds upon which the Christian is forbidden to love the world and its three characteristic activities, we must first of all make sure what those grounds are. Two orders of things are contrasted; the one is centred in ὁ κόσμος and ἡ ἐπιθυμία, the other in τὸ θέλημα τοῦ θεοῦ. The former is ephemeral, the latter eternal. The Christian whose life centres round the will of God is forbidden to love the world and its lusts, lest he lose the prize of eternity which belongs to him as the doer of the will of God, lest he become a partaker in the transitory nature of the world and pass away with it. Now there is no question here of a deluded expectation of the end of the world, such as Mr. Garrod finds in the Synoptic Gospels. This epistle is generally agreed to be quite probably the latest document in the New Testament; and in any case it was written, like the Fourth Gospel, after the Church had ceased to expect an immediate end of the world.[1] This passing of the world, then, is not apocalyptic, but rather something which answers to mystical experience. This is just what we should expect in a Johannine document. Ὁ κόσμος, too, does not mean the natural order of the universe or of earthly life as the creation of God, but, according to the universal Johannine use, the natural order of human society as constituted in alienation from God through sin. With respect to the social order, it is parallel to St. Paul's phrase "the natural man" with respect to the individual. Ἐπιθυμία is the characteristic activity of individuals who are of ὁ κόσμος. It is the perverted natural activity which characterizes an individual when his life is rooted in a natural order estranged from God. Further, it cannot be true to say that the hostility of this writer to ἐπιθυμία is due to a failure to appreciate the goodness of the natural order. This very letter is full of opposition to the docetic heresy. This means that the writer is sternly opposed to those who in his day were most conspicuously guilty of undervaluing the goodness of the natural order; for by refusing a real body to our Lord they implicitly declared that matter was too evil to be redeemed. It is not then the natural order in itself which is here attacked, but something which has found its way into that order and which is in violent opposition to τὸ θέλημα τοῦ θεοῦ. There are here depicted, in fact, two moral spheres in either of which it is possible for a man to dwell. The one to which the Christian must cleave is that of which God is the centre and His will the ruling principle of action; in other words, the otherworldly sphere.

[1] See above, pp. 172–174.

The other sphere is the direct opposite of this.   Its
materials come from the natural order, but everything in it is perverted from its original use.   Desire
is so perverted, for it has here become the ruling
principle ; it has taken upon itself functions which
it was never intended to exercise.   Its place in the
created order is properly that of a servant ; but in
the corrupt sphere of "the world" it has become the
master.   Thus, corresponding to these two hostile
spheres, two ruling principles stand opposed to one
another, Desire and Will.   To speak more exactly,
they are the degraded desire which constitutes
ἐπιθυμία on the one hand, and that divine manifestation of will-activity which constitutes τὸ θέλημα τοῦ
θεοῦ on the other.   Now in the sphere where
ἐπιθυμία dominates human life, it is literally true to
say that there is a continual "passing away" of
things.   "The world passeth away and the lust
thereof."   At every moment the man thus mastered
by desire strives to possess the natural goods of life.
He can, however, never attain the full possession of
them ; for they are all the while withering under the
corrupting atmosphere of the world.   Thus he is
in pitiable plight.   Because his will is enslaved to
desire, he is utterly dependent upon that desire
which feeds itself remorselessly through all the
activities of life, and yet is ever doomed to poison
the fountain from which it drinks.   Thus every
natural thing which is approached by the human will
through the medium of ἐπιθυμία is thereby vitiated
and "passes away," like fruit turned to dust.

In contrast to all this there is offered to man the
life of him that "doeth the Will of God."   Here
the ruling principle is that which is the extreme

antithesis of ἐπιθυμία. Instead of desire in its most degraded form, we here find will raised to its highest power. Will is at the centre of human personality, whereas desire is on the outskirts. Personality is at its lowest when desire is dominant, at its highest when will controls all else. Let us, then, picture a man passing right across from the one sphere to the other. He moves not merely from the prevalence of desire to that of will, but from the dominance of ἐπιθυμία, which is desire diseased and degraded into a curse, to the dominance of τὸ θέλημα τοῦ θεοῦ, which is the highest form of will-power which we can conceive. It is not that he has merely cut ἐπιθυμία out of his life and left a vacuum there— a thing which of course is utterly impossible ; but that by the planting of his will in the otherworldly sphere, it has been united with the Will of God. Accordingly, just as formerly the desire element in him was dragged down and dragged all else with it, so now the will element in him has been raised to its highest power—a power, indeed, of which there is no measure. Thus we reach the answer to the question, Will not the elimination of ἐπιθυμία involve the impoverishment of human nature ? The answer is No. For, whereas ἐπιθυμία destroys the true worth of desire, the transfigured will which takes the place of ἐπιθυμία restores order and value to all the once-perverted activities by relating them to the Will of God. The identification of the will of man with the Will of God does not enslave it, but sets it free to realize itself ; and the will thus strengthened becomes master of all the activities of the man's life. Desire now recovers its proper place. All the passions and emotions of life are now secure in their natural goodness; for the will is able to use them in the interests of the whole personality. Thus the true Christian ascetic has less of the machine about him than anyone else. His life still possesses all the richness of natural desires—only, they come forth under the control of the will. The man is therefore able to use each desire in the interests of his truest self, instead of being used by the desire. He can enjoy the true sweetness of what is natural and good, without finding it turn sour ere he has finished tasting it. For instantly, by the otherworldly will-power in him, the goodness which he has culled from the natural order is caught away from the danger zone and attains an abiding worth in the sum-total of his life.

It is, then, ἐπιθυμία or lust, taken in the sense of the whole sinful attitude of the natural man towards the phenomenal order, against which the ascetic principle rightly hardens into fierce antagonism. Here there can be no sort of compromise for the Christian, but a stern war of extermination. The two moral spheres, those of God and the world, are vividly portrayed for us in St. Paul's metaphor of the old Adam and the new. St. Paul speaks of the old Adam or the old man being destroyed, crucified, and buried, and the new Adam or the new man being created and growing to completion in its place. This is most literally the universal Christian experience; it is as if one personality were gradually destroyed and another sprang up out of its ashes. The whole false growth of character, habit, and desire, which once grew up unchecked, is first arrested, and then slowly and surely cut down, uprooted, and finally effaced. As this process of destruction proceeds, another growth of character, habit, and desire springs up in its place—that of the Spiritual Man. But the new can only come according to the measure in which the old is being destroyed. To cling secretly to one single thought which is inspired by the sinful ἐπιθυμία of the Natural Man is to arrest the whole movement of the man's personality towards the otherworldly sphere. He is borne back once more into the confusions of a dualism in which flesh and spirit are at war. On the other hand, to renounce such a thought proceeding from the Natural Man is to make room in the life for an opposite thought which contains in germ the whole worth of the otherworldly values. The flash of a suggested thought is followed at once by one of two things : either the sinking of natural desire into ἐπιθυμία, or the bearing up of the desire, while it is still untainted, into the atmosphere of a God-centred will-activity. Desire is really the natural instrument through which otherworldly activity realizes itself in the phenomenal world ; since everything in the phenomenal world which is a natural good has an otherworldly value proper to it. The God-centred will, therefore, is able so to transmute the desire which it controls, that, through the very desire itself thus transfigured, it enters upon the possession of that otherworldly value which lies behind the phenomenal object of desire. Such, then, is the ascetic warfare which our Lord initiated. It is in the region of the first suggestion of a thought that the real battle lies. By carrying conduct back to its fountain source, our Lord showed us how to destroy the Natural Man from the very roots upwards.

Now it is just this uncompromising hostility to the first stirrings of evil desire which seems so deeply exaggerated to those who have not accepted the ascetic principle, and who cling to the old Greek idea of a beautiful mean between passion and austerity.   Let us take as an illustration a passage in the Gospel which is criticized from this point of view by Strauss[1] and by Mr. Garrod: "Whoso looketh upon a woman with an eye to lust after her hath already committed adultery with her in his heart."[2]   Strauss remarks that if the implied injunction were literally obeyed all sexual attraction, and therefore all marriage, would be impossible. Mr. Garrod places this saying into the class of "precepts which may be described as the exaggerations of all the ordinary virtues"; and he adds: "Men in a world of men cannot live by these precepts: but they can and must live towards them." In a note he remarks: "It is a typical Christian exaggeration.   Few would be saved were the sentence true: and what would become of the virtue of the ἐγκρατής?   Do not most of us prefer the ἐγκρατής to the σώφρων?"[3]

In the first place, let us examine the statement above: "Men cannot live by these precepts; but they can and must live towards them."   If the meaning of this is that men are not perfect and must attain purity and other virtues gradually, it is a truism of Christian teaching.   But this does not

---

[1] For Strauss' treatment of the Christian Ethic see his *The Old Faith and the New*, vol. i. pp. 70–107 ; and vol. ii. pp. 56, 66–71.

[2] St. Matt. v. 28.

[3] *The Religion of All Good Men*, pp. 72, 73.   The ἐγκρατής and the σώφρων are respectively the self-controlled man and the chaste man.

seem to be Mr. Garrod's meaning. A man lives by a precept when he is straining every nerve to obey it. To live *towards* a precept, therefore, without living *by* it can only mean to try and carry it out *to some extent*, without any intention of attempting to reach full conformity with its spirit. If this is what Mr. Garrod means, it must be replied that partial obedience to such a precept as the one under consideration is a miserable and wretched alternative to choose, when the pathway to perfect purity is open and ready to our hand. It is like saying that when a man has weeds in his garden he should cut off their heads when they get to a certain height, but that it is unnecessary to root them out altogether; or that if a man has a cancer, it will do him no harm so long as it is kept within certain limits, and need not therefore be cut out. The truth is that if men cannot live *by* this precept they most certainly will not live *towards* it. Strauss' comment that all sexual attraction would be rendered impossible is based upon a misunderstanding. He confuses ἐπιθυμία or lust, in which the senses dominate the whole man, with desire itself, which was never intended to be dominant, but to be a pure and sacramental instrument whereby spiritual ends are attained. For when sexual attraction is entirely dominated by spiritual appreciation of the otherworldly value in the other's personality, it is itself the germ of a pure human love and can therefore become the gateway to an otherworldly love. It is πρὸς τὸ ἐπιθυμῆσαι which constitutes the sin. It is perhaps just at this point that we may be able to see a little more clearly why the elimination of ἐπιθυμία, instead of impoverishing the natural dispositions of human nature, actually brings with it a priceless enrichment. For this destruction of ἐπιθυμία cuts nothing away from the fulness of the natural human personality. It does not, for example, remove passion, and leave only an æsthetic or intellectual power of appraising beauty, such as that which the artist seeks to attain. The change does not take place in the first instance, in the region of sense at all. The will-activity lying behind sense must first be purified. Then, as a consequence, the objective reality, lying behind physical beauty, which is sought as an end by that will-activity, becomes capable of a sacramental relation to the will. This may perhaps be made clearer if the exact relations of desire and beauty to one another, when they are treated sacramentally, are defined. Physical beauty, then, appears in the divine plan to be the phenomenal expression of an ideal otherworldly value, "the image of God" in man or woman. Physical beauty thus has a high office to fulfil; its function is nothing less than to convey to human consciousness in the phenomenal world that otherworldly value which belongs to every human personality. Now the highest relationship of human beings is one in which there is a reciprocity of otherworldly will-power. But this relationship must originate in the phenomenal sphere; and here physical beauty comes in to make manifest to the one the otherworldly value of the other. Where it is absent, that otherworldly value can still be made manifest : because love, if it be ever so little of the other world, has such power in it that it can fashion its own means of sacramental self-realization out of materials which might at first seem poor and unpromising. Yet still physical beauty remains the phenomenal means pre-eminently fitted to disclose the ideal worth of human personality. But now, just as beauty mediates other-worldly value from the one side, so it must have something complementary to it in the phenomenal order whereby a corresponding movement of appreciation may from the other side reach out towards beauty and the value lying beyond it. This complementary something is desire; and it is the interaction of beauty and desire upon one another which constitutes natural sexual attraction. Desire, then, is the proper means whereby the will of the one personality reaches the phenomenal beauty of the other. Now when men and women behold one another in the pure atmosphere of the other world, the current of otherworldly love-power completes its circuit through the phenomenal order safely and blamelessly. The otherworldly will-activity of the one, using and controlling desire, appreciates the phenomenal beauty of the other; but, by the power of its impetus, it passes on un-arrested, and reaches through to the otherworldly value behind. This circuit of will-activity is effected by both personalities; and thus the reciprocity of otherworldly will-power is complete. In each case the otherworldly value of the other is possessed by the one who has thus reached it, and its worth passes up to the enrichment of his own personality.

Finally, what is the truth as to the comparative merits of the ἐγκρατής and the σώφρων, of self-control and chastity? It will be readily seen from what has been said about living *by* a precept or *towards* it, that to accept deliberately a partial conformity to the ideal of purity as sufficient is not worthy of the name of self-control. It means that a man is unwilling or unable to strive after perfect purity of thought, and contents himself with a standard which demands *less* self-control. Such partial self-control is, as a matter of fact, a totally unpractical and impossible ideal; and in any case it has no right to the name of ἐγκράτεια in comparison with that complete self-control which Christianity requires. For it is quite a delusion to think that in the case of the σώφρων there is no place for self-control. Perfect purity is attained by the maintenance of a constant warfare. It is the crown of self-control, not a pale and unreal substitute; and its attainment does not mean freedom from struggle, but power always to be victorious. The pure are those who have attained a state of ἐγκράτεια through repeated exercise of the ascetic principle in successive acts of self-control. This is indeed the universal method of the ascetic principle; thus it gradually replaces dualism by a harmony in which the natural order is the instrument of the spirit. The unsacramental use of any earthly phenomena means enslavement to the plane of nature. In each case this wrong use must be utterly abolished in order that the right use, the sacramental, may come into existence. One cannot use the natural order in these two ways simultaneously, for they are utterly opposed to one another; nor can one gain any harmony or settled power of dealing with the phenomena of life, if they are used first in one way and then in another. The only true power of dealing with the natural order is that which comes from relating one's whole personality to it in one way to the extinction of the other.

It is now possible, in the light of this exposition of the method of the ascetic principle, to understand that intense opposition to "the world" with which the Church entered upon her task in the early centuries of Christianity. Paulsen has paid special attention to this primitive hostility to the world.[1] He has sought to show (1) that in those early centuries of persecution Christianity set itself against all the virtues which make civilization possible, and (2) that in this the early Christians were true to the New Testament. He thinks that the Church of later generations has found herself obliged to make a compromise between the teaching of Christ and the spirit of the world. This latter idea is also to be found in Mr. Garrod's book. Let us consider the first point. Christianity entered a world in which the whole of human life was lived upon the natural plane without reference to any higher principle. The Natural Man was the centre of gravity for the whole field of human conduct. To those, therefore, who had the secret of the otherworldly principle, all human life was thus seen to be built upon a false foundation. In the light of the otherworldly values it is clear that virtue should be the fruit of the otherworldly activity of the Christ-self. It should become the permanent adornment of that higher self. But in the old classical world exactly the reverse was the case. There was no recognition either of humility or of any sense of sin, because the Natural Man was the magnetic centre round which virtues and vices alike were ranged side by side. The virtues of the classical world were thus centred in the lower ego and adorned it, instead of

(iv.) The Ascetic Principle and the Natural Virtues.

[1] _A System of Ethics_ (English trans., pp. 67–87).

adorning the Christ-self. If they did not actually grow out of self-conceit, they inevitably fostered it; for they were referred to man as their source. They therefore glorified man, and promoted the worship of self instead of God. Thus Paulsen says: "The Greek is proud of his virtues, he has acquired them himself, they are the fruits of hard labour. In one respect, says Seneca, the wise man excels God; the latter owes it to His Nature that He fears nothing, the wise man owes it *to himself*." [1] As he goes on to point out, "we discover a kind of heathen counterpart to" the Christian virtues; but the difference between them is really an impassable gulf. The Christian virtues are the energies of the otherworldly power in its various relations to the phenomenal world, and are practised with reference to God and to His glory. The pagan or natural virtues may be the counterpart of the others; they may be derived from the divine image in every man; but as soon as they leave their source, they become tainted and corrupted by being related to the natural centre of gravity, instead of to the spiritual. A good example of this is to be found in Paulsen's contrast of Christian pity with pagan "liberality" and its "intensified form . . . magnificence ($\mu\epsilon\gamma\alpha\lambda\sigma\pi\rho\epsilon\pi\epsilon\iota\alpha$)." After quoting Aristotle's definition of this pagan virtue, the writer remarks: "Here the important person is not the recipient of the gift, but the giver; the object is not to alleviate suffering, but to glorify the name of the benefactor. Not a single word . . . is said of the neediness of the recipient; compassion plays no part as a motive. . . . It is obvious that this virtue has nothing in common with Christian pity. The

[1] *Op. cit.*, p. 82.

fundamental characteristic of Christian charity is
self-denial, while liberality[1] is a form of self-enjoy-
ment.   Pity contemplates the wants of others, and
makes sacrifices to help them ; liberality has for its
object the glorification of the giver. . . . Christian
charity does not spring from the natural impulse to
enjoy one's own superiority by giving help. . . ."[2]
As Paulsen's main charge against Christianity is
that its virtues are not favourable to social life, it
is fair to ask whether he can ever have fully considered the significance of the passage just quoted.
The general conclusion would seem to be that a
virtue should be considered good if it proceeds
from a natural impulse, irrespective of its actual
results in society.   That point of view is intelligible
in Nietzsche and his school.   Their conception of
nobility includes a generosity which proclaims the
magnificence of the giver without regard to the
recipient.   Such "nobility" found its climax, as
Paulsen himself points out, in the "liberality" of
the Roman Emperors, who ruined the Roman
populace with their doles of bread and games.   It
is difficult to see what lasting value for civilization
can be found in virtues which take no account of the
welfare of the recipients, that is, of society.   In short,
the fundamental defect of all virtue which is centred
in the Natural Man consists in this, that it is not
directed towards social ends.   On the other hand,
that which makes the Christian virtues essentially

[1] Of course this pagan liberality is entirely distinct from the
Christian liberality referred to towards the end of Chapter V.
pp. 201-203, above.

[2] This, however, was exactly the charge which Nietzsche
levelled against it.   The quotation is from *A System of Ethics*,
p. 83.

social is that both their source, and the goal towards which they are directed, are entirely outside the vicious self-centred circle of the lower self. Moreover, the whole exercise of these virtues is preserved from that fatal circle by the constant operation of the ascetic principle. It is this consideration which justifies some stern words of St. Augustine, which Paulsen quotes : "And the virtues themselves, if they bear no relation to God, are in truth vices rather than virtues; for although they are regarded by many as truly moral, when they are desired as ends in themselves, and not for the sake of something else, they are, nevertheless, inflated and arrogant, and therefore not to be viewed as virtues but as vices."[1]   These words, no doubt, sound hard to our modern ears, accustomed as we are to an exaggeration of the Alexandrine point of view. But it is well to notice that the important words here are "if they bear no relation to God." In so far as any such virtue takes its origin from some spark of the divine in man, it justifies its claim to the title virtue and gives promise of untold possibilities. It is a germ which, if brought back into relation with God in the regenerate life, will blossom ultimately into a Christian virtue. But in its present condition, bearing no actual relation to God, but adorning instead the Natural Man, it ministers to natural pride, and is a support to self-righteousness, that sin which above all others separates a man from God. Thus, while we shall look eagerly for the divine germ hidden away in others beneath these natural virtues, we shall, with St. Paul, count it right to reckon all our

---

[1] *A System of Ethics* (English trans., p. 69); quoted from *De Civitate Dei*, xix. 25.

own righteousness as filthy rags, and to desire a
wholly new righteousness which is of God by faith.
We shall know, too, that this attitude is necessary
for all men. It follows, then, that the early Church
was justified in this condemnation of the pagan
virtues. It would indeed be a serious mistake to
suppose that she was moved to condemn them out
of envy, because she had nothing adequate to
put in their place. The precise reason why they
were to her but splendid vices was that she was
conscious of having in her treasure-house something
vastly superior to them all, namely, the whole
hierarchy of virtues which proceed from the otherworldly centre and from the Spirit of Love. So
conscious was the Church of her natural right to
claim the whole field of virtue and make it her own,
that we find—strange paradox it seems at first
sight—the Fathers quietly incorporating the four
cardinal virtues of pagan antiquity into their systems.
St. Ambrose, a Latin Father, and a contemporary of
St. Augustine, whose words have just been quoted,
is perhaps the most remarkable example in this connection.[1] In reality the paradox lies only upon the
surface. The Fathers had at first no vocabulary
which could be used to bring home adequately the
new social virtues of Christianity to the people of
the Empire. The phraseology of the New Testament was rich; but it came as a new and strange
tongue to the pagan world, and had to be translated
into a language which they could understand. The
Church accordingly did what most wise missionaries
do. She took the best materials she could find,—in

---

[1] In his *De Officiis*; see T. B. Strong, *Christian Ethics*,
lecture iv. pp. 138, 139.

this case the names of those virtues which ranked
highest in men's eyes,—and gradually filled them
with an entirely new meaning. Her mission was,
indeed, to rescue all that was good in the ancient
world, little as that might be. Whilst she cried out
to men to flee from their boasted virtues as from a
city of destruction, she was ready, when these outworks of the Natural Man had been pulled down, to
enter the ruins and dig deep for the original corner
stones, overlaid as they were with a mass of corruption. There upon those precious remnants she would
strive to rebuild the city of God.

This method of destroying in order to build anew
will be found to be the explanation of everything
in the Christian outlook which to some
Wisdom.
seems mere weakness, and to others
fanaticism and vandalism. It is the explanation
of the whole attitude of the Church towards wisdom
and knowledge. Worldly wisdom is frequently a
one-sided development of the reasoning and logical
faculties which have lost their relation to life as a
whole, through a failure to keep their use in due
proportion to that of the other faculties. More
especially is this the case when there is no corresponding development of the moral activity proper
to the will. But with Christianity the will takes
its place as the most important factor in the shaping of human conduct. If the will is weakened
or corrupt, the moral vision is obscured; and thus
the whole man is handicapped in his pursuit of truth
in a way which no development of the reason or
piling up of knowledge can remedy, so long as the
moral defect remains. It was not therefore wisdom [1]

[1] See Paulsen, pp. 67, 68.

against which St. Paul warned the Corinthians, but "the wisdom *of this world.*" When a man's intellectual outlook is tainted either with pride or with cynical pessimism, his deepest need is that he should be brought to a profound sense of his ignorance, especially in respect to moral and spiritual questions. In this way the intellectual side of his nature may be detached from its bondage to the Natural Man, and may become the instrument of a regenerate will in bringing the vision of truth to the higher self. It is this method which the Church has always had in view. The Christian experience constitutes a kind of heavenly wisdom. Earthly wisdom can receive its proper significance only in the light of this heavenly wisdom, just as the whole life of man is lighted up with new meaning by the otherworldly principle. The earthly forms of learning and knowledge are valuable instruments which the Christian seeks to use sacramentally, as means whereby the heavenly wisdom may express itself to mankind. The method of our Lord's teaching shows great respect for the human intellect. He threw that teaching into forms most calculated to make men think. He blamed His disciples again and again for their slowness of understanding, and for suffering the children of this world to be wiser than the children of light; He bade them be wise as serpents, and as scribes made disciples to the Kingdom of Heaven to bring forth out of their treasures things new and old.[1] So to all the wealth of earthly knowledge is added the new treasure of heavenly wisdom, whereby the former is sanctified and turned to its highest

[1] *E.g.* see St. Mark viii. 17–21; St. Luke xvi. 8; St. Matthew x. 16; xiii. 51, 52.

17

possible use.   But earthly knowledge is only so
sanctified by the method of the ascetic principle, by
the rooting out of intellectual pride and all idolatry
of mere cleverness.

We have already considered to some extent the
manner in which the otherworldly values actively
Courage and influence and transform both individual
Justice.   and social conduct.[1]   We have seen that
love is really strongest when it appears to be weakest.
The highest courage is that of the Christian martyrs,
—a patient endurance born of an intense realization
of the otherworldly values of Christ-self and Neighbour, which must be sacrificed to no lower thing.
We have seen, too, that right conduct necessarily
flows from the essential righteousness of Love,
which will not allow the highest interests of either
Self or Neighbour to be overlooked.   Paulsen, however, in his treatment of the relation of Christianity
to the virtues of Courage and Justice, urges that the
whole attitude of the early Christians to the State
and its activities was one of violent negation.   He
instances such institutions as the law-courts, war,
and the public service.   There is not the slightest
doubt, indeed, as to their general attitude.   It was
one of absolute opposition to the prevailing standards of conduct which gave character to these institutions ; and consequently it was one of cautious
detachment from the institutions themselves.   Christianity had entered a decaying world ; and every
important institution in that world must have been
tainted with corruption.   If, for example, a Christian
served as a public officer, he would be required to
perform heathen rites, and perhaps to condone all

[1] Chapter V. (iv.) (*b*), esp. p. 189 to the end of the chapter.

manner of social customs intolerable to his higher standard.   As a soldier he would be the paid hireling of an emperor, who was often utterly depraved, and almost always a tyrant.   We have all heard the story of the legion of St. Maurice, which is said to have been decimated for refusing to take part in what was thought to involve a butchery of their fellow-Christians.   Whether it really happened or not exactly as tradition asserts,[1] is a matter of small importance.   Such stories do not usually grow up unless there is something corresponding to them in the actual facts.   Paulsen remarks that even as late as the year 305 the Synod of Elvira discouraged the holding of public offices by Christians.[2]   He fails, however, to balance this statement by recording the fact that at that very time the fiercest of all the persecutions was raging against the Church; to have held office, then, at such a time must inevitably have meant to further in some way the task of the persecutors.   Then, too, could they forget that the emperor was worshipped as a god, and sat in the seat of antichrist?

Was it, then, seemly for Christians to go to law with one another before heathen courts?   Our Lord had recommended a suitable method of obtaining satisfaction from an offending brother without resorting to this.[3]   In the last resort he might have to be treated as a heathen and a publican—that is, as one outside the fellowship of the Church.   Yet even so he would still be treated from the point of view of

---

[1] See *The Christian Church in Gaul*, by T. Scott Holmes, pp. 85–88, where the historicity of the story is contended for, and the documentary evidence is given.

[2] *A System of Ethics*, p. 74.

[3] St. Matt. xviii. 15–17; *cf.* Paulsen, *ibid.*, p. 72, note.

the otherworldly values in accordance with the principles already laid down.[1]   On the otherworldly plane
love alone constrains men without any machinery of
justice.   But in the world at large the love-values
are recognized only partially or not at all.   Here,
then, where the plane of rights predominates, any
institution which can be made a means to win men's
respect for the personal dignity and worth of the
individual—though grounded upon rights and not
upon love — is notwithstanding, like the Jewish
Law, a schoolmaster to bring men to Christ.   For
in the case of those who still lack a full Christian
recognition of the otherworldly values, and who cannot as yet move upon that otherworldly level of
conduct, which is perfect freedom,—for such there
is still need of the institutions of law and justice.
The necessity will remain, too, just so long as
society is only imperfectly Christian.   But in the
primitive Church under the Empire, when numbers
were still small, and there were few nominal Christians, it was impossible for the faithful to attach
much value to legal institutions which were founded
on the basis of the natural virtues.   There was, it
is true, a certain tradition of justice, for which Rome
had in the past earned a noble reputation ; but to
Christian eyes it appeared to have been built up
without any conception of that absolute standard of
values which was lifted so high in their own hearts.[2]

[1] Chapter V. (iv.) (*b*).

[2] These considerations help to explain St. Paul's treatment of
the question in 1 Corinthians vi. 1-9.   At the root of this
passage is the thought that corporate Love of the Brethren is a
sacred thing to be kept bright and beautiful and so to be a revelation of the heavenly life to the world.   When, therefore, through
the imperfection of Christian Love in this dispensation, disfigure-
ments and wounds appear upon its surface, very shame should

Our Lord was concerned to raise the whole spirit
and temper of society on to a higher level. He
substituted the positive principle of love, with its
power of meeting every set of circumstances, for
the barren and stilted assertion of rights. The man
who studies our Lord's teaching without having
grasped love's unbounded possibilities of transforming every situation, is continually liable to misunderstand the individual precepts through looking at
everything from the narrow basis of rights. This
seems to be the reason why Paulsen has completely
misunderstood one passage in the Gospels; [1] he has
taken it to mean that our Lord formally abolished
law-courts, whereas in that passage He is in reality
inculcating the love-spirit. The true exegesis is
made unmistakably clear by the verses which immediately precede. In St. Matt. v. 21–24, a spiritual
interpretation of the Sixth Commandment is given,
culminating in an urgent exhortation as to the need
of immediate reconciliation with an offended brother.
The matter will not wait; it must be set right
at once. This necessity of reconciliation becomes
paramount when a solemn approach to the presence
of God to offer Him gifts is contemplated. For
otherwise such an approach to God with a spiritual
debt upon the conscience would be like entering into
the presence of a judge in a debtors' court with an
aggrieved creditor pressing for justice.[2] The words,
"Agree with thine adversary quickly, etc.," are a
piece of worldly wisdom used in metaphor to convey
a spiritual lesson. To delay paying one's debt may

make us wish to hide these blots upon our corporate witness from
the gaze of the world around. See Paulsen, p. 74.

[1] St. Matt. v. 25, 26.　　　[2] *Cf.* St. Matt. xviii. 21–35.

land one in a debtors' prison ; so to delay paying
the debt of love [1] may bring one to the prison-house
of selfish callousness and hatred, and so shut one out
from the presence of God.   Thus everywhere the
words of Christ about conduct bring one into an
atmosphere where the fire of holy Love glows.
Society and its institutions, if cast into this fire, are
purged of their dross, and—unless indeed all be
found to be dross—they are transformed and not
destroyed.

Let us turn now to Paulsen's second main criticism
of Christianity.   Primitive Christians, it is said, set
(v.) The perma- themselves in opposition to the virtues
nence of the which make civilization possible, and in
Revolutionary
Element in so doing they were acting in accord-
Christianity. ance with New Testament principles.
Modern Christianity, on the other hand, has deserted
its true principles, because they have been found
in the course of the centuries to be unpractical and
dangerous to society.[2]   If this criticism were justified, the implication would be that since the Christian
ethic has apparently been found impossible even by
Christians themselves, some new ethic must be
evolved, including perhaps, as Paulsen suggests,
the best elements in Hellenism and Christianity.[3]
There is, however, one important factor which
seems to have been forgotten here.   It is contained
in our Lord's parable of the leaven " which a woman
took and hid in three measures of meal until the
whole was leavened." [4]   The working of the spirit of

[1] *Cf.* Romans xiii. 8.
[2] See p. 251 above, and Paulsen, *A System of Ethics*, Chapter II.
Cf. also H. W. Garrod, *The Religion of All Good Men*, p. 65, etc.
[3] See Paulsen, *ibid.*, ch. v., " The Modern Conception of Life."
[4] St. Matt. xiii. 33.

Christianity is like the working of leaven. The first insertion of the leaven into the meal stirs both to an activity which is all the more noticeable in comparison with the inertness of the meal before its contact with the leaven. These first stirrings of the leaven, before it has become mixed with the meal, are of necessity strongly marked. But the case is different when the whole cake has become in large measure leavened. The violent contact between two alien elements gradually subsides as they become mingled and the one penetrates the other. Now primitive Christianity had to face a situation entirely unlike any other which has since existed. Its intensely revolutionary spirit was in part due to two features of those earliest days. In the first place, it entered a civilization entirely dominated by pagan ideas, like the unleavened meal. Secondly, owing to the fact that this pagan system was in possession, the whole force and authority of the Roman Empire, the highest concentration of worldly power ever yet seen, was actively on the side of the unadulterated pagan view of life as against the humble claims of Christianity. The old classical civilization represented the most complete and mature expression of human society as it is when organized wholly upon the natural plane. Within it, therefore, the natural man also had reached his full development in every direction in the use of the phenomenal world for purely natural ends. In entering such a world, then, Christianity had from its very nature to express itself by way of contradiction and negation at every turn; only so could it clear a space for itself in which to build up its own ideal on the earth. Never again could the same situation recur. Missionaries of the Church in modern days—even though they go to the ancient heathen civilizations of the East—are able, notwithstanding, to point to the history of a Christian civilization. This civilization, too, while it bears deeply impressed upon it the influence of Christian ideals, holds at the same time a predominating position in the possession of earthly power. Thus the whole situation is almost reversed. Christianity enters these new fields as something which has already passed the violence of its first impact with the world-forces; it comes now as something already in possession. Nevertheless, though the leaven has spread, the meal is still largely unaffected. It does not require much study of modern Christian missions to know that, in spite of the changed circumstances, the leaven of Christianity shows all the old revolutionary characteristics when it comes in contact with the unleavened mass.

The truth of the matter is that Christianity is always essentially revolutionary. So it must remain as long as sin continues to exist in the world. It is also true, however, that this revolutionary character has been manifested in varying forms and in difference of degree in every age; while sometimes the fiery flame has come nigh to dying out altogether. Yet the long series of recoveries recorded by history,[1] the continual recurrence of the spirit of the Cross at almost every stage in the progress of Western civilization, would seem to give no countenance to the theory now advanced that civilization actually holds together through our practical abandonment of this revolutionary element

[1] As, for example, in the repeated appearance of new monastic orders during almost the whole length of Christian history.

in the Gospel. During the age when the pagan view of life had to be attacked and dethroned from its imperial seat, the Church was the society of martyrs and confessors. When Christianity became fashionable and the Church became the mother of nations, hermits, monks and friars arose in long succession to bear witness in unmistakable terms to the primitive gospel of revolutionary self-sacrifice. Moreover, it was always under the direct influence of those who adhered most closely to this revolutionary spirit that the old order passed away, and the new civilization was established. The Roman Empire bowed to the martyr spirit; the monks, the direct successors of the martyrs, took up their mantle, and were everywhere foremost as leaders in building up the new order. Those who of all men were most emphatically committed to the other-worldliness of the Gospel, accepting most literally its sternest precepts, were foremost in turning wild and desolate places into centres of all the arts of civilization.[1] Often, indeed, the spiritual power became spent; but always a fresh wave gathered force and followed at no great interval. The ascetic principle has repeatedly shown itself in history to be the instrument whereby earthly goods are turned to the highest—and therefore the most social—uses. Paulsen himself has clearly stated the truth of the matter. He says: "Christianity now and then becomes conscious of its original negative relation to the 'world,' and the kingdom which is of this world, and so, in my opinion, regains some of its pristine essence and strength. A Christianity en-

---

[1] See Montalembert, *The Monks of the West* (6 vols., English trans.).

tirely reconciled and at peace with the world is a
weak and powerless affair, and surely not the real
and original Christianity. True Christianity may
always be recognized by the fact that it seems
strange and dangerous to the world."[1] Such sentiments as these are to be welcomed. As long as
men will condemn Christianity on the ground that
it is dangerous, Christians will have every reason
for thankfulness. For although the peculiar circumstances of the first centuries have passed, the "world"
—that is the unleavened mass of meal—remains.
We shall not, then, be alarmed at the disturbance
created by the leaven, if we believe that the unleavened state of the meal leaves something seriously to be desired.

As a fact, however, some will be disposed to allow
a far more important place in history to the revolutionary aspect of Christianity; the leaven tends to
be lost to sight amidst the violent disturbances
which it has brought about. The whole controversy,
for example, between Popes and Emperors may be
said to have been one form which the Christian
revolution took; for at bottom the issue at stake
was no less than the supremacy of spiritual over
secular things.[2] Here was the fundamental claim
of Christianity making itself felt—the claim to be
all or nothing. The Inquisition, and the religious
wars of the Reformation period, the Reformation
itself on its religious side, and indeed all theological
controversy, have the same ultimate significance.
All these things are, in however perverted and
unworthy a fashion, the reiteration—by Christians

[1] *A System of Ethics*, p. 66.
[2] See B. Kidd, *Principles of Western Civilisation*, ch. viii.

of every sort through successive generations—of that same divine intolerance. The spirit of Christianity will not brook any obstacle to the realization of the otherworldly values so firmly rooted in the Gospel. The renewal of religious devotion during the past century has been rapidly bringing back the revolutionary character of the Gospel into something of its rightful prominence again. Once more it begins to seem "strange and dangerous to the world." This revolutionary spirit has, no doubt, been perverted into a mere fanaticism, such as the unreasonable defiance of ultramontanism or the gloomy negations of puritanism. Apart from such perversions, however, Christianity has nothing to fear from it ; nor indeed has humanity, for it is only by the strength of its opposition to the world-spirit that Christianity can bring home to man his true worth. Only, then, through the ascetic principle can man attain those otherworldly ideals in which he shall truly find his life.

CHAPTER VII

THE SUPERNATURAL SYNTHESIS

So far our argument has been somewhat as follows. For various reasons there has been growing of late (i.) The Need a movement taking many forms, which of a Synthesis. has sought to reinstate the natural life of man as an adequate basis for human conduct. Supernatural religion having been rejected on other grounds, this movement was sooner or later inevitable. It was also natural that from the new point of view—ruling out, as it did, all experience of revealed religion—the Christian ideals based upon that experience should lose their significance. It has, however, been found on examination that typical naturalistic schemes leave upon the mind an impression of complete failure to provide the desired basis for conduct. They serve only to draw attention to the incompleteness of the natural plane of life, its irreconcilable dualism, its vagueness, fatalism, and uncertainty, its lack of clear principles and power of progress. It has therefore been found necessary to seek the foundations of conduct outside and above the natural plane in the Will of a transcendent God. This Will is manifested, first as an objective standard of Right, and then as a power of Love, whereby the individual is enabled to transcend the sphere of law by fulfilling it, and thus to escape from all the tyrannies of the natural order. The principle now planted in him gives a deep significance as well as a strong and clear direction to individual conduct. In short, it provides a means whereby progress is possible to increasing harmony and fulness of life.

In this chapter the significance of the Christian solution to the problem of conduct will be emphasized in contrast to the other attempts which history records. Probably all schools of ethical thought would agree on one point, namely, the pressing need for a satisfactory synthesis. In no other department of thought can so many well-meant efforts have been expended as over this perpetual problem of conduct; and surely nowhere else can such an extraordinary diversity of unsatisfactory and partial results be shown.[1] At the centre of the problem has always stood the question, What is the meaning and worth of the individual? This is the question of questions; and in the end it always resolves itself into a further question, viz., How is the dualism of life to be met? At every point in our personal experience we are met by a conflict of motives— pleasure and duty, happiness and virtue, flesh and spirit, the present and the future; these are some of the terms in which the antinomy may be expressed. How are these conflicting elements to be brought into harmony? Many have sought to solve the problem by subordinating the one set of motives to the other. Again, another group of moralists

---

[1] Since writing the above, I have read Professor Eucken's valuable little book, *The Meaning and Value of Life*, in which the same conclusions are reached, especially with reference to the modern situation.

may be distinguished who have yielded a place to each set of motives the one beside the other, content if they could thus be held together within tolerable bounds, like a pair of horses under harness. Neither of these methods is satisfactory ; indeed it may be laid down as an axiom that all such partial and one-sided answers to the problem stand self-condemned. They are not solutions, but short-cuts and make-shifts, which will not stand the wear and tear of human needs.

A serious attempt was made in the Græco-Roman world to find a solution.[1] The ideal which the (ii.) The Classi- ancient Greeks set before themselves cal Systems. was εὐδαιμονία (eudæmony)—something which cannot be identified with happiness, still less with virtue. It was, however, intended to provide a synthesis of these two. Eudæmony is a certain noble state of life, the highest earthly ideal possible, in which happiness is experienced through the proper exercise of virtue. It is important to notice, however, that the possibility of attaining eudæmony was strictly limited to those for whom nature had rendered it possible by certain fortunate circumstances, that is, to the citizens of the ancient city-state, the aristocratic minority. These required a far larger number of people, an "inferior" class, together with property and some natural gifts, to make their ideal possible of attainment. Thus while virtue and duty were recognised, they were based upon a certain minimum of good fortune already provided. Moreover, the virtue of the

---

[1] See Paulsen, *A System of Ethics*, ch. i. ; Kidd, *Principles of Western Civilisation*, esp. chapters vi. and vii. ; and G. Lowes Dickinson, *The Greek View of Life*.

citizen was not exercised with a view to the progressive attainment of character. It had a far more
limited and negative purpose than that. It was not
individual perfection in any sense which was sought,
but simply an equilibrium within the narrow limits
of the existing city-state.[1] "The Ruling Present had
made virtue and enlightened pleasure synonymous
for the individual . . . virtue and enlightened self-
interest synonymous in the State."[2] The ideal of
eudæmony, then, was simply a static harmony of the
individual with the conditions of life under which he
had grown up, and these were in themselves purely
temporal, local, and accidental. Thus there could be
no progress beyond a certain point, that of adaptation to a very limited environment. In reaction
against the Sophists, first Socrates, and then Plato
and Aristotle proclaimed the reality of justice, and
uplifted the ideal of the just man who lives according
to reason. But this delicately adjusted harmony of
happiness and virtue, based upon reason, was overthrown by the fall of the city-states and the disappearance with them of the necessary conditions of
security which the old citizen virtues presupposed.
To the Stoics fell the task of readjustment; and
in their hands the earlier conceptions were found
inadequate to meet the larger problems of the Roman
Empire. The attainment of harmony by means of
virtue based on nature and reason was still the ideal;
but in this dogged pursuit of virtue men found it
increasingly difficult to find happiness in the ill-
assorted world of the Empire. To seek virtue meant
a growing estrangement from the atmosphere of
ordinary life, and at length mere sullen endurance,

[1] See Kidd, *op. cit.*   [2] *Ibid.*, p. 198.

servile submission to an inexplicable law.   Thus the
Stoic sought more and more to become αὐτάρκης—
independent of the external goods of life; virtue,
in fact, became the sole good.   The revolt of the
Epicureans stood for happiness.   If virtue does not
bring happiness, it is not worth practising.   In so
far as Epicureanism meant this, it was natural and
even healthy, despite all the disinterested humani-
tarianism preached to-day.   The individual was
never intended to be a slave of duty, to work for
work's sake.   Life should be a joy to him and not
merely a duty.   He must have happiness as well as
virtue.   But if virtue was not intended to be an end
in itself, neither was it right that virtue should be
submerged in the pursuit of happiness.   Neither a
gloomy pessimism nor a superficial optimism is good
for human nature.   In this way the classical world
travelled along two opposite lines of thought, neither
of which provided a solution of the problem of
conduct; and thus it proved its failure to abolish
that fundamental dualism which was to be the test
problem of all subsequent thought.   The worth of
the individual remained an unknown quantity, and
consequently no solution was reached.

Then Christianity came and reconciled the conflicting elements in human nature by means of
(iii.) The Chris- what may be called a Supernatural
tian Solution. Synthesis.   In the place of earthly
eudæmony it put otherworldly blessedness as the
goal to be attained, and the significance of this
change was immense.   The whole value of life for
the individual became intensified a thousandfold.
The individual must have a personal end after
which to strive.   Such an end is to be found in

earthly happiness, but it is an end upon the natural plane; and to seek such a natural end is to enlarge the natural egoism, that very element which has no possibility of social development except an "enlightened self-interest." For the natural ego is isolated and unable to relate itself to social ends except of the narrowest and most fortuitous kind, such as those of the aristocracy of a city-state. But if the end set before a man be otherworldly blessedness, his outlook is at once completely changed. There is now no longer a dilemma of choice as between virtue and happiness. Virtue is still made the means to the end; but as the end is not earthly, it is not, like happiness, affected by every change in external goods and circumstances. Virtue therefore does not undergo the baffling experience of being the means to an uncertain, shifting, and unstable end; it grows in robustness as it partakes more and more of the unchangeable reality of that towards which it is directed. Again, as virtue is braced by a right orientation, so happiness no longer runs to waste, but becomes the symbol of that higher blessedness in whose light it is transfigured. If on the other hand the tide of earthly happiness recedes, this very deprivation may by the ascetic method be made a means to more whole-hearted concentration upon blessedness, which is the real end. This blessedness, again, though to be revealed in its full consummation hereafter, is known and experienced now; and the knowledge, though partial, is ever increasing. Even this fragmentary experience of the otherworldly treasure, therefore, suffices to transcend the dualism of the natural order. Virtue is practised, however imperfectly, yet with joy; not merely in anticipation of a future reward of blessedness, but because an increasing store of blessedness is found in the very practice. In this way virtue and happiness meet in a mysterious harmony, because both are lifted to a higher level; both are purged and sanctified by becoming the ever-open gates of blessedness. On the one hand, virtue is purged of all slavishness and the drudgery of mere dutifulness for its own sake, and so becomes the way of entry into joy. Happiness, on the other hand, being no longer a final end to rest in, becomes truly natural, simple, and innocent—a window, as it were, through which the joy of the soul flashes forth upon the world, or a body which blessedness takes to itself that it may be more freely manifested on earth. In this way Christianity secures the truths of both the Epicurean and the Stoic. On the one hand, it ensures to each individual a supreme significance for his own life and a goal to work for, by giving to his personality as such an absolute value. On the other, it asserts just as strongly that society also is a final end, and therefore that the individual may only attain his self-realization socially. It renders the individual αὐτάρκης; and in this way, lifting him above an all-engrossing pursuit of happiness, it sets him free for virtuous activity on behalf of society. The harmony of the two ends, self and society, is found in that blessedness wherein both the self, and society through its individual units, find their consummation.

In his *Principles of Western Civilisation* Mr. Benjamin Kidd has given a most fascinating exposition of the way in which these principles of the supernatural synthesis have worked themselves out in the history of Western Christendom. His testimony is all the more weighty because the subject is treated strictly from the scientific standpoint. He is concerned only to examine the *method* of the Christian ethic, whose entrance into history he is content to regard simply as the appearance of a new principle in the evolutionary process. The subordination of the natural to the spiritual order is treated by this writer as a subordination of the present to the future. For his purpose this was doubtless the most suitable method of expression ; but from the point of view of the Christian experience it is inadequate.[1] Doubtless the method of Christian conduct is seen externally to be a rejection of the easier and the immediate use of the phenomenal order for present satisfaction, in favour of a higher use. Also, this Christian use of the phenomenal order, while more difficult, bears within itself the promise of a greater ultimate satisfaction upon the natural plane, if not for the individual, at least for society. But this future justification of conduct upon the natural plane is *not* actually the deciding factor in the Christian consciousness. The subordination of the present to the future is the rule of Christian conduct *not in the first instance* because the future outweighs the present in the mind, but because the present which belongs to the natural order is outweighed by another and greater Present which belongs to the spiritual order.[2] Some measure, therefore, of passing happiness is surrendered for the sake of the *immediate* experience of blessedness. Thus the

---

[1] *Cf.* what has been said in Chapter V. (iii.), (*c*) and (*d*).

[2] Kidd expresses the substantial truth of this idea when he speaks of the principle at work as "transcending the limits of political consciousness."

struggle of the Church against the domination of the State, in so far as it was conducted in the spirit of the otherworldly ideals, constituted a sacrifice of worldly compromise and all its attractions for the sake of the immediate blessedness which belongs to those who stand true to the spiritual needs of society. The controversies of the Reformation period have the same significance. In so far as men on either side stood for the vital importance of a true and living faith or sought to safeguard the way to a personal realization of holiness, they were actuated by a desire for the immediate blessedness of standing true to their convictions on these great matters. They preferred such fidelity to the worldly ease of inaction or conformity to the way of the majority. In each case the moving force was the sense of individual responsibility to realize the otherworldly ideal and so enter upon the immediate experience of blessedness. The growth of toleration again was due to the same causes. As there is a divine intolerance of evil to be practised,[1] where the otherworldly blessedness of the individual is at stake, so there is a divine tolerance of individuals towards one another, and of society towards all. Such tolerance involves a mutual recognition of the sacredness of personality, and of the convictions of the individual soul. Christians hold to a belief that man is made, not merely for earthly happiness, but for eternal blessedness. They hold, also, to a conviction attained by actual experience that this blessedness can be realized now in the midst of all the earthly activities, and in spite of every obstacle. Moreover, this belief and this conviction are the

[1] See p. 267.

foundations of that supernatural view of the individual which bears the whole weight of whatever is sound and healthy in our modern civilization. The individual in this supernatural setting has an abiding worth, which includes inalienable rights before God and man; it also involves fundamental duties towards his fellow-men, since they too have in each case the same abiding worth and the same inalienable rights. Thus the whole of society, in so far as it is Christian, rests upon an otherworldly basis; and this is its only sure foundation.

It was these great ideas which lay behind the political progress made in England during the (iv.) Modern seventeenth century.[1] But in the course Systems. of the past two hundred and fifty years or so the religious basis of social and political theory has been silently pushed into the background, until it has been lost to sight altogether. From the French Revolution onwards, through the Utilitarians to the most modern writers, the process has gone on until the logical result has been reached—a complete revulsion from the traditional ethic. The whole theory of the rights and duties of man, based upon the worth and equality of all individuals, which makes up our modern democratic outfit, has been, so to speak, stolen from a Christian pedestal without acknowledgment, and set up as a thing self-evident and able to stand by itself. The climax of this process was reached by the Utilitarians; and it is hardly a thing to be wondered at that Nietzsche turned his big guns upon them, and blew their flimsy castle sky-high. "The greatest happiness of the greatest number"—that was the

[1] See Kidd, *op. cit.*, esp. ch. iv.

formula against which he revolted, and rightly ;
against a smug millennium of universal comfort.   In
this work of destruction Nietzsche was doing
Christian work, little though he suspected it.   A
great part of the attack which he levelled at
Christianity is justly merited by the utilitarian
doctrines which he wrongly identified with the
Gospel.   It is not surprising that he found them
obnoxious.   The great ocean bears along many
goodly living things in the current of its waters ;
but when the tide casts them high upon the beach
they become decaying corpses and stale rubbish,
foul and poisonous.   Even so the great tide of
otherworldly Love, because it is sacrificial, bears
along with it all the goodness of the natural order
and brings forth continually out of its broad bosom
rich materials for earthly happiness.   Yet, if these
treasures, so hardly won for mankind by the sacrificial power of love, be stranded high and dry upon
the beach, they will at once turn to decay.   Earthly
goods, ideals of earthly comfort, if separated from
that tide of spiritual power which brought them
into being, become at once desacramentalized, and
so lose their worth.   Nay, more, these cast-up leav-
ings of the spiritual world have something peculiarly
offensive about them.   Men hailed the " greatest
happiness of the greatest number " as their watch-
word, confident that all men could be and ought
to be made happy.   Yet at the same time they repudiated that otherworldly equality of souls, which
alone provides any sort of justification for the
attempt to bring happiness to all men.   The
Christian's world is one in which otherworldly
love seeks the happiness of all in the phenomenal

sphere, just because such love cannot stop short of realizing the good of every human life which it touches. It seeks to realize the whole good proper to such a life, natural as well as spiritual ; and what we call happiness is the experience of realized natural good. When, therefore, a man actuated by otherworldly love seeks the earthly happiness of all men, his activity is an otherworldly movement energizing sacramentally towards the natural good of others ; it seeks to win for them that natural good in order that they in their turn may use it sacramentally for otherworldly purposes. In the Christian scheme, therefore, happiness remains the product of a virtuous activity within the otherworldly sphere. Even as it comes forth, it becomes the means to something greater than itself. The Utilitarian, on the other hand, in making the earthly happiness of all his highest end, is as one who, lacking faith or courage for the fisherman's art, is content to gather dead things from the rubbish thrown up by the tide.

Well might Nietzsche prophesy the speedy coming of the " Last Man," the sleek and contented devotee of comfort :—

" Alas ! there cometh the time of the most contemptible man who can no longer despise himself. Behold, I show you the *last man*.

Then earth will have become small, and on it the last man will be hopping, who maketh everything small. His kind is indestructible, like the ground-flea ; the last man liveth longest.

'We have invented happiness'—the last men say, blinking.

They have left the regions where it is hard to live, for one must have warmth. One still loveth his neighbour and rubbeth one's self on him ; for warmth one must have.

A little poison now and then : that causeth pleasant dreams. And much poison at last for an easy death.

They still work, for work is an entertainment. But they are careful, lest the entertainment exhaust them.

They no longer grow poor and rich ; it is too troublesome to do either.

. . . They still quarrel, but they are soon reconciled—otherwise the stomach would turn.

One hath one's little lust for the day and one's little lust for the night : but one honoureth health.

'We have invented happiness,' the last men say, blinking." [1]

So wrote Nietzsche ; but here we see how on the natural plane both sides fall into the old dilemma of Epicurean and Stoic. The Hedonist said man has only to seek happiness and all will be well. The Utilitarian, finding that this maxim would not hold, shifted the point of view slightly and declared that man must seek the happiness of all, because that will mean universal happiness, the highest end of man. Nietzsche, in his revolt, stood for virtue. Man is here to be great and powerful rather than happy, to strive and achieve, no matter what the cost. In Nietzsche's outlook there is no place for individual happiness, but only for a kind of grim satisfaction in the consciousness that one is fulfilling the universal Will to Power ; for the exaggerated individualism of the superman is only the blind instrument of this Will to Power. In this way happiness is crushed out, and virtue is consequently robbed of all personal meaning ; the activity of the individual has no more meaning for himself than its movement down a swollen stream has for a floating chip of wood. Schopenhauer and Nietzsche merely

[1] *Thus Spake Zarathustra*, English trans., edited by A. Tille, pp. 11-13.

swung the pendulum back from the superficial optimism of the seekers after happiness to the dour pessimism of Stoic philosophy. The horns of this dilemma have remained unchanged in modern times. Not one of the writers whose theories have been criticized in the present volume has offered any solution of the problem. Each in his own way, Mr. Shaw and Mr. Wells have set before themselves the ideal of a social millennium, in which all are to be happy; and to this end they have tried to relate the individual's conduct. Mr. Shaw declares that the individual must spend his life in virtuous striving to further the Life-purpose. With him the perfection of this Life-purpose is seen to be a state in which Life has ceased to bungle and fail, and cause misery—in other words, a state of happiness. Poverty must be abolished because it is evil; comfort, then, must be good, and the object of virtuous striving must be universal happiness. This Utopia will not be reached without long struggles. The individual, therefore, is to spend his life in the exercise of virtue in which he finds only a tolerable satisfaction, in order that future individuals may, relieved of the annoyance of having to be virtuous, live in mechanical comfort. The whole trend of Mr. Wells's books is in the same direction. We must first devise a means whereby all can be free from distress and privation, and then all can really begin to live. The highest individual life is thus made to consist of a sleek happiness, to which virtue is only a tiresome preliminary. What ground is there for hoping that humanity will accept this strange ideal of an extravagantly disinterested virtue, the only object of which is to provide ready-made ease and comfort for future generations? It does not seem likely that the individual of the immediate future will be attracted by the call of this evolutionary-monist fatalism.[1] Mr. H. W. Garrod goes so far as to suggest that we are bound to hold the individual responsible for failure, even though we are convinced that he has no free will at all.[2] In one chapter he calls men to the higher Teutonic virtue, and in the next he tells them that they are weak slaves of necessity. The fact is that on the natural plane not only are virtue and happiness irreconcilable, but also the true instincts both of egoism and of altruism become shrivelled, stunted, and perverted things. As the ego shrinks into the isolation of the natural self, it loses all connection with the general stream of human welfare. Yet there are those who still accept the fatal argument that the general pursuit of individual happiness must necessarily increase the sum of universal happiness. The extremes to which this mistaken idea leads people may be seen in such writers as Miss Ellen Key.[3]

Such people have not unnaturally found no attraction in the idea that this generation must be virtuous in order that future generations may be happy. It is more pleasant to persuade oneself that the cultivation of one's own happiness to the fullest extent will enlarge the amount of general happiness in the world, and is therefore altogether good. So the pendulum swings to and fro. Either the individual is submerged in his own altruism,

[1] See Chapter I.
[2] *The Religion of All Good Men*, pp. 211–213.
[3] See Chapter VIII. below.

because there is no personal incentive to virtuous effort, or again he is submerged in his own egoism ; his true self is lost in the pursuit of individual ends. In both cases what is wrong is the absence of any-thing which can inspire a true self-respect for the absolute worth of the nobler self. The otherworldly ideals show a man that his personal worth is too great to allow him to dissipate it in a mere culture of earthly happiness. On the other hand, in the light of these same ideals it would be an equally foolish waste to expend energy solely that others may thereby be enabled to dissipate *their* personal worth in the same shallow pursuit of happiness.

CHAPTER VIII

THE SEX IDEAL

THE consideration of the ethics of sex has been reserved to the last place in this discussion. The (i.) Application greater part of our space has inevitably of Principles. been taken up with an examination of the foundation principles upon which conduct is based respectively by Christianity and by the systems which are offered in its place to-day. All conduct is inevitably based upon what a man believes, and not least upon his beliefs about human nature. This is nowhere more true than in the delicate problems of conduct which belong to the sphere of sex. It has been felt necessary to devote a special chapter to this one department of practical ethics, because it is probably the most important of the ethical questions over which society is being asked to make up its mind to-day. Moreover, it seems almost certain that in this matter, more than in any other, the actual tendencies of the opposing groups of principles which we have been considering—the Christian and the non-Christian—will be manifested respectively in their full significance for good or evil. In the first chapter it was stated that all the principles under discussion would be found to be involved in the different views held to-day about this question of sex.[1] It would seem

[1] See p. 22, above.

clear that the key to the solution of this question is to be found in the acceptance of the conclusions reached in the preceding pages. If the view taken here of the insufficiency of human nature upon the natural plane, and its inability to provide itself with a satisfactory subjective morality, be accepted, then the condemnation of the new anti-Christian sex "morality" follows at once. For the whole literature of this new "morality" is nothing but a feverish output of innumerable subjective schemes, each differing from the last. The writers themselves sometimes change their ground; but all agree that human nature is strong enough to experiment freely in this dangerous sphere. The new sex "morality" represents a return from fixed objective standards to the hazardous choice of individual licence. The traditional Christian forms of sex relationship, like everything else which is fundamental to Christian morality, are presented to the conscience as authoritative law. But when the ideals lying behind that law have faded out of men's minds, and the experience which enables a man to transcend law in love is lost, then it is inevitable that such authoritative forms should become irksome. They appear as fetters instead of safeguards; and thus there arises a demand that questions of sex morality should be solved upon the natural plane. Such a return to nature for the solution of sex problems is the necessary result of a wholesale rejection of the Christian foundations of conduct. To those who have been able to accept the main conclusions reached in the preceding argument this return to nature will seem disastrous. If conduct as a whole must rise from the plane of nature through the discipline of law to the otherworldly sphere, then certainly no solution of the sex problem can be accepted which does not place sex morality upon the same otherworldly basis. The Christian solution of the sex problem is therefore the immediate corollary of the principles enunciated in the preceding chapters. Of these the following are specially important :—the supreme worth of the Christ-self in each individual soul, the relationship of otherworldly love which must be realized between all individuals, the ascetic method of realizing these ideals, and the higher synthesis which transcends the conflict of virtue and happiness. Not by way of nature is the solution to be reached, but by way of a supremely high ideal, based upon the otherworldly values and embodied in an objective standard, with unchanging forms. Such forms supply the external lines along which individual conduct must move, and within which that same high ideal can alone be protected and realized.

In the last chapter it was pointed out that no system of ethics formed on the natural plane suc-
(ii.) Sex on the ceeds in providing for all the needs of
Natural Plane. the individual. One instinct or another of human personality is usually pressed into a one-sided and unmeaning prominence, while no reconciliation of conflicting tendencies is reached. This is conspicuously true of the new schemes of sex morality. It was natural that Nietzsche should favour a more or less oriental view of the relations between man and woman. The morality of "masters and slaves" would naturally be disposed to accept that age-long tyranny of man over woman which the working of the Christian leaven has always

tended to mitigate. He disliked the movement for emancipating woman ; it was to him a manifestation of that Christian democratic spirit which he abhorred. Thus he wrote : " A man who has depth of spirit . . . can only think of women as Orientals do ; he must conceive of her as a possession, as confinable property, as being predestined for service. . . ."[1] The same point of view appears in the Dedication of *The Testament of John Davidson*.[2] Extreme individualism of this type, however, which lives by crushing other individuals, is not likely to find favour amongst the new sex moralists. The danger at present lies not in the direction of oriental tyranny, but of extreme licence under the name of freedom. Under a regime of Nietzsche morality, women would once more become the slaves, and men the masters ; but the other alternative which is being sedulously preached to-day is not less dangerous. It is certainly more deceptive ; it fits in so fatally with that weak utilitarian doctrine of happiness for all as the highest ideal which has taken such a hold upon the modern world. According to this doctrine the principal rule of conduct is—" Let everyone seek his own happiness, and the result will be the general happiness of all." Again and again one comes across the assumption that in dealing with sex problems the only thing to be considered is the pleasure and comfort of the individual. For example, it is urged that all the present miseries of unhappy marriages could be removed by the

---

[1] *Beyond Good and Evil*, by F. Nietzsche, § 238 (English trans. by Miss Helen Zimmern ; T. N. Foulis) : *cf.* the whole of §§ 232–239, and also *Will to Power*, § 943 (vol. ii. p. 355, English trans. by A. Ludovici).

[2] See Chapter II. ii. above.

granting of divorce on the slightest possible grounds ; as though the attainment of immediate happiness by individuals at the expense of all responsibility could possibly have any but ruinous social results. It is this doctrine of a social value to be found in an individualistic pursuit of happiness which vitiates the whole literature of the new "moralists." Such writers as Professor Karl Pearson, Mr. Bernard Shaw, Mr. H. G. Wells, Miss Ellen Key, and C. Gasquoine Hartley, have all in one degree or another advocated the setting aside of the old restraints, under a specious plea for the free development of individuality. Moreover, they appear to be entirely blind to their own delusion in this matter.

These writers display the greatest differences amongst themselves. Mr. Wells, for example,

Exponents of the New Morality. seems to have returned in his more recent works to some realization of the value of the traditional sex code.[1] Miss Ellen Key, again, advocates a most extreme theory of the rights of "love" to be free from all forms ;[2] whereas C. Gasquoine Hartley frankly shrinks from this inevitable conclusion of the individualistic standpoint which all of these writers profess.[3] Professor Karl Pearson has propounded the idea that absolute freedom of intercourse between the sexes should be combined with a state supervision of births. Men and women are to be allowed unlimited intimacy with one another ; yet no child is to be born without permission from the state.[4] Something of the

---

[1] E.g., *Marriage* and *The Passionate Friends.*
[2] In her *Love and Marriage.*
[3] *The Truth about Women* (concluding chapters).
[4] *The Ethic of Freethought*, ch. xv., "Socialism and Sex."

same kind would seem to be involved in Mr. Shaw's advocacy, on the one hand, of divorce on the easiest terms, and, on the other, of a careful state breeding of children.[1] Such loosening of individual restraints as these writers desire does not fit in well with their eugenic proposals. Once again we have Miss Ellen Key declaring for "love's freedom," and advocating illegitimate connections, on the ground that "love" cannot decide whether it can assume the permanence of the married state until it has first been consummated in a free connection.[2] On the one hand the sex passion is treated as a thing which can easily be made to bow to state laws of breeding; and on the other it is exalted into the position of a religious inspiration which must be allowed to work out its own destiny without restraint. Two main points may be noticed, both connected with the idea of individual happiness adopted by all these writers : (1) their theory of self-realization, and (2) their amazing over-estimation of the human power of controlling the sex-instincts.

It has already been found necessary, in the case of Mr. Wells, to examine the theory that self-realiza-

Their Theory of Self-realization. tion consists in embracing all possible experiences, and that all refusal of experience must be wrong. Writers of this class do not seem able to grasp the fact that to embrace any and every experience is the easiest thing in the world, whereas to refuse some experi-

---

[1] See the Preface to *Getting Married*, and "The Revolutionist's Handbook" in the volume, *Man and Superman*.

[2] *Love and Marriage*; see the chapter entitled "Love's Freedom."

19

ences for the sake of possessing others is an infinitely harder but truer method of attaining self-realization.   Moreover, it is fatal to talk smoothly of the necessity of self-realization without taking the slightest thought as to *what sort of self* is to be realized.   The usual argument put forward in favour of giving up lifelong monogamy and making divorce as easy as possible, is that the man and woman each have " rights " which they cannot hand over to one another irretrievably.   They cannot, therefore, be bound to one another if that involves the sacrifice of individual happiness on the one side or the other. Marriage, it is therefore held, must be increasingly of the nature of a contract terminable as easily as possible, since each of the parties must retain a maximum of personal independence.   From the side of the movement for the emancipation of women it is argued that marriage must be a contract of rights, in order that the wife may be delivered from the humiliation of dependence upon her husband's good will.   It is certainly true that everything possible should be done to guard the rights of wife and children.   One must, however, point to the conclusion reached in the last chapter, that the whole modern theory of individual "rights" to happiness or anything else is drawn directly from Christian presuppositions as to the worth of the individual as an end.   Accordingly when the "right" of the individual is brought forward as an argument in favour of loosening the marriage bonds, one must ask, What sort of right is this?   Miss Ellen Key answers that the "spiritual" nature of men and women must be preserved from the crushing fetters of obsolete forms. But she habitually uses this word "spiritual" to

mean, not the higher self which Christianity values
so much that it declares it to have inalienable
rights, but the earthly self which seeks pleasure
and happiness in culture of mind and æsthetic sense.[1]
The whole doctrine of individual rights grew up on
the basis of a belief in the value of the otherworldly
self. But the right to self-realization is now used as
an excuse for every kind of exaggerated egoism of
the Natural Man. Thus Miss Ellen Key, discuss-
ing the fate of the children in the event of a divorce,
writes : " Children receive with life a right to the
conditions which may make them fully fit for life ;
no less than this, but at the same time no more.
What their parents may be willing to sacrifice of
their own lives beyond this must be reckoned to their
generosity not their duty. . . . Great love may thus
be admitted to possess a right superior to that of the
children." [2] On the other hand, several exponents
of the new morality have commented adversely upon
the grasping and self-centred character which sexual
love so easily assumes. They are eager to point
out that lifelong monogamy is based upon an
antiquated theory that the wife is the property of
the husband, and they propose instead a friendship
of man and woman, in which each preserves his or
her independence.[3] Mr. Wells brings an indictment
against jealousy as the curse of strong sexual love ;[4]
and Miss Ellen Key refers to this self-centredness
of the sex passion as a kind of erotic kleptomania.[5]

[1] See, e.g., her book, The Women's Movement.
[2] Love and Marriage, pp. 341, 342.
[3] E.g., see Professor Karl Pearson, The Ethic of Freethought,
p. 427 (2nd ed.).
[4] The Passionate Friends (last chapter).
[5] Love and Marriage, p. 325.

But it does not seem to have occurred to the latter that to make such a self-centred passion the supreme and only standard of self-realization is fantastic. Such an idea would be laughable were it not that this perilous doctrine will be accepted only too readily by young people of to-day. The peril is all the greater because the method of this self-realization in sexual love is declared to be an entirely subjective matter for each individual to decide for himself. Thus we are told: "This mighty emotion seizes a man, without asking whether he is bound or free. He who feels strongly and wholly enough need never wonder what it is he feels. . . . Nor does he who feels strongly enough ever ask himself whether he has a right to his feeling. He is so exalted by his love that he knows he is thus exalting the life of mankind."[1] In reality the exact opposite is the truth. Passionate erotic feeling, when it is allowed to be the supreme motive of conduct, does *not* enable a man to think more unselfishly about "exalting the life of mankind." It does not allow him to consider the interests of mankind at all; for it is wholly self-centred, and blinds a man utterly to all other interests outside the realization of itself. The ancients understood this well enough when they depicted Eros as blindfolded. It has been left to the twentieth century to restore the idol to its old pedestal, and to justify the act by declaring that their god is really gifted with special powers of vision! This then is what is meant by the cultivation of individual happiness and the "enrichment of life," upon which the whole welfare of society is to be hazarded.

[1] *Love and Marriage*, p. 343.

Nevertheless, when this pursuit of happiness is concentrated in its most highly self-centred form of blind erotic passion, an amazing con-

Their Over-
Confidence in
Human Nature. fidence is expressed in a supposed inherent stability of human nature. It is imagined that this natural stability will control the instincts at will in the interests of social welfare. Thus we read : " Marriage has made such sure allies in man's psycho-physical conditions of life that one need not be afraid of freedom of divorce becoming equivalent to polygamy." [1] Again : " When every life is regarded as an end in itself from the point of view that it can never be lived again . . . then also the erotic happiness or unhappiness of a human being will be treated as of greater importance, and not to himself alone. No, it will be so also to the whole community—through the life and the work his happiness may give the race or his unhappiness deprive it of. For himself as well as for others, the individual will then examine the right of renouncing happiness as conscientiously as he now submits to the duty of bearing unhappiness." [2] But the community is composed of individuals, each of whom is, under the new morality, to be dominated by the self-centred erotic passion ; and this, as we have seen, is held to be above all law and every consideration of right—" Nor does he who feels strongly enough ever ask himself whether he has a right to his feelings." Will a community, in which every individual is so dominated by blind passion, consider the right of others to erotic happiness, or indeed to any happiness at all ? Will the individual be able to renounce his happiness ? It is not

[1] *Love and Marriage*, p. 311.   [2] *Ibid.*, p. 396.

likely; especially as we are told that in this new order of things the race needs people with courage to sacrifice others in order to win their own lives.[1] This presumptuous confidence is not to be found in Professor Karl Pearson, an earlier writer. For all his belief in the power of knowledge to abolish ills, he writes with reference to prostitution and other problems: "Put aside all dogmatic faith, all dogmatic morality, regard the sexual relation as in itself neither good nor evil, but only so with the misery it brings to the individual or to the race: and then try to influence the average human being! If you have sufficient Hellenism in you to regard all exercise of passion as good in moderation, provided it be productive of no mediate or immediate misery: if you see no virtue in asceticism, but only something as unworthy of humanity as excess, then how infinitely difficult you will find it to influence the average mortal!"[2] That is a significant confession to come from the pen of a thorough-going rationalist, who starts from the point of view that the sole object of man's existence is to attain earthly happiness.[3] But the rationalist is not altogether blind to facts as is the case with the devotees of "the religion of life." Such people assume that the moral progress achieved by centuries of Christian influence is due solely to the processes of evolution. They are, therefore, ready to make the wildest experiments. They are unable to relinquish the delusive hope that man is just about to reach a stage of progress when the fundamental dualism of life will vanish

---

[1] *Love and Marriage*, p. 347.
[2] *The Ethic of Free Thought*, p. 376 (2nd ed.).
[3] *Ibid.*, p. 303.

and there will be nothing henceforth to disturb the pursuit of happiness.[1]

But this reckless confidence of the new moralists in the natural power of controlling the erotic passion at will is probably due more than anything else to the extraordinary ignorance they display as to the volcanic character of the whole sexual side of human nature. Miss Ellen Key everywhere takes for granted that what is needed is a "union of soul and sense," in which these two elements are to be nicely balanced in proper proportions. This kind of talk is about as foolish as an attempt, let us say, to keep a small fire burning in a magazine filled with lyddite shells, with trains of powder laid loose all around, on the plea that as long as the fire is kept within certain limits no harm can come! What is wrong with these writers is that, having given up the Christian ideal of asceticism—the subordination of sense to spirit—they are infatuated with that idea of balance and moderation which has already been examined when the system of Mr. H. G. Wells was under discussion. They desire that "soul and sense" should meet one another on equal ground. They have, however, forgotten the truth, which the Middle Ages knew so well, that in the interests of the whole personality the sensual side of human nature cannot be allowed an equal place with the spiritual, but must be brought into complete subordination to it. Only so is there any hope of the senses being trained to take their right place in furthering the development of human life. In the later novels of Mr. Wells there seems to

---

[1] See, for example, *The Truth about Woman*, by C. G. Hartley, pp. 337–339.

be a growing recognition of something like this truer point of view.[1]

To make erotic passion the arbiter of life is to give the predominance to something which has in it possibilities both of higher and of lower development. But when it is placed in the autonomous position advocated by Miss Ellen Key as supreme above all the higher interests of the personality, this very right to freedom from restraint which is bestowed upon it will inevitably make it a prey to all the lower instincts. It will give them the encouragement which they are ever ready to take, and will set the senses in a position of advantage over the soul which can spell nothing but ruin for the whole personality. It is amazing that it is necessary to say these things ; but doubtless there are already plenty of people hailing the "freedom of love" as a new gospel. As soon as it is seen that individual happiness, in the shape of erotic passion, cannot, without infinite peril, be placed in the seat of authority, all the tirades levelled against lifelong monogamy are understood for what they are worth. Mr. Wells, for example, says with reference to divorce : "I want to get just as many contented and law-abiding citizens as possible ; I do not want to force people who would otherwise be useful citizens into rebellion . . . because they may not love and marry as their temperaments command, and so I want to make the meshes of the law as wide as possible."[2] It must be replied that, to alter the laws of social restraint to suit erotic tastes is to place the latter in the seat

[1] E.g., *The New Machiavelli*, *Marriage*, and *The Passionate Friends*.
[2] *First and Last Things*, p. 217.

of authority. To subordinate all social welfare to blind individual passions would be about as useful a process as to open wide the floodgates of a great river-dam in obedience to the pressure of water behind, when to do so would involve the sacrifice of thousands of human lives. So again when Miss Ellen Key declares that the permanence of the outward form of marriage should be entirely conditioned by the continuance of love between husband and wife, she fails to understand that the outward form is in itself a great bulwark of true love. It serves as an actual protection for the individual man or woman, keeping him or her from becoming a prey to their own undisciplined emotions and desires.[1] To adopt Miss Ellen Key's principles in this matter would be to give active encouragement to sexual passion, not to train itself up to a great and disciplined loyalty lasting for life, but to become a prey to its own moods and to the ebb and flow of instinct and emotion. In fact, the most fickle and unstable tendencies in human nature would gain the ascendency.

Earlier in this chapter it was said that "not by way of nature is the solution to be reached, but by (iii.) The way of a supremely high ideal, based Christian Ideal. (a) The Other- upon the otherworldly values and em-worldly Signifi- bodied in an objective standard, with cance of Marriage. unchanging forms."[2] With subjective evolutionary moralists it is a natural consequence of their presuppositions that they agree to reject

[1] *Cf.* Foerster, *Marriage and the Sex Problem*, chapters iii. and v. The writer's criticism of the "new morality" in this chapter owes much to Dr Foerster's book, especially pp. 292–297, above.

[2] See p. 286 above.

the idea of a permanent form of sex-relationship holding good for all time. We have seen that, when pushed to its logical conclusion, this rejection means the placing of sexual passion in the seat of authority over the whole of human life. Now the Christian view of sex starts from the opposite pole of thought. The Christian institution of lifelong monogamous marriage is the necessary and permanent expression of a sex ideal based entirely upon the otherworldly principle. Christian marriage is the outward form through which the otherworldly love-values are realized in the sex relationship; it is because of this that lifelong permanence is of its essence. Christianity is always in every department of conduct intensely personal. In every detail of the Gospel rule of life which has entered into this discussion, we have found that the otherworldly value of human personality as such is the starting-point; and the same principle holds good in determining the principles of the sex relationship. Sexual love upon the natural plane is not of itself necessarily personal; it has great possibilities in that direction; but it is equally possible for it to become predominantly sensuous. The new moralists do not realise that the strongly personal character of sexual love in modern times is a thing which we owe entirely to the long influence of Christian ideals upon this side of life. *Sexual love cannot rise to a pure appreciation of the spiritual personality of the one loved unless it is made the sacramental channel of the otherworldly love.* Herein lies the value of the emphasis which lifelong monogamy places upon the element of personal loyalty between husband and wife. The method of the Christian marriage ideal is to make the whole sexual life depend upon something far higher and more stable than itself, namely, the love of the Christ-self in each to the Christ-self in the other. We have seen already how this otherworldly neighbour-love is the proper basis for all the social relationships of humanity. If anything, the importance of such otherworldly power is greater in the sphere of sex than in any other department of human life, because there it has stronger and more elemental forces to bring under control. Only Goliath can wield Goliath's spear; even so the power of otherworldly love alone can bring the natural sexual love under full control. But more than that: it, and it alone, can use sexual love sacramentally. By so doing it lifts it into the otherworldly sphere, there to be transfigured, so that the sex relationship has a lasting spiritual value for the development of the Christ-self in both husband and wife.

It is the greatest possible mistake to think that sexual love is of itself a spiritual power. One sees the truth of this nowhere more clearly than in Mr. Wells' novels. In relation to the world of spiritual activity sexual love is of itself strictly neutral like all other instincts which belong to the natural order.[1] There is therefore no greater mistake possible than to put it in the place of that otherworldly love which alone can raise it to its true dignity and value. Even Mr. Shaw's dislike for romanticism bears witness to the same truth. Earthly love of any kind, and not least sexual love, loses its attraction and freshness and becomes eventually a dull weight, or else at least leaves a

[1] See pp. 177–180 above.

vacant space in the life unfilled, unless it is made a means to something higher. That is what is wrong with the family relationships depicted by Mr. Shaw in his preface to *Getting Married*. He declares that intimate family life is a failure, and that this is largely so because it has been smothered in an excessive attempt to realize family love, of which in reality we want less and not more. Now what is true of sexual love is true also of family love. Its intimate character makes it all the more necessary that it should be absolutely dominated by the higher otherworldly love; otherwise it may easily suffer from an excess of itself. But the remedy is not, as Mr. Shaw suggests, that we should do away with unreal attempts to keep up a belief in family love. Rather we should continually bring fresh life and significance into this natural sphere by the deepening of the otherworldly love. In this way alone can its purity and freshness be sustained.

It follows from all this that neither marriage nor family life ought ever to become ends in themselves. All earthly social relationships are so many means whereby the love of the Christ-self in each is to be realized towards the Christ-self in the other. Lifelong monogamous marriage is the principal and most fundamental of the earthly relationships which are to be so used. It is the most fundamental; for it is the most intimate form of human fellowship, and therefore it serves as a centre round which all other social relationships are grouped. Moreover, the greater stability of the more intimate relationship of marriage serves to strengthen and solidify the less intimate relationships of social life. Christian marriage occupies this central position, whereby it binds together the whole of society. It does so by virtue of the fact that the medium of its intimacy, namely sexual love, is the strongest instrument for drawing human beings together which exists throughout the whole natural order. Regarded from this point of view, the spiritualizing of sexual love for the proper fulfilment of its social task is seen to be by far the most powerful method of spiritualizing the relationships of society. Christian marriage is therefore the sacramental means whereby the otherworldly love of the self to the other is to be realized in the most permanent and intimate manner possible on earth. When marriage is made such a means to the otherworldly ideal, it embodies that ideal on earth so impressively that it becomes itself the most fitting symbol of all otherworldly love. It concentrates the light of that love in itself, and then gives it forth again—a steady flame to enlighten all around.

Once more, when married life passes into family life its otherworldly value is enlarged. The presence of the child intensifies the sacramental value of the marriage as a means to the realization of the otherworldly ideals. All natural values attain their full significance only when related to the otherworldly values. To say therefore that marriage exists solely or even primarily for the propagation of natural life is as false as to say that sexual love may be made an end in itself; for it is to give to something which belongs to the natural order an absolute value which belongs rightly to the spiritual order alone. This is the danger which lies in the path of the eugenic movement. The propagation of natural life has a moral value only as a means to a higher end. The whole natural order is moral only as it becomes a basis for the spiritual life. The propagation of natural life fulfils this principle only as it is made a means to the cultivation of a sphere of spiritual personalities knit together by the otherworldly love-values ; this, then, is the significance of the Christian family. For here again, just as sexual love is the most intensive natural instrument whereby the otherworldly love of the self to the other is realized, so family affection is a powerful instrument—more powerful than the ordinary social affinities of human nature—whereby the same otherworldly love is realized in a larger and more complete social grouping than that which is formed by husband and wife alone. Family life therefore comes next to marriage itself in its value as a binding social force. Moreover, the Christian institution of lifelong consecrated monogamy is the only means whereby family life may universally attain this otherworldly value. For if children are to learn to recognise the absolute otherworldly value of each personality in the family, they can only do so in two ways. They must learn it first by seeing that recognition of the supreme worth of the other actually existing in the relations of the parents to one another and to themselves, and secondly, through the direct teaching of the parents, to whom they look as their examples of what the otherworldly love ought to be in its earthly manifestation. This is the ideal of the Christian family ; the realization of the otherworldly love between parents is the soil out of which the same realization is to grow up amongst children. When through selfishness the otherworldly transformation of sexual love has been lost between husband and wife, the whole family life has lost its principal internal bond and source of inspiration. Yet this loss can never justify divorce ; for divorce deliberately breaks before the very eyes of the children that solemn pledge of loyalty, made by each to the other, which is the symbol of the supreme worth of the otherworldly love-values, not only to husband and wife, but also to the children themselves. Divorce, moreover, defames the outward form of marriage ; and this by its sacramental use has in itself the otherworldly value of that love of the Christ-self in each to the other, to the realization of which it is the one and only means in the sphere of sex.   Divorce must by its very nature be excluded from the Christian life, for it constitutes *a deliberate renunciation of the otherworldly ideal,* which is infinitely more damaging to the moral sense of the children than the vision of that ideal imperfectly realized.   Even when the ideal has been lost, the continuance of the marriage tie is a promise that it may be recovered ; whereas divorce is a final denial of this possibility of recovery.   Such a denial must leave in the soul of the child a deep sense of violence done to human personality far exceeding any harm wrought by the quarrels of parents, who have, however, not yet turned their backs upon the ideal for good.[1]   The Christian forms of marriage and family

[1] To repudiate divorce does not mean to deny the rightfulness in some cases of a separation, that is, a discontinuance of the common home life, without, however, the right of either party to remarry being allowed.   This separation without power to remarry keeps the way always open to a recovery of the lost ideal, and guards the pledge of mutual loyalty as something still sacred, notwithstanding past failure to observe it.

Cf. Foerster, *Marriage and the Sex Problem,* p. 37 note, especially the opening words :—" We do not overlook the fact

life are, then, the central means whereby the other-worldly love-values are mediated to mankind; and we have seen that these values are the source from which proceed the whole range of social virtues which bind society together.

It will be well perhaps, in this connection, to say something about that virtue which is most closely Christian connected with the sexual side of human Purity. nature, namely Christian purity. In criticism of the Christian exaltation of this virtue, Mr. Wells has written: "I do not believe in negative virtues. . . . Our minds fall very readily under the spell of such unmitigated words as Purity and Chastity. Only death beyond decay, absolute non-existence, can be pure and chaste. Life is impurity, fact is impure . . . we are born impure, we die impure, . . . the chastity of monk or nun is but introverted impurity."[1] Two things are to be noticed here: first the idea that "Life is impure," and secondly the conception of purity as something negative. "Life is impurity, fact is impure"—who does not feel the pathetic force of such words as these? Yet they really proceed from a complete misapprehension of those facts of human nature which determine the meaning of Christian purity. For purity does not begin with the external bodily life; that is where its effects are manifested finally. There is doubtless a natural tendency in human nature to conceive of moral issues which ultimately affect the material and physical sphere as though

that there may also be very deep and serious reasons for separation —we are merely demonstrating the effects which the annulling of the sanctified form must have, and has been proved to have, on the lower and weaker side of human nature."

[1] *First and Last Things*, p. 182.

they started from and hinged upon the material and physical phenomena. This is probably due largely, if not wholly, to the effects of sin. In our sin-tainted nature we are unable to realize to the full the perfect goodness of all that belongs to the natural order; consequently the material and physical world ever appears to us under the darkening shadow cast upon it by our own sinfulness. Here lies the origin of the Manichean heresy and all kindred errors. Purity like all other virtues begins with the will. In the sphere of the will it takes its origin; thence it flows outwards in a cleansing stream which covers thoughts, words, and deeds, and all the circumstances of the bodily life. It can, then, be said with truth that "Life is impurity, fact is impure," only when the will has deliberately allied itself with evil. The will is the key to the life in matters of conduct; and the facts of the physical life only become contaminated through being under the direction of a contaminated will. If the will is pure, it cannot be defiled by any fact of life; and this remains true even though some physiological facts may in themselves be due wholly or in part to the effects of past sin upon the life.[1] The body, then, cannot defile the will, unless the will use it unsacramentally. Christian purity is that virtue by which the sacramental use of the body for purely spiritual ends is specially upheld. To turn now to the other point raised by Mr. Wells' words—the idea that purity is a "negative virtue." This mistake follows, of course, directly from the other. If "Life is impure," then death alone can be pure. In this case Buddha was right; for purity can

---

[1] For some further consideration of this subject, see the Appendix.

only be won by fighting against life. Here again
purity is pictured as something which starts its crusade
from the surface of things, from without. The life of
man is conceived as something fatally involved in a
fixed routine of physical fact and material circumstance, fast closed in a circle of nature from which
there is no way out, having no power within which
is capable of transcending it. Purity, then, can only
be a destroyer summoned from without to break the
walls of this prison of life—a vandal who destroys
good and bad together, who heaps up wreckage
and offers nothing in its place. But if we correct
the initial mistake and picture purity as something
coming down from above into the heart of the
stronghold, the whole appearance of things is
changed. The purified will at once transcends its
natural prison, bursts all bonds, and takes possession
of the whole order of fact and circumstance, so that
life becomes what the will makes it to be. How,
then, is Christian purity to be actually defined? It is
the virtue which corresponds to the duty of bringing
the sexual side of life into sacramental relationship
with the otherworldly love-values. Like every other
virtue it has both a negative and a positive aspect.
Negatively it is the absolute repudiation of all
unsacramental use of sexual passion throughout
the entire range of the personal life, both inwardly
and outwardly, in thought, word, and deed. Posi-
tively it is the maintenance of the atmosphere of
otherworldly love between men and women always
and under all circumstances. This definition covers
equally both the married and the celibate life. For
the celibate man or woman, in whom sexual love is
dormant, purity will mean the complete subordina-

tion of the whole range of sex-instinct to the higher atmosphere of otherworldly love in which the Christian moves. If a legitimate sexual love arises, then the true self of man or woman will at once make it a means to the furtherance of otherworldly love. Whether there be sexual love or not, men and women can behold within the otherworldly sphere the pure and unsullied beauty of the Christ-self in each other;[1] only in the one case this vision will be enhanced by the sacramental use of sexual love. In Christian marriage, where the whole sexual life finds its proper and legitimate fulfilment, purity will still be in principle exactly the same virtue, though related to a different set of circumstances.

The Christian sex ideal, as it has just been defined, is one which calls for a strenuous and incessant discipline of the whole life in each (b) The Ascetic Principle and individual. Nowhere, therefore, is the the Sex Ideal. ascetic principle more emphatically important than in this sphere of sex. So clearly has the Church realized this in the past, that Christian asceticism has come to be regarded as very largely identical with ecclesiastical celibacy. The ideal of celibacy as a religious ideal has played an important part in the history of Christian morals. It is, therefore, impossible to treat the Christian sex ideal adequately without endeavouring to understand the significance of this particular manifestation of it.

As the sex instincts are among the strongest instincts in human nature, they can be made means to the realization of the otherworldly ideals only by

[1] See p. 249 above.

a very great exercise of the ascetic principle, which must be both individual and corporate. Individuals vary enormously as to the degree in which their sexual nature asserts itself; but for society as a whole the strongest possible exercise of self-discipline is necessary, and that not only individually but also corporately. Since marriage and the family are social institutions, and the sexual side of human nature is so clearly linked to the whole social life of man, society needs to have the ascetic principle constantly at work within it and before its eyes. Just as the individual must exalt the ascetic principle into an ideal of self-control for his own life before he can enter into the otherworldly possession of himself, so it is indispensable to the spiritual welfare of the whole body that the ascetic principle should be raised to the level of a corporate ideal within the general life of society. It is this principle which is embodied in our Lord's words: "There are eunuchs, which made themselves eunuchs for the kingdom of heaven's sake. He that is able to receive it, let him receive it."[1] The ascetic principle is capable of an infinitely greater use as a means to the realization of the otherworldly ideals than the mass of mankind imagines. A general decline into worldliness, luxury, and undisciplined habits, an imperceptible sinking back from the plane of spiritual ideals into a contented misuse of the natural order as an end in itself,—this is probably the most dangerous temptation, the most widespread cause of moral failure in every age and in every civilization which bears the name of Christian. It is the perhaps unconscious abandonment of the ascetic principle

[1] St. Matt. xix. 12.

which will be more likely than anything else to lead
to a general collapse of civilization. As a barrier
against this perpetual danger the Church has in
every age set forth the Ascetic Ideal; and with it
the celibate life has always been found as one way
in which the ideal rightly and properly expresses
itself. For even marriage and the family may be
made natural ends, instead of means to a more intense appropriation of spiritual ideals. It is against
this perversion of things that celibacy stands forth
as a perpetual protest, when it is deliberately adopted
as a religious ideal "for the kingdom of heaven's
sake." In the age of primitive Christianity, when
the conflict of the otherworldly ideal with the gross
spirit of paganism was at its full height, the Fathers
of the Church were not slow to understand this.
Disgusted with the widespread immoralities of the
decaying Empire, they were passionately enthusiastic
for that complete revolution with regard to sex ideals
which Christianity was destined to accomplish. It
is not, then, to be wondered at that St. Jerome and
others gave way at times to exaggerated language
in exalting the celibate ideal which they had chosen,
and which has proved such an inestimable benefit
to Christendom. For it needs to be repeated that
society lives by spiritual ideals and by nothing else;
yet nothing is easier to lose than these ideals.
The preservation of spiritual ideals, such as that of
Christian purity, is the hardest task which is set to
every generation and every age; and this is not less
the case but more so when civilization and culture
are as highly developed as they are at the present
time. Engrossment in material progress and ac-
cumulation of luxurious ways deaden the corporate

sense of the value of a sternly disciplined life. Yet
without the maintenance of this ideal of discipline,
personal life tends to become increasingly selfish and
dependent upon comfort at every turn. Moreover,
since the sexual side of human nature is closely
related to all the rest, it quickly feels the effect of
this downward tendency. An evidence of this to-
day is the fact that the increased demand for divorce
and for freedom from the restraints of Christian
marriage has followed rapidly upon the general increase in the means of material comfort. The task
of counteracting this downward process has always
fallen in a special way to those who have adopted
the monastic life. It was pointed out just now that
the ascetic ideal needs to be perpetually manifested
before the eyes of men not only individually but
corporately ; and if the witness of history counts for
anything, it would appear that it is only some form
of monasticism which is capable of giving this corporate manifestation of the ascetic ideal to the world.
We have already seen how in one of his books
Mr. H. G. Wells has actually pictured an ideal
order living on essentially monastic lines for the
benefit of the race.[1]

The Christian monastic community exists, then,
to keep the otherworldly and ascetic ideals ever
fresh before the eyes of the world. Over against
Christian marriage it sets the ideal of a family of
celibates. It does this in no sense with a view to
depreciating marriage, but in order to *preserve* it
by exercising a strong influence on behalf of self-
discipline, the only means by which the sex ideal
can be maintained in its full purity and beauty.

[1] *A Modern Utopia*, see pp. 100 ff. above.

The individual Christian from time to time withholds himself deliberately from a full enjoyment of the natural order by the method of the ascetic principle, in order that he may strengthen his hold upon the spiritual world and his power of using the natural order sacramentally. In the same way it is good for the Christian society that some of its members should deliberately withhold themselves from the lawful use of marriage and family life, from sexual love and the whole range of natural enjoyments which belong to it. Thus the society will, through some of its members, be enabled to realize the otherworldly ideal as something to which the cycle of natural experience belonging to the sphere of sex must always be subordinated.

The significance of the Christian sex ideal and the indispensability of the ascetic principle in connection with that ideal have recently been set forth with great clearness and vigour by Dr. F. W. Foerster in his book *Marriage and the Sex Problem.*[1] His strongly Christian point of view is all the more valuable because he was brought up in a non-religious atmosphere. Starting from a purely secular point of view, he was led by a study, first of social problems, and then of moral education, to the conviction that Christianity alone provides an adequate basis for morals. "Totally uninfluenced by any religious training or by any atmosphere of belief, but following only the inner necessities of his own social and educational work, Foerster drew nearer and nearer to Christianity, until, after a still further development, he became convinced that the Christian

[1] This is the title given to the English edition (translated by Dr. Meyrick Booth).

religion was the sole foundation for both social and individual life."[1]   Moreover, by "the Christian religion" he came to understand that he must mean Catholicism.   Although not apparently himself claiming the name of Catholic, he declares that Protestants cannot "afford to neglect the *psychology and pedagogy* which lie behind the Catholic system."[2] Again, he quotes with approval Schopenhauer's remark that "Protestantism killed one of the vital nerves of Christianity in combating the value of celibacy."[3]   His chapter on "The Indispensability of the Ascetic Ideal" is a strong independent witness to what Catholic Christianity has always believed and taught upon this subject; for he sees clearly the dangers which are gathering about our present civilization through the neglect of the ascetic principle.   Thus he writes: "To secure the mastery of man's higher self over the whole world of animal desire is a task which demands a more systematic development of will-power and the cultivation of a deeper faith in the spiritual destiny of humanity than are to be found in the superficial intellectualistic civilization of to-day. . . . The contempt which has been poured upon the idea of asceticism in recent times has contributed more than anything else towards effeminacy.   Nothing could be more effective in bringing humanity back to the best traditions of manhood than a respect for the spiritual strength and conquest which is sym-

---

[1] Translator's introduction to *Marriage and the Sex Problem* (p. vii).   As Dr. Meyrick Booth points out, Eucken shares Foerster's conviction as to "the doubt and indecision of the modern world," which make it so essential that it should find some rallying centre such as Christianity affords (p. viii).

[2] *Ibid.*, p. 133.   [3] *Ibid.*, p. 154.

bolised in ascetic lives."[1] He fully understands the value of the monastic ideal for the realization of this side of truth. The purpose of this ideal is, as he says, "Not in order to make a more natural life appear contemptible, but with the express purpose of enriching life and preserving it from degeneration by means of heroic examples of spiritual power. Properly to understand the significance of asceticism, it should be remembered that natural life does not flourish unless the spirit retains the upper hand; and since we are surrounded for the most part by striking examples of lives in which the spirit plays anything but a leading part, it is in the highest degree desirable that living and striking examples of men and women, who have fully freed themselves from the distraction of the world and the domination of natural desires, should be continually before our eyes. The vast majority of modern men will see nothing but matter for laughter in such an ideal as this. Even earnest and spiritually minded people regard it as an obsolete and erroneous view, which must soon give place to a more harmonious conception of life. I am, however, profoundly convinced that this attitude is the product of a shallow understanding of actual human nature. Ignorance of the awful dangers latent in our weak nature is very commonly to be met with in epochs still powerfully influenced by great traditions of moral discipline. Those born in such periods are apt to be lacking in personal acquaintance with the darker side of human nature, owing to the very state of discipline into which their fellow-citizens have been brought. Hence they fail to realise what a labori-

[1] *Marriage and the Sex Problem*, pp. 127, 128.

ous taming of passion has preceded the comparative security they find around them." [1]

Reference has already been made to the real danger which exists in all ages of making even such sacred institutions as marriage and the family ends in themselves.[2] It was the understanding of this danger which impelled some of the great saints, such as St. Elizabeth, and some of the devoted women of royal blood in the early days of English Christianity, deliberately to take the remarkable step of separating themselves from husband and children to enter the cloister.   Such action, strange as it may seem to our comfort-loving civilization, was in the highest interests of marriage and the family.   Dr. Foerster well describes the true significance of such unique actions: " The spirit which animated the great saints was one of pure devotion to God.   With the penetrating gaze of the purified soul they saw that a family life not based upon anything higher than earthly love may be no more than a species of extended self-interest ; they perceived that blunting of all higher needs which so often accompanies the mere worship of motherhood, that naïve self-expansion and self-reflection in the offspring, that character-destroying exaggeration of outward care, that growing indifference to everything except the welfare of one's own circle, that idolatrous cult of the work of human propagation, without any true and consistent worship of God." [3]

It is apparently one of the most convincing marks of the inherent power of the Christian ethic to meet the needs of human life at every point, that,

[1] *Op. cit.*, p. 129.   [2] See above, pp. 300, 301.
[3] *Marriage and the Sex Problem*, p. 138.

while it raises the ideal of married life to a higher
level, and gives it a greater and more dignified place
at the heart of the social system than is suggested
by any other religion or scheme of morality, it also
points with deep and impartial sincerity to the
dangers of its misuse.   Christianity takes its stand
neither with the pagan worship of the natural life
nor with oriental nihilism; it comprehends the
truth of both, whilst rejecting their errors.   It
honours both marriage and celibacy, as two different
but equally honourable paths by which the highest
ideals may be realized.   The function of celibacy as
a religious ideal which supports the true dignity of
marriage is well expressed by Dr. Foerster in the
following passage : "Celibacy is an extremely valuable means of representing the independence of
higher aims in life against the ascendancy of family
impulses and family cares, thus safeguarding marriage
against being degraded from a sacrament to a mere
matter of gratification. . . . The oath of voluntary
celibacy, so far from degrading marriage, is a support to the holiness of the marital bond, since it
gives material shape to the spiritual freedom of man
in the face of natural impulses; it also acts like a
conscience in respect of all passing moods and en-
croachments of the sensual temperament.   Celibacy
is a protection of marriage in this sense, too, that
its existence prevents married people, in their relations to one another, from feeling themselves as the
mere slaves of obscure natural forces, and leads
them to take their stand against nature as free
beings able to command.[1]   Those who mock at

[1] To this Dr. Foerster appends this significant note : "Anyone
wishing to convince himself completely how necessary this is, need

celibacy as unnatural and impossible, know not, in very truth, what they do. They do not see that the attitude which induces them to speak thus must lead, as its logical consequence, to prostitution and to the dissolution of monogamy. . . . Consistent monogamy stands or falls with the esteem in which celibacy is held. It is no accident that Luther, by his fight against celibacy, was led to the secondary result that breach of marriage is permissible in cases where the physiological aim of marriage cannot be fulfilled." [1]

Dr. Foerster's book has been quoted at some length, because he appears to have gone to the very heart of the Christian point of view with regard to the sex ideal. This point of view must be maintained with regard to the whole range of ethics. Too often one comes across attempts to meet the neo-pagan criticism of Christian ideals by timid compromising arguments, as though one needed to apologize for the Gospel. Such an attitude of apology can only be possible for the Christian if he allows himself to be dazzled by the imposing outward display of our modern civilization ; whereas in reality the opinions of those who are contented with its superficial valuations are not worthy of any great respect, since they are based upon ignorance of the heights and depths of spiritual experience. We cannot expect the worshippers of material and mechanical power to understand the value of humility and poverty of spirit, or to grasp the significance of otherworldly values and the delicate

only inform himself through experienced medical men and women what misery is caused in so-called happy marriages. . . ."

[1] *Op. cit.*, pp. 151, 152.

dignity of spiritual personality. But one thing is certain. Christianity will not win their respect but earn their contempt if, in our anxiety to commend it to the world, we are eager to conceal or deny its revolutionary character, and to repudiate its strongly ascetic tendency. Smug Lutheranism could not hide from Nietzsche the fact that asceticism, the principle of conquering the world by opposing it, is, and always has been, one of the hall-marks of genuine Christianity. The whole strength of the Christian position lies, not in repudiating those features in it which are most unlike the temper of the world, but in emphasizing them. If the Christian ethic were of this world and like unto it, there would be nothing more to be said. Its distinctive character is its very otherworldliness. For Christianity, so far from being a system or a code, is the manifestation in the world of a Life which draws all its power from a supernatural religious experience—an experience which in its turn is based upon a supernatural creed.

APPENDIX

THE RELATION OF CHRISTIAN ASCETICISM
TO ANCIENT PHYSIOLOGICAL THEORIES

IN this appendix Christian asceticism will be considered
in relation to one special point, raised in a private
criticism passed upon the original draft of this essay.[1]
The question to be considered is briefly this : How far
can the traditional asceticism practised in the Church,
the "ascetic principle" approved in this book, be held to
have depended in its origin and subsequent development
upon physiological theories current at the time of the rise
of Christianity ? The question is obviously an important
one. Since modern science has given us an entirely
new knowledge of physiology, ancient theories have
become obsolete ; and if the early Christians built up
their ascetic view of life upon such obsolete theories,
that fact would go far to undermine our belief in its
permanency. Now it will be well first to see clearly
what it is exactly that we have to decide. It is evident
that, whatever physiological theories were current in the
Roman Empire, they must have been shared to a considerable extent, at any rate, by the Christians ; and,
further, that such theories must have been *one* factor in
the shaping of their views of life. So much we may
concede at once. But it would be a long step from this

[1] By Professor F. C. Burkitt of Cambridge. In the statement made
in the next paragraph about the ancient theories, I have followed
closely his private communication to me, which he has very kindly
allowed me to make use of in this way.

318

to conclude that such theories were the *dominating* factor. Yet that is what will have to be shown before their truth or untruth can be held to impair the validity of a view of life which has proved itself to be such a permanent feature of Christianity as Catholic asceticism.

This, then, is the problem to be considered. In the ancient classical world the universal fact of decay and corruption was a serious difficulty to many minds. The things which have most to do with life, they observed, tend to "go bad" and putrefy. Πνεῦμα was a form of substance (or "matter") which did not putrefy like "flesh and blood." "Eternal life" is life that does not go bad. The life nourished by ordinary food was a life subject to φθορά (corruption); all the passions issued in φθορά, and so the ascetic attempted to nourish himself as little as possible from this "corruption." All this doctrine of πνεῦμα (as the heavenly *material*) and of φθορά is strange to modern science. Does not all this make a difference in our views about asceticism? Most early Christian writers considered a virgin, male or female, more perfect, less "corrupted," than one who was no longer virgin— and so on. It is obviously impossible within the compass of an appendix, even if the writer had the necessary learning, to come to any conclusions as to whether the above statement gives a correct account of the matter. I shall confine myself to the more general considerations already indicated; granted for our present purpose that such views were prevalent, can it be said that the traditional asceticism of the Church is bound up with them?

Before we pass to consider what other factors were brought to bear upon such questions by Christianity, let us make sure that we understand what significance they were likely to have for the heathen world. Paganism of the Hellenic type stood for the truth that the natural order is good. This was the passionate assertion of all that was best in the life and religion of the Greeks. But for them this natural order was a final end. Since, then, the

material had an absolute worth, the universal phenomenon of the corruption and decay of material goods with
what seemed like ruthless disregard for their apparent
worth was a positive evil in the most absolute and final
sense.   They strove, therefore, to make the best possible
use of the material world before its goodness passed
out of their grasp.   In the East, however, a different
result was obtained from the same facts.   In a world
where the natural order was final, this fact of corruption
was so overwhelming that the Oriental reached an opposite
conclusion ; if matter is so corruptible, it cannot be good.
The fault of corruption must lie in that which is corrupted ; matter therefore is evil.   Now when we turn
to the New Testament we find new and powerful factors
coming in, which change the whole face of the problem.
The old facts are still there ; matter is emphatically pronounced to be good, for "every creature of God is good
and nothing is to be rejected."[1]   Yet the fact of corruption
is just as clearly recognized : earthly treasure corrupts,
the world and its lust pass away.   Both Hellenist and
Oriental are seen to have been justified in their conclusions, so far as they went, though the scales were
certainly in favour of the positive view of life.   But something new has taken possession of the problem, and appears always as the deciding factor.   There has come a
great inrush from the spiritual world.   Spirit henceforth
is to direct and determine the use of the material.   All
use of matter is good, if it is dominated by spirit for its
own purposes.   In matters of conduct the stress has
shifted from the outward to the inward, although not to
the detriment of the outward.   The reverse is the result :
our Lord pronounces all meats clean and exalts marriage
to the highest level of sanctity.

St. Paul passionately denounces those who would reverse
these decisions.[2]   The outward and bodily is determined
by spiritual needs.[3]   All is in complete contrast to such

---

[1] I Tim. iv. 4.
[2] I Tim. iv. 3 ; *cf.* Romans xiv. and Coloss. iii.   [3] *Cf.* Acts xv.

sects as the Pharisees and Essenes, which were largely engrossed in external taboos. The Son of Man came eating and drinking, for the material is good. Yet its goodness is only realized by the dominance of spirit ; and to that end asceticism is necessary. Thus, for example, virginity is deliberately exalted by our Lord and by St. Paul on spiritual grounds.[1] What, then, of corruption? Φθορά is still the mark of matter, whereas ἀφθαρσία is the mark of πνεῦμα. Whether πνεῦμα is thought of in the New Testament as a kind of heavenly material substance or not does not seem to matter at all. Even though a material category be employed, it provides a very vivid and suitable image. The problem of physical φθορά is solved by the Resurrection. "Flesh and blood" are under the law of φθορά ; but for Christians what does that matter? we have something else to fall back upon, namely πνεῦμα, the indestructible matter. Where spirit dominates body, the material particles of the body may become corrupt ; but its worth has already been conserved by spirit, which can thus take to itself again the "spiritual body" proper to it ; and this shares in the "incorruptible substance." In our use of matter, therefore, though there be physical corruption, it is no loss ; but a *spiritual* corruption through misuse of matter is to be shunned, and a spiritual conservation of matter through spirit is to be attained. The early Christian solution of the problem would thus seem to be that matter, though corruptible, is good, because by its association with incorruptible spirit it has the potentiality of becoming incorruptible. Physical corruption is thus in the first place a reason for concentrating upon the spiritual, through which alone the physical life can be redeemed. But for the Christian it must always be something else as well. For him it is a symbol of the fact of sin, and a sign of the opportunity of sin's entry which is ever at hand when we make use of the material order. Corruption of matter can only be an absolute evil for man when

---

[1] St. Matt. xix. and 1 Cor. vii.

his relationship to matter is unsacramental ; but the very
fact of corruption must remind us of the imminence of
this evil.   Now all our use of the material world is under
the cloud of sin's possibility.   Thus there is a real sense
in which matter may " go bad " in the using, not merely
physically, but *spiritually*.   Matter used unsacramentally
is so much matter lost to the spiritual world ; its worth
does not pass up into the spiritual sphere where it would
become incorruptible.   May not this be the real ground
upon which Christian thinkers held virginity to be a more
perfect state than marriage ?   In the heathen world,
where virginity was held in high repute, as in the case
of the Vestal Virgins, this attitude would doubtless be
explicable on the purely physical theory, which they
held, of a perfection belonging to " unused " matter.
But in view of the dominating position given to " spirit "
in the New Testament, where, notwithstanding, asceticism
is firmly rooted, it does not appear conceivable that the
early Christians could have honoured virginity solely, or
even mainly, on physical grounds.   It would be hard
perhaps to appraise the influence of the physiological
theory ; but surely the thing they were really concerned
to guard against was the *spiritual* corruption involved in
a misuse of matter.   The line of thought followed would
perhaps be something like this :—In the use of the material
world ἐπιθυμία is ever at the door, ready to enter, for
original sin has weakened the defences.   This is specially
true in matters of sex ; who can deny that this is pre-
eminently a case where for fallen human nature a right
sacramental use is never completely realized ?   Moreover,
if this be so, is it not entirely natural that many with
high ideals should be strongly moved to refrain from that
which would inevitably involve *for them* some spiritual
loss ?   St. Paul had found sufficient reason for giving a
high place to virginity in the fact that marriage and family
cares inevitably distract attention from the things of the
Spirit ; here, as always, it was the dominance of spiritual
interests which decided the matter.   It is better not to

use than to use and suffer spiritual loss. The natural is good ; but original sin always makes *our use* of the natural to be a doubtful good in practice, a good not wholly pure in the using ; such we realize it to be as we look back upon it. Something of this kind would seem to have been in the mind of the Early Church ; and who will dare say that she was wrong?

The physiological theory, which we have been assuming to be prevalent at the time when Christianity was first propagated, would appear to have been by no means productive of the same ethical results in all cases. We are told, on the one hand, that the typical ascetic refrained as far as possible from nourishing the life which issued in "corruption"; and yet we have, on the other hand, to take account of the case of antinomian Gnostic sects such as the Carpocratians. *Ex hypothesi* they must have shared the current opinion that the use of passion leads to physical "corruption"; yet as a fact they believed that spiritual liberty was to be obtained by an unbounded use of the bodily passions! Clearly the kind of asceticism which should have issued from the physiological theories of the day had no place in their system, and this fact must surely put us on our guard against supposing that such theories would have a determining influence, where other important factors were at work. Here was a sect which took the oriental view that matter is bad, and upon that ground its members sought to justify unbounded licentiousness. Christianity deliberately allied itself with the Western belief that matter is good, and in opposition to these antinomian Gnostics venerated virginity and asceticism. Yet here is the remarkable thing. Both Christians and Gnostics alike held their opposite theories *primarily on spiritual grounds* ;— so the evidence would seem to show. The Gnostics said : We have learnt the secret of spiritual liberty ; we are independent of the body and can defile it without injury to our souls. The Christians replied: Body and spirit cannot be separated into two moral spheres ; if the spirit is to dominate, the body must be used sacramentally for spiritual ends ; and upon that ground asceticism is to be honoured and used as our chief weapon. Now, where in all of this is the evidence that physiological theories were the determining factor that we should expect, if the criticism we are considering is to hold good ?

There is one more important consideration to be weighed. If the physiological theories referred to were in possession of the field when Christianity began its work, Christian thinkers may well have found themselves obliged to think and speak in the phraseology of their day. But it does not in the least follow that the thought in their minds, which lay behind such phrases, was identical in content with the ordinary pagan thought of their day. As we have already seen in the case of the cardinal virtues,[1] they were obliged to use the materials they found to hand ; but surely a great dynamic force like that which moved in primitive Christianity could not use such materials without powerfully remoulding them and bringing them at length into conformity with its own genius. An obvious illustration of this is to be found in the use to which the Greek Fathers put current philosophical terminology. Such terminology may be now obsolete ; it may seem to us very materialistic, like the doctrine of $\pi\nu\epsilon\hat{\upsilon}\mu\alpha$—the heavenly material substance which does not corrupt. Yet the Fathers managed to use it in such a way as to make it the vehicle of great dogmatic verities, which have been handed down to us unchanged, even though, it may be, through an imperfect and obsolete medium. It is very important that we should not set aside ancient thought simply because in its expression there is involved some element, which may now seem to be unscientific, but which, because it is only a medium, cannot destroy the efficacy of the belief which lies behind it. In some such way as this it would seem that, if the language of primitive

---

[1] See above, chapter vi. p. 255.

Christian asceticism be proved to bear a close likeness to the language of contemporary physiological theories, we can never quite gauge to what extent these external physical conceptions may be used, for lack of better material, to convey truth which has its roots much deeper. If this be the case we cannot securely build arguments upon such use of a particular phraseology.

INDEX

PRINTED IN GREAT BRITAIN BY NEILL AND CO., LTD., EDINBURGH.

16.11.15